Understanding
Media Industries

Understanding Media Industries

TIMOTHY HAVENS
University of Iowa

AMANDA D. LOTZ
University of Michigan

New York   Oxford
OXFORD UNIVERSITY PRESS

Oxford University Press, Inc., publishes works that further Oxford University's
objective of excellence in research, scholarship, and education.

Oxford   New York
Auckland   Cape Town   Dar es Salaam   Hong Kong   Karachi
Kuala Lumpur   Madrid   Melbourne   Mexico City   Nairobi
New Delhi   Shanghai   Taipei   Toronto

With offices in
Argentina   Austria   Brazil   Chile   Czech Republic   France   Greece
Guatemala   Hungary   Italy   Japan   Poland   Portugal   Singapore
South Korea   Switzerland   Thailand   Turkey   Ukraine   Vietnam

For titles covered by Section 112 of the US Higher Education Opportunity Act,
please visit www.oup.com/us.he for the latest information about
pricing and alternate formats.

Published by Oxford University Press, Inc.
198 Madison Avenue, New York, New York 10016
http://www.oup.com

Library of Congress Cataloging-in-Publication Data
Lotz, Amanda D., 1974–
    Understanding media industries / Amanda Lotz, Timothy Havens.
        p. cm.
    Includes bibliographical references.
    ISBN 978-0-19-539767-3 (pbk. : alk. paper) 1. Mass media. I. Havens, Timothy. II. Title.
    PN90.L68 2011
    302.23—dc22
                                                                                        2010030017

Printing number: 9 8 7 6 5 4 3 2 1

Printed in the United States of America
on acid-free paper.

CONTENTS

PREFACE

—

Understanding Media Industries guides students through an introductory exploration of the complex and rapidly evolving media industries in the United States. The origins of this book are in the classroom. It grew out of our frustration with existing materials for our introductory media industries courses, which we've taught at various universities, in classrooms large and small, each of us for more than a decade. We found that existing textbooks tend to have *either* thematic and conceptual consistency *or* a thorough and nuanced understanding of the complexities of media industry operations, but none achieve both. Rather than simply cobble together an array of material from media economics, political economy, and more concrete explanations of actual industry practices (usually in collections with a chapter focused on various industries), we wanted to provide this material with a center—a core conceptual framework particularly crucial in an introductory class. Research and perspectives on media industry operation have grown tremendously in recent years, yet we have also found that frameworks of study or distinctive theoretical approaches (beyond that of political economy) remain lacking.

The Unique Approach of this Book: Industrialization of Culture
Among the key challenges of designing a media industry class are the variation among industries and national contexts and the impermanence of information as industry practices and structures change constantly. Consequently, we felt a conceptual framework would be the most valuable contribution we could make to the existing literature, with the idea that such a framework would provide a map for students becoming aware of media industries for the first time. In designing it, we interrogated many of the previously unexamined assumptions that have driven our own scholarship and findings. Rather than the prescriptive form we associate more with the creation of "models," we believe our "framework" brings a looser, yet productive, order to the variation characteristic of media industry operation and a language for speaking about media industries in a manner that has wide application.

Thus, after many long discussions about vocabulary and the relationships among media industries and their practices, we developed the Industrialization of Culture framework that provides the core organization of this book. The framework is a synthesis of many ideas that are now well established in media studies; its innovation is primarily its articulation and explanation of these ideas. Our primary goal was to allow for the complexity of media industry operation while nevertheless making these operations understandable at a conceptual level. For example, we sought to explain different payment schemes and how they can affect media content, while not providing a detailed listing of every variation of advertising or direct payment that can be found in contemporary media industries. We hope we offer a starting point that introduces novice students to the basic processes and components of media-making while setting forth a vocabulary and set of relationships (the framework) that more advanced students can use to begin to make applications.

Throughout, this book introduces and explains the Industrialization of Culture framework, which identifies the key areas and aspects of media industries that we must consider when analyzing how they function and why they do the things they do. The first three sections of the book develop this framework in considerable depth with extensive examples and illustrations. The last section then examines three developments—the rise of the symbolic economy, digitalization, and globalization—that are causing significant adjustment in media industry operation and explores how prior norms of operation are changing in every level of the framework.

We openly acknowledge it is impossible to write a concise text that explains all media industries, everywhere. Thus, we try to be succinct and provide only enough examples to make the point—allowing instructors to introduce further applications in their teaching or through assignments. We rely heavily on the framework as an organizing force in the hope that it provides a malleable tool for instructors that can be applied to a variety of teaching and media contexts. Certainly, valuable intellectual insights will come from identifying limitations of the framework and contexts in which its components have less explanatory value.

Scholars in a range of fields study media industries, and as a result there is considerable variation in the assumptions, methods, and goals of different types of research. The approach we take might be best described as that of "media studies." As media studies scholars, we believe that media and media industries are important because of their central role in the production and circulation of culture. We are interested in understanding the interaction between commercial industry realities (regulations, profit-maximization strategies, pricing, and so on) and the products of media industries (films, TV shows, music, and so on).[1] We seek to develop understandings of the media industries that make it clear they are "complex, ambivalent, and contested"[2]; we find that claims and theories about "the media" that suggest uniformity and consistency in their operation are simply not realistic.

Certain conditions may encourage media companies to perform in certain ways, but situations are often far more complicated than most grand theories about the media industries imagine. We are much more intrigued by exploring the situations that lead media companies to react or behave in unique or unexpected ways that force us to re-examine our basic assumptions. This is not to say that we'd describe our approach as acritical. Rather, we acknowledge the considerable capital and power of global media industries, but believe it productive to consider how their complexities and inconsistencies create opportunities for critical intervention. We are generally wary of the influence of commercial media culture on society, though we are by no means willing to dismiss commercial media outright. Unlike analysts we would characterize as "free marketeers," who believe that commercialization inevitably leads to a vibrant "marketplace of ideas" that best serves democratic societies, we begin with the assumption that capitalist societies are inherently unequal, as certain groups have more money and power than others; consequently, commercial media systems tend to suffer from the same kinds of inequities that permeate capitalist democracies.

Features of this Book

- **Application and Discussion Questions**. At the end of each chapter we've included some application and discussion questions. We've offered questions that are less about rote recall of information and instead provide the basis for group discussions. Many ask the students to begin from their own interests and experiences in such a way as to be useful as writing exercises as well. Whether your course is a large lecture with smaller discussion sections, or a smaller, discussion-driven class, we hope you will find these useful.

- **Suggestions for Further Reading**. Each chapter also includes suggestions for further reading. For the most part, our suggestions are established books that provide greater depth on the topics necessarily skimmed in this book. These are designed to be useful as a starting point for student research for assignments. Any of these books would also provide an excellent source for a book report. We also included a longer list of readings at the conclusion of Chapter 1. Here, we have listed a number of publications that offer overviews of specific industries, sorted by industry. These sources will be helpful for students who want to learn more about a particular industry.

Companion Website at www.oup.com/us/lotz

One of the joys—and challenges—of teaching about media industries is their ever-shifting nature. In this book we've deliberately focused on ideas and concepts likely to remain valid as long as this book is in print, leaving contemporary applications to the instructor. Instead of detailed listings and extensive data about who owns what, with what valuation, what circulation, etc., we provide a conceptual framework and encourage the instructor to supplement this book with whatever current information the semester brings. We'll keep links to recent information and developments on the book's website, along with annotations.

Annually Updated Instructor's Manual

Finally, we have created—and plan to update annually—an Instructor's Manual available as a PDF on the book's website at www.oup.com/us/lotz. While the Further Readings emphasize books and established literature, the Instructor's Supplement offers media links, ideas for application, and brief readings taken from recent articles. The book's website offers even more up-to-date links (with notation of which textbook material it relates to) that we hope will help you engage your students with the dynamism of contemporary media industry operations.

Acknowledgments

We'd like to thank many colleagues who have shared ideas with us throughout the drafting process, particularly Alisa Perren, Aswin Punathambekar, Douglas Schules, Serra Tinic, and Joe Turow. Also, sincere thanks to our anonymous reviewers as well as Jennifer Holt, University of California, Santa Barbara; Vicki Mayer, Tulane University; Paul Mihailidis, Hofstra University; Susan Moeller, University of Maryland; Kimberly Ann Owczarski, University of Arizona; Ann Savage, Butler University; and Sharon Sharp, California State University, Dominguez Hills, for their many thoughts and helpful suggestions. Also, we owe a considerable debt to our outstanding editorial assistant, Jimmy Draper, who helped us maintain consistency across the chapters and provided most of the magazine-industry examples throughout the book and supplementary materials, including the glossary, further readings, questions, and the teaching supplement. Our thanks as well to Peter Labella for his excellent editorial guidance, and Caitlin Kaufman for helping us through the editorial process.

We hope you enjoy this book! We welcome suggestions and comments from you.

Amanda D Lotz
lotz@umich.edu

Timothy Havens
timothy-havens@uiowa.edu

Notes

1. *See also* Timothy Havens, Amanda D. Lotz, and Serra Tinic, "Critical Media Industry Studies: A Research Approach." *Communication, Culture and Critique* 2 (2009): 234–53.
2. David Hesmondhalgh, *The Cultural Industries*, 2nd ed. (Thousand Oaks, CA: Sage, 2007), 4.

Understanding
Media Industries

CHAPTER 1

Key Concepts in Media Industry Studies

In an episode of the animated series *South Park* entitled "Gnomes," we meet an entrepreneurial group of gnomes who steal underwear for profit. They explain their business plan with the slide shown in Figure 1.1. None of the gnomes is sure what "Phase 2" is, but they all are certain that others know and, more important, that profit can be generated from stolen underpants.

The wisdom, or folly, of the Underpants Gnomes—their belief that they can somehow turn stolen underpants into hard cash—is similar in some ways to the commercial media's efforts to generate profits from cultural endeavors. The process of building and maintaining an industry on the commercial exploitation of cultural expression is a challenge. Unlike other industries specializing in the production of goods and services, such as the food industry or tax preparation services, none of us *needs* the kind of popular entertainment that the media industries provide. For generations, cultural activities, especially the kinds of domestic amusements that characterize the majority of our media consumption today, were nonprofessional, spontaneous, and free of charge. In addition, people's cultural tastes are far more fickle and unpredictable than their tastes in other goods and services, making media production a particularly risky business. Finally, media consumers are left with little but their memories afterwards, whereas consumers of wheat will be full, consumers of tax preparation services will have held off the IRS for one more year, and consumers of a cleaning service will have a clean house to come home to.

The fact that media do not fulfill essential human needs is often called the "nonutilitarian" feature of media. At the same time, while we may not *need* media, in the sense that we need food, many people nevertheless see media as central to the proper functioning of a democratic society—because democratic societies require public forums for discussion, and because media are widely available to the public in industrialized societies. Debates abound about the media's role as a forum for public communication, and the second section of this chapter introduces these debates. A related issue—the autonomy of people working in the industries to create media products as they see fit—is the focus of the third section

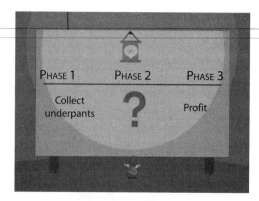

Figure 1.1 A gnome on South Park explains their business model.

of this chapter. And, finally, we explore the general economic and organizational principles by which the media industries operate. First, however, we introduce our own framework for understanding media industries, the Industrialization of Culture framework, which organizes the book.

UNDERSTANDING MEDIA INDUSTRIES

Despite the fact that most of us have spent many hours of our lives consuming media—perhaps as much as half of our waking hours—we may still know very little about how and why the media we enjoy are made. We are most familiar with the **media texts**—the shows, songs, films, magazines, and games that we watch, listen to, read, or play. We also may be quite savvy users of media. We know where to look for the texts we want and have established elaborate rituals of media use, such as reading a newspaper at breakfast, carrying portable music, or relaxing with particular television shows in the evening.

The one aspect of media that most people know the least about, however, is how they are organized into and operate as industries. Most of the media consumed worldwide are created by businesses aimed at making money, and media industries have been very profitable indeed. In 2008, for example, *Advertising Age* reported that the top 100 media companies in the United States brought in more than $300 billion in net profits.[1] The normal functioning of media industries may be outside of our general awareness, but understanding media industries is an important component of being an educated citizen and consumer in today's world.

WHY STUDY MEDIA INDUSTRIES?

By analyzing how media industries operate, we can better appreciate how and why the texts we interact with come to be created. Perhaps in other classes you have studied how the media can have social and cultural consequences. Studying media industries also intersects with such questions, but we begin looking at texts earlier in the process, before they reach audiences, before they are even created. One of the key questions in the study of media industries is how and why texts are created in the first place.

In most of the world and in most industries, media today are created primarily for profit, and for some observers, this is all we need to know: commercial media, they argue, operate like any other industries. While it is true, however, that most media industries are rooted in such profit motives, this is only part of the story. In the process of making money, the media industries also contribute to dialogues and discussions about important issues in a society and even to the enabling or disabling of democracy, a process we take up in more detail below.

Think about other industries: packaged food, automotive, furniture. How they operate their businesses does contribute to material culture, and their goods also produce meaningful cultural products, but there is something different about the role media play. Whether intentional or not, in the process of conducting their business, the media industries circulate ideas, attitudes, and information in society. Their products are important in framing civic discourse and perceptions of different cultures in ways that can affect public policy, elections, and our everyday lives. Thus, although in many cases the media industries operate with the goal of making money, they are significant cultural and political institutions as well. Balancing these two realities is necessary, and it is probably the most difficult aspect of engaging in serious and fair examination of the media industries.

So media industries warrant understanding for several reasons: first, they are increasingly important sectors of the American and world economies; second, they contribute to political discussions and even, at times, set the ground rules for political debate; and third, they contribute to our everyday lives in ways that are sometimes obvious and sometimes subtle.

Defining Media Industries

The following pages will offer you many ways to classify media based on various industry characteristics. When people say "the media," they often mean something far more specific, such as news outlets, television news outlets, or the local television news station in their community. A crucial part of understanding media industries requires that we identify precisely what media or medium we are talking about when examining a specific issue. One of our key tasks here is to illustrate the great variety of conditions and practices that lead media outlets to behave in certain ways.

With that said, this book would be far too long and heavy if we took an encyclopedic approach to explaining each aspect of every relevant media industry. Instead, throughout the book we write about the economic, regulatory, industrial, organizational, and creative practices that shape many media industries. Our main examples of media industries include those of television, radio, film, magazines, music, video games, and newspapers. We also attend to the situation of various "new media" when possible. Although these industries are clearly growing in importance, their short histories and fluid practices tend to frustrate efforts to write about them in current and insightful ways. Newspaper and radio may seem like old, and perhaps fading, media industries from the vantage point of today's media environment, but their long histories of adapting to various changes in industrial conditions are precisely what make them so useful for illustrating concepts of media industry operations.

Significant discrepancies also exist within any one industry. The economic norms of the magazine industry vary considerably among magazines that are entirely advertiser supported, those paid for exclusively through reader subscriptions, and others that blend advertiser and subscriber financing. Similar variation can be found in the television industry among broadcast television (networks such as NBC, ABC, and CBS), "basic cable" (channels such as ESPN, TNT, or USA), and "premium cable" (channels such as HBO and Showtime). Likewise, differences in production financing distinguish independent films from those produced by the Hollywood studios. To deal with this complexity, our framework identifies key operating conditions and business practices that influence the functioning of media industries, although the significance of each influence varies considerably in different contexts.

The Industrialization of Culture Framework

The framework we use for explaining the operation of media industries, shown in Figure 1.2, features three different levels of influence. The first level addresses the **mandate** of the media outlet under analysis, or the organization's foremost goals, its reason for operating. The second level of the framework examines the various **conditions** under which the media industries operate, which are typically broader than an individual company and regulate the behavior of an entire media sector. Finally, the third level addresses the day-to-day **practices** of the organizations and individuals who work in the various media industries. We often imagine the mandates, conditions, and practices organized vertically, but not necessarily in a

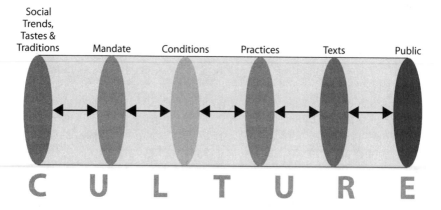

Figure 1.2 How media industries shape texts.

hierarchy. Instead, each of the levels influences all of the others as well as, crucially, the working conditions of the people in the media industries and the texts that they create.

We begin with the assumption that just about anything could *in theory* appear in the media, from the most abstract expressions of high art to the most offensive forms of pornography.

The uppermost portion of the framework, labeled "Social Trends, Tastes, and Traditions," identifies the range of social and cultural resources that media producers might possibly draw on when creating texts. Every culture possesses cultural and aesthetic traditions, such as genres, that shape the kinds of texts a media producer is likely to imagine, even before the operations of the media industries begin to influence the process. In addition, political traditions, such as freedom of the press in the United States, bear on how journalists envision their jobs and the kinds of stories they seek out. Each of the ensuing levels of the framework shapes the media text until we wind up with the actual texts that get produced and circulate within society.

Notice that culture forms the background for the entire Industrialization of Culture framework, suggesting how culture influences the industries' mandates, conditions, and practices. We use the term **culture** in two related senses throughout the book: first, in an aesthetic sense, to refer to the texts that the media industries produce, such as films, newspapers, and the like; second, in an anthropological sense, to refer to the specific social practices, values, mores, and hierarchies associated with a particular group of people. The anthropological sense of culture explains why some nations favor public or commercial mandates, why they enact particular laws governing the types of content that can be broadcast, and a whole host of other conditions and practices. More commonly, however, we will use the anthropological definition of culture to address the ways in which the people who work at all levels of the media industries exist within industrial cultures that shape their views of themselves, the texts they produce, and the audiences they engage.

Our use of the term "culture" in the framework also includes members of the public in a variety of different roles that relate to the media industries: as members of political pressure groups, as consumers of commercial products, as audiences for media texts, and as citizens. Groups of citizens banded together can influence the regulatory conditions of the media industries, as well as the industry's economic conditions through advertiser boycotts. As consumers, members of the public are divided into demographic groups by the advertising industry and persuaded, often through commercial media outlets, to buy products. While audiences for media texts do not get direct input into the practices of the media industries, commercial media producers always have audiences in mind when making production decisions. In a sense, the audience functions as a ghost that haunts every level of our framework. Thus, although we don't focus much upon how audiences consume media, what importance it plays in their lives, or the economics of media consumption, our framework accounts for the variety of ways that members of the public influence media industry operations.

Mandates

The first level in the Industrialization of Culture framework asks, "What is the mandate of the media industry?" A mandate is the primary goal or the reason for being of the media industry—and this contributes significantly to how the media industry is likely to behave and what texts it is likely to produce. Almost all large-scale media operations today function under a **commercial mandate**. Such media primarily value the earning of profits and thus make decisions based on the perceived consequence of the profitability of content, whether such content is sold directly to audiences or as supported by advertisers. With the exception of the Public Broadcasting System (PBS) and National Public Radio (NPR), nearly all media of nationwide scale in the United States operate with a commercial mandate. Commercial media systems tend not to be democratic—in other words, some audiences are considered more valuable than others. As a result, some people, typically those who are younger and/or have higher incomes, enjoy far greater choices of media texts designed for them.

There are exceptions to media with a commercial mandate, as we'll explain in more detail in Chapter 2. Various **noncommercial mandates** include public, community, alternative/DIY, and governmental mandates. Media operating with these mandates primarily value something other than commercial profits. In the case of the British Broadcasting Company (BBC) and PBS, that priority is serving the needs of the citizens of the nation that support those media outlets with tax money. Media with a community mandate are similar, but they exist to serve far more specific groups, as in the case of community radio or a community newsletter. Media produced with an alternative, or DIY (do-it-yourself), mandate often seek to fill a void in existing media outlets or are primarily vehicles of self-expression for creators. Finally, media produced with a governmental mandate are characterized by tight governmental control over content and are typically exercised by a totalitarian regime. In fact, most totalitarian regimes of the past century have exhibited this tendency to use media outlets as mouthpieces, including South Africa's South African Broadcasting Corporation during apartheid, the Soviet Union's TASS news service, and Myanmar's film industry since 1988.

Conditions

The next level in our framework encompasses what we call **conditions**. Conditions are larger than any individual entity and organize how media industries can operate. The available **technology**, for instance, contributes considerably to defining the possibilities available to media industries. Technology can affect how professionals produce media, as in the case of digital publishing and recording equipment. Technology can also affect the distribution of media, as in the case of Internet music distribution leading to piracy and the undermining of traditional music industry business models. Technology also governs how we exhibit media, enabling us to freely move texts among various display devices.

Regulation also functions as a condition—often particular to a specific country and industry—that encompasses the legal rules within which media companies operate. There are many different types of regulation that govern media industries, but most can be categorized as regulations on business structure and practice; regulations on technical standards; or regulations on content. Media industries face some of the same regulations that every industry faces; however, we emphasize those regulations that have developed to deal with the unique social and political qualities of media.

Economics provide another significant condition that affects how media industries operate. Economic considerations include how the ownership norms of a specific media industry might affect the content it produces. Two of the most significant changes in media industries over the past few decades have been the steady **conglomeration** of many different kinds of companies under a single corporate umbrella, and the **consolidation of ownership** of the conglomerates into a few global behemoths. Additionally, economic matters such as norms for funding media production or whether consumers pay for media through subscription, direct pay, advertiser funding, or other methods also function as economic conditions.

One final point about each of these conditions is that they rarely operate independently. That is, changes in one of the conditions typically alter each of the others. For example, the introduction of digital distribution technologies has eroded the typical distinction that the Federal Communications Commission (FCC), the primary governing body in the United States, drew between broadcasting and telecommunications companies and the regulations that applied to them. Today, broadcasters, cable providers, and telephone companies all carry voice, video, and data services, and the FCC increasingly regulates these industries in similar ways. In today's media world, each of these conditions is in a period of transition due to a number of factors that we detail in the later chapters of this book, including globalization, technological digitization, and the shift from an industrial to a symbolic economy.

Practices

The final level of our framework encompasses a myriad of professional roles, people who are responsible for the day-to-day operation of media industries, and the content they produce. We designate these as **practices**, an umbrella term that can include a broad range of workers and activities. In one of the classic textbooks about media systems, Joseph Turow identified at least thirteen different "power roles" that describe the duties and activities of media industry workers (see Table 1.1).[2]

For the sake of clarity, we have organized these roles into three distinct types of practices: creative practices, distribution and exhibition practices, and auxiliary practices.

Creative practices encompass the tasks and workers involved in the making of media texts. Distribution and exhibition practices include workers and activities that bring finished media texts to the audience. Auxiliary practices comprise numerous other practices that exist somewhat outside the media industries, but that remain crucial to their functioning and contribute meaningfully to

Table 1.1 Turow's "Power Roles"

TUROW'S "POWER ROLES" OF A MASS MEDIA INDUSTRY	
Set conditions of media-making	Authorities
Make, fund media	Producers
	Creators
	Investors
	Clients
	Auxiliaries
	Unions
	Facilitators
Make media available	Distributors
	Exhibitors
	Linking pins
Consume, respond to media	Publics
	Public advocacy groups

circumscribing textual possibilities. These auxiliary practices include the advertising industry, audience measurement services, promotion and criticism of media products, and dubbing, among others.

Our framework is intended to be multidirectional, by which we mean that each level influences the others. In most instances, we imagine the Industrialization of Culture framework functioning sort of like an old-fashioned pinball machine, in which every individual ball travels a unique path through the playing field, as determined by the skill of the player and the various objects that each ball encounters. In our metaphor, illustrated in Figure 1.3, the particular culture within which the media industries operate determines the placement of the bumpers, spinners, chutes, flippers, and special bonuses that each ball (or idea) must negotiate.

The large bumpers that deflect the balls, determining their speed and trajectory, represent the "Mandates" in our model. The various smaller bumpers, spinners, ramps, and chutes that alter a ball's speed and direction in less dramatic ways represent "Conditions." Finally, the "Practices" of the industries and the people who work in them are represented by the players themselves, who demonstrate varying degrees of skill operating the plunger and the flippers to initiate and redirect each pinball. Even though all of these features are the same every time, each ball (or each idea for a song, news story, film, TV show, game) travels a unique path through the playfield, making the impact of the Mandate, Conditions, and Practices on each text unpredictable. Any thorough analysis of how a particular text came into being must account for the ways in which all of the conditions and practices represented in the framework influence one another and the final text, and these insights are not inevitably transferrable to other texts, industries, locations, or historical periods.

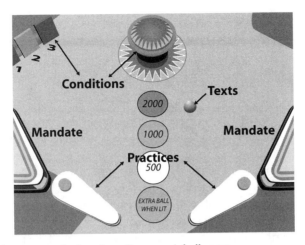

Figure 1.3 The process of cultural creation as a pinball game.

The discussion of media systems' mandates, conditions, and practices offered here is meant as a quick introduction to these concepts. The next chapters focus on each level and their components in much greater depth to better explain what they are and why they are important to understanding the operation of media industries. Our hope is that the Industrialization of Culture framework can be useful for establishing an understanding of many different media industries in many different contexts. After we explain all of the components of the framework, we turn our attention to three developments—the rise of the symbolic economy, digitization, and globalization—that are redefining the operation of media industries. Understanding how these developments are leading to changes in different aspects of the framework and the media industries will prepare you well for assessing the current state and future operations of the media.

MEDIA INDUSTRIES IN SOCIETY

As we have already mentioned, media texts are simultaneously nonutilitarian *and* socially important in industrialized societies. In the final section of this chapter, we will explore some of the basic strategies that the industries have developed to try to generate predictable profits from such nonutilitarian commodities. In this section and the next, however, we examine the main debates about the role of media industries in society. In particular, we focus on media operating with commercial mandates, which have been the commonest forms of media in the United States for nearly a century. And, for nearly just as long, the impact of commercial media on democracy, cultural diversity, and the autonomy of creative workers have been important topics of debate among scholars.

Communications technologies have fascinated politicians, business people, philosophers, and poets since their earliest incarnations in the late nineteenth century. These observers tend to veer between utopian hopes about the capacity of mass communications to enhance democracy and cultural understanding, to fearful condemnations that the media are brainwashing the masses and destroying individuality. Such extremes may seem normal to us in an era of instantaneous, global Internet communications, but it is important to remember that the hopes and fears that communications technologies engender have a much longer history. We can see these traces as far back as the nineteenth century, when Rudyard Kipling wrote of deep sea cable technology in 1897, "They have wakened the timeless Things; they have killed their father Time;/ Joining hands in the gloom, a league from the last of the sun./ Hush! Men talk to-day o'er the waste of the ultimate slime,/ And a new Word runs between: whispering, "Let us be one!"[3] Here, we see effusive praise and hope for a technology that most of us today would consider pretty mundane. The point remains, however, that communications technologies stir deep human passions, and for this reason, the organizations that operate them and the cultural products that they circulate have long been objects of concerns for society.

The utopian versions of communications technologies got a significant boost with the introduction of radio **broadcasting** in the early decades of the twentieth century. Broadcasting permitted a single transmission to reach hundreds, even thousands, of listeners with the same message at the same time. In many ways, this development was the beginning of modern-day **mass media**, or the creation and distribution of information and entertainment to mass audiences. Once again, philosophers and poets saw this ability to reach unprecedented numbers of people as an opportunity to increase understanding and democracy. Politicians, meanwhile, saw a chance to bring their perspectives and arguments to large swaths of the voting public. And businesspeople saw great opportunities to reach across the nation with their promotional messages.

Alongside the soaring hopes about the democratic potential of the mass media has run an equally powerful sense of fear, having to do with their unknown persuasive powers. Various anecdotal accounts of the powerful effects of radio broadcasting on listeners' perceptions and actions abounded as these technologies emerged, perhaps most notably in relation to the 1938 broadcast of Orson Welles' radio adaptation of the H.G. Wells novel *The War of the Worlds* (1898). Reportedly, after hearing this broadcast, which was performed as a series of news flashes that interrupted "regular" programming, thousands of listeners fled in horror from New York City as "Martians" invaded. Although the accuracy of these reports is debated, the incident still served as an example of the persuasive powers of the relatively new medium of radio broadcasting. Moreover, the broadcast took place in the midst of Nazi movements in Germany and elsewhere, which strove hard to influence citizens' opinions and actions through mass **propaganda**. Radio became a favored tool for Nazi propaganda, as were films and parades, again adding to widespread fears about broadcasting's social influence.

This example from the early years of radio illustrates that the media industries and the texts they produce have typically been treated differently than other industries because of widespread perceptions that their "products" possess the potential for great social good and harm. For this reason, governments have tended to regulate the media industries differently, and the relationship between commercial forces and the media industries has been more controversial than in most other industries. Take, for instance, the automobile industry. While numerous individuals and groups protest the commercial control of the media industries, the public at large accepts a commercial automobile industry without question, because cars are not seen as having the kinds of social and political potential that media products do.[4]

All Media Matter in the Public Sphere

Understanding exactly how media industries—particularly commercial industries—influence society and politics has been a matter of some debate. Many observers distinguish between entertainment and information services, with the latter typically identified as more serious and more important for the proper functioning of democratic societies. This perspective emerges from the belief that noninformational media are "only entertainment" and thus unlikely to play a significant role in shaping attitudes about political and social issues. We disagree strongly with this position, and sketch out below our reasons for those beliefs. First, however, let us examine information-oriented media industries and their special social and legal status.

The idea that information is central to the proper functioning of democratic societies dates back to the days of the American Revolution and earlier. The unique position of informational media was enshrined in the Constitution of the United States, which guarantees "freedom of speech, or of the press," and this idea of a free press has, more recently, been recognized as a universal human right by the United Nations. The presses of eighteenth- and nineteenth-century America differed significantly from what we today associate with newspapers; in particular, they were more frequently a place for extreme partisanship rather than objective news. One newspaper, for instance, persistently referred to President Rutherford B. Hayes—whose election victory many people doubted—as "his Fraudlency," while another called Andrew Jackson's wife a "whore" on numerous occasions.[5] Despite these excesses, press freedom enjoyed protected legal status because of the widespread recognition that vigorous, even vulgar, debate is necessary if democratic governments want to try to respond to and represent the interests of the public at large.

The German social theorist Jürgen Habermas coined the phrase "**public sphere**" to refer to the unique space for public debate that the mass media can provide in modern societies. His ideas have been clarified, critiqued, and expanded by a large number of other theorists over the years, but the basic concept has remained and become quite popular, even outside academia: that functioning democracies need to create a public space for the expression and debate of important social ideas, and that the mass media provide one powerful, *potential* vehicle for such discussions. For this reason, most public sphere theorists agree, media industries need to be free of substantial control by either governmental or business interests if they are to fulfill their proper public sphere functions.

Notice that we included interference from both government and commercial forces as possible threats to the vibrancy of the public sphere. In the United States, we are more likely to think about the dangers of government influence on the press—or what we have called a **governmental mandate**—than about the dangers of commercial influence. This may have to do with the history of enemy propaganda during WWII, greater faith in the democratic potential of free markets than in most other nations, or a host of other reasons. Regardless of its origins, however, in both cases the concern is that journalistic **objectivity** in investigating and reporting stories might be compromised by meddling institutions that stand to gain or lose from whether and how stories are reported. Indeed, numerous examples of interference in editorial integrity and decision-making litter American history, some of which we recount in the pages that follow.

The metaphor of the public sphere has also been extended to include entertainment media based on an argument that entertaining texts are also significant in forming our worldviews and perspectives about society, but its main emphasis has been journalism, and most discussions about the public sphere tend to either ignore or short-shrift thorough discussions about entertainment. Instead, most scholars who work with entertainment media adopt something closer to Horace Newcomb and Paul Hirsch's metaphor of the "cultural forum."[6] In this conceptualization, media are not judged for their degree of independence from government or industry, but rather assessed for the **ideologies** they incorporate.[7]

The term "ideology" conventionally carries derogatory connotations of overly politicized attitudes toward subjects or issues that are seen as apolitical. Because critical researchers believe that no topics or areas of human endeavor are free from political considerations, however, ideology is a far more neutral term in their vocabularies, referring simply to the worldviews that lie behind and give meaning to those endeavors. We think of ideologies as lenses that we use to interpret the world around us. Just as with contacts or magnifying glasses, the ideologies that structure our belief systems influence *what* we see, and what we see influences *how* we understand the world. Whether we recognize them or not, all of us believe in countless ideologies, some of which are well thought through, others of which we may be almost completely unaware.

The focus on ideology in media studies comes from a revision of conventional theories of Marxism, which tries to examine how we come to understand the world, our place in it, and our relationships with others, as well as whose interests are served and ignored by those understandings. **Dominant ideology** is the term used to refer to the social common sense of our time, and the capacity to define that common sense can be a powerful political tool. Moreover, most media scholars believe that the media are important purveyors of social common sense.

We can begin to get a clearer idea of what this social common sense is and the role that both informational and entertainment media play in constituting it if we think about contemporary definitions of terrorism in the United States.

Without getting into explosive political debates, we think it safe to say that, in some instances, one person's "terrorist" is another's "freedom fighter." How do we come to believe that a particular incident is the work of terrorists rather than freedom fighters? Certainly the way in which news media and government sources frame and explain the attack has a lot to do with it, but it also matters whether the person fits our general idea of what a terrorist looks like. And, more likely than not, some of our ideas about what terrorists look like come from entertainment media.

The terrorism example makes reference to contemporary politics, but ideology is also political in a much broader sense, in that it influences our ideas about what societal groups we do and don't belong to, and what the traits of those groups are. In these instances, scholars typically evaluate media based on whether they support or challenge social inequities. For instance, African-American women in 2004 earned only sixty-eight cents for every dollar earned by a white male. While we cannot attribute the entire wage gap to media representations, the conventional image of African-American women in music videos as brainless sex objects may well contribute to a mindset that understands these earning differences as either natural or unimportant. Where the scholarly analysis of media texts tries to identify the ideologies present in media texts, the processes whereby various ideologies get embedded into media texts, how they get framed, and how they are organized, silenced, privileged, or dismissed vis-à-vis other ideologies are a primary focus of much of the research on the media industries.

AGENCY OF MEDIA PROFESSIONALS

The question of the ideologies present in media texts brings us quickly to debates about the autonomy or **agency** of the people who work in the media industries. To put the matter bluntly: are they talented individuals expressing their creative visions for clear political and ideological ends, or are they merely cogs in corporate machines trying to satiate the masses by producing texts full of ideological messages that maintain the interests of those in power? Given the massive number of stories that demonstrate neither of these extreme positions is accurate, it is safe to say that most observers today think that the truth of the matter lies somewhere in between, but little agreement exists on how we can assess autonomy and its consequences.

Some scholars argue that, by the time creative workers in most industries achieve a degree of autonomy, they have already internalized the worldviews of the corporations they work for. This includes journalists at major news outlets who wield editorial authority. What is more, these powerful creative and editorial workers are among the most elite members of society, and they consequently tend to share the same worldviews as one another and the elite owners and executives of the corporations they work for. In other words, while these creators may not simply be cogs in the corporate machine who reproduce the ideologies that serve corporate interests, their ideological orientations may not fall very far from the corporate tree.

At the same time, in order for media texts to become popular—and therefore profitable—they cannot merely rehearse ideologies that serve the interests of society's elites, because elites make up a tiny fraction of the American society, and most of them consume very little popular media. Likewise, with regard to journalism, stories and outlets that are persistently biased toward elite points-of-view would carry very little influence or interest with most of the public. Therefore, both entertainment and information media have to include a wider range of ideological positions in order to survive and thrive.

Again, while most scholars recognize that popular media contain a range of ideologies, their interpretations of the significance and consequences of those inclusions differ markedly. Some believe that popular media include nondominant ideologies as a way to domesticate the threats they pose to the dominant order. That is, popular media essentially work to inoculate the social system against significant threats to the status quo. For instance, in the 1970s, feminism posed a challenge to the traditional male dominance of American society, and many critics believe that television programs helped prevent more significant social changes by channeling feminist political critiques into personal relationships and the private sphere. On the other hand, some scholars believe that including nondominant ideologies in popular media gives those ideologies recognition and potentially increases their capacity to change society.[8]

Of course, these debates about the ideological impact of popular media on society go beyond the immediate concerns of a textbook about the media industries. Still, our recognition of these larger issues influences how we understand the role of workers in the media industries, their relationships to the organizations they work for, and our assessments of their general autonomy with regard to creative expression and editorial independence. For these reasons, it is important that we specify our take on these issues from the outset, because they will influence how we assess and explain the media industries throughout the book. First, we believe that media workers consistently strive for, and frequently achieve, some degree of autonomy with regard to editorial and creative decisions. In fact, most media organizations have tended to give creative people wide berth when it comes to creating texts, because those in charge of the organizations recognize how impossible it is to predict quality and popularity. Still, when a large number of people have varying degrees of creative control, which is often the case with media texts, the nature of that text is, to some degree, a product of the negotiations among all who participate in producing it.

Second, we believe that, once nondominant ideologies are included in popular media, those texts have very little capacity to influence their broader social uptake and impact. In this way, it is probably less important whether media workers are looking to change or inoculate society with their texts, and more important what people do with those texts and—especially—how the audience's uptake of those texts and their ideologies ricochet back into the practices and ideologies of media workers themselves.

Because of our perspectives on ideology and worker autonomy, we place media workers at the center of our analyses of media industry operations. For others, particularly scholars working from a **political economy of media** perspective, the main issues are the economics of supply and demand or the drive of large conglomerates to control risks by dominating markets and destroying competitors. While we also attend to these issues in the Industrialization of Culture framework, we mainly try to understand them in terms of how they shape the perceptions and working conditions of people in the media industries. For this reason, it is worthwhile to pause for a moment and explain how we understand the issue of individual autonomy in a little more detail.

Debates about individual autonomy revolve around the question of how much agency we have to make our own choices. We work from a perspective of **circumscribed agency**, which assumes that the choices we make in our lives are not wholly our own, but neither are they simply imposed upon us by outside forces. While it is a widespread idea in American culture that all of us are free-thinking and free-acting individuals who have complete control over our lives, our opinions, and our tastes, few serious thinkers believe that such an extreme theory of individualism is an accurate characterization of contemporary societies. Specifically, a host of modern institutions and cultural traditions encourage us to think and act in similar ways, and to cultivate tastes that reflect our particular social locations and aspirations. In general, we internalize these attitudes and tastes so deeply that they seem to us as though they spring spontaneously from ourselves. With regard to media production, three main influences work to mold creative workers' individual visions into socially sanctioned forms: the general culture itself, formal and informal professional expectations, and specific organizational practices and norms.

Forces that Circumscribe Agency

One of the clearest ways to think about how cultural traditions circumscribe individual creativity is to consider the case of music. Anyone who has learned to play an instrument through formal instruction knows that mastering scales is crucial. Scales get you used to how notes should sound in relation to one another and which notes and chords do and do not go together, and scales allow you to anticipate developments and changes in a musical piece. At the same time, conventional scales privilege certain types of music and musical expression that predominate in Western music, but are sometimes absent in music from other parts of the world, including the preference for harmony and consonance. By the time you become a concert virtuoso or composer, you will have internalized these structures so thoroughly that it will be nearly impossible to play or write music without them. While the aesthetic dimensions of the music example are clear, it is more difficult to see how this process works with regard to ideology, because the ideologies of music are generally more subtle and intuitive than the ideologies of other media texts. Still, if we think about the ways in which various artists, cultural institutions, and schools privilege certain types of musical expression over others, and how musical practices from foreign or nondominant groups can get suppressed because they don't fit dominant models, we can begin to get a sense of how what might seem to be objective, conventional, and natural ways of expressing oneself can, in fact, be political and domineering.

When it comes to popular media texts, a wide range of **conventions** typically restricts both aesthetic and ideological creativity. **Genre**, a French word that simply means "type," is one of the main restrictions, because popular media texts must generally fit conventional genre definitions before they can get made. Genres help guarantee that a new text will find an appropriate and willing audience. For instance, band members who decide to release a death metal album are not only choosing to work in a conventional genre, but are also typically choosing to write music for suburban, white, male teenagers and young adults. Conventions often carry the illusion of quality, professionalism, or inevitability. What we mean is that particular ways of doing things, such as the editing of a situation comedy or norms of composing music, come to be seen as the only way of doing things—or the way that professionals do them. As you might suspect, these technical or aesthetic issues always have ideological dimensions to them, even if they are often subtle and easy to ignore. For instance, in Hollywood films of the 1940s, it was conventional to shoot dialogues between male and female leads with a low camera angle that made the man look tall and powerful and a high camera angle that made the woman look short and vulnerable, thereby reinforcing patriarchal gender roles.

Professional organizations can also circumscribe the autonomy of media professionals. One of the clearest examples of this influence comes from organizations such as the Society for Professional Journalists, which publishes a code of ethics that members are supposed to follow, influencing both what stories journalists report and how they report them. In most media professions, however, such codes of ethics are less common and less specific. Instead, the main sway that those organizations have over members comes through trade journals and conventions that reward and teach industrywide "best practices." While these best practices are primarily technical and aesthetic in nature, as we have already suggested, they also operate as bearers of ideology.

Finally, different organizations have different rules, practices, and cultures that tend to influence how media professionals ply their trades. Formal and informal, these influences include the degree of job security people feel, ideas about the corporate brand, the degree of formality in dress and decorum around the office, and so forth. For instance, when General Electric took over NBC in 1986, it established far more job security for programming executives than was the norm for American broadcasters at the time. As a result, programmers felt that they could nurture underperforming series longer without fear of losing their jobs due to poor ratings. The big television hits of the 1990s, including *Friends* and *Seinfeld*, benefited from this strategy, because it took them a long time to build audiences, and both series would probably have been cancelled in their first seasons if it weren't for the change in corporate culture at NBC that GE inaugurated.[9]

We focused in this section on three main theoretical principles that explain our perspective on how much autonomy—or agency—media workers have. The first principle is what we've called "circumscribed agency," which conceives of the people who work in commercial media organizations as agents with some degree of individual autonomy, even though their autonomy is delimited by a range of forces, including the cultures from which they come, the conventions of the media they work in, and the priorities of their organizations and superiors. The second principle is ideological uncertainty, which suggests that, no matter how much media creators may try to control the ideological content of the programs they produce, the political volatility of that content, the unpredictability of audience interpretation, and the collective nature of production make it impossible to pre-ordain the impact of media texts on society. The final principle is the relative isolation of media producers, which explains that, to the extent that media workers and organizations care about the political impact of their texts, only those issues that find their way back to them—usually through advertiser or activist pressure—have an influence on production practices and decisions.

KEY ECONOMIC ASPECTS OF
THE MEDIA INDUSTRIES

As we have said, conventions of genre, camerawork, editing, scale progression, band composition, etc., are rampant in popular media industries. Likewise, journalism tends to have equally numerous and rigid conventions. To some extent, these conventions ensure quality, but more than that, they help diminish the economic **risk** that commercial media organizations face. Along with a host of other **adaptive strategies**, conventional practices help to make commercial media production more predictable—or, at least, they help media executives to feel that the business is more predictable. In this section, we trace out some of the unique aspects of the commercial media industries before detailing some of the adaptive strategies that the industry has developed to help defray risks.

Economist Richard E. Caves identifies some of the particularly challenging aspects of media industry operation that make them financially riskier than many other industries.[10] First, he recognizes an issue he calls **nobody knows**, which describes how much more difficult it is to predict what products will succeed than it is in most other industries. Countless times, media producers have developed texts with every characteristic of a previously successful one, only to see the new one fail while an idea that has never before succeeded unexpectedly draws record crowds. While every industry faces financial risks, the nature of cultural commodities prevents many of the tactics that reduce risk and uncertainty in other industries from being effective.

One of the unique aspects of the commercial media industries is the high level of **sunk costs**. If you are making a movie, for instance, you need to spend the entire budget of millions of dollars before you have any sense of whether it's any good. Consequently, media industries typically have what are called high **first-copy costs** and relatively low **reproduction costs**. In other words, nearly all of the money that goes into media production must be spent to shoot the film, record the album, or make the show (first-copy costs). After that, the cost of distribution—or getting the content to millions of homes, theaters, or retail outlets—is comparatively low (reproduction costs).

Due to high sunk costs and low reproduction costs, economists consider most media texts as **public** or **semi-public goods**. Despite what the name suggests, public goods are not things that are good for the public, but rather commodities that are not destroyed or used up in the process of consuming them. An expensive dinner is a good example of a **private good**, because once you've eaten it, no one else can enjoy it. By contrast, when you watch a television show or see a film, it typically doesn't prevent someone else from also doing so. Compare the media industries with the automotive industry, for instance. Carmakers also have extensive first-copy costs, as millions of research and development dollars are required to design a new car model. Although those expenses can be amortized over the millions of cars built in that model, each car still has pretty substantial reproduction costs—the steel, glass, materials, and labor necessary to build each car. The result is a private good: when you buy or lease a car, no one else can benefit from the labor and goods required to manufacture it. In contrast, the cost of burning a CD or DVD or distributing a television show by broadcast or cable is comparatively insignificant compared to the cost of making the original text. Moreover, that text may be consumed by millions of fans, all of whom can enjoy the music, program, or film without preventing anyone else from doing so as well.

The high sunk costs associated with media production create their own challenges for media companies, because larger production budgets do not always lead to greater revenues. Producers can always spend more money on a product— perhaps in more costly special effects or in paying for a bigger star—but those expenditures are less guaranteed to pay off than in many other industries.[11] For example, in crafting a chair, a furniture maker might face a choice between using pine, a light and fairly inexpensive wood, or oak, a dense and more expensive wood. The furniture maker knows the decision to use oak will make it a stronger chair and that consumers will recognize that strength and be willing to pay more for it. Media consumers, by contrast, typically pay the same amount for media products (a ticket to a first-run film costs the same regardless of its production cost). Instead, media producers must try to calculate how many more people might see a film if more expensive special effects are used, and whether those additional people will provide enough additional revenue to balance the cost.

An issue related to the questionable benefits of additional costs is the **A-list/ B-list issue**.[12] Selecting talent to star in or record media texts defies norms that govern the economic decisions of many other industries. A relatively unknown actress may offer just as good of a performance as an established star with a salary ten times higher, but sometimes featuring the star is what makes people see the film. Unlike the example of furniture construction above, in which oak will always be heavier than pine, the popularity of actors and directors can wane without cause, or an actor who had previously offered top performances may turn in below-par work. It is very difficult to assign value to the status of creative staff in the media industry in a manner similar to tallying the production costs of many other industries.

Sometimes, the products of the media industries also require a long period before they begin returning profits. In the case of television production, for instance, it has been commonplace for studios to lose money on network shows for the first three to five years, and some movies do not begin to turn a profit until they are released on DVD. On the other side of the equation, companies may continue earning profits on a media text for decades after production is completed, a phenomenon known as the "**ars longa**," or the long economic life of media industry products.[13] For instance, Apple Records, a label founded by the Beatles in 1968, continues to receive revenues when a consumer buys one of its Beatles CDs today.

Finally, the creative products that the media industries produce lead to what might be considered irrational behavior in other industries. Many of the creative workers who supply the lifeblood of the media industries pursue their crafts with an "**art for art's sake**" attitude. Indeed, there are many who work in these industries whose primary incentive is to make the types of shows, music, games, or movies that are likely to make the most money, but there are also many who would willingly give up some of the profits in order to have more control over the production, to make the story they really want to tell, or to work on a schedule that better matches their creative process. As a result, those involved in the media industries often do not behave in the same profit-centered manner as workers in most other commercial industries.

Media Industry Responses to Risk

In response to the unique economic conditions that distinguish the media industries from other commercial endeavors, practitioners have developed a number of strategies to balance or compensate for the challenges. First, media industries engage in **intentional overproduction** in an effort to offset inevitable miscalculations against a broad repertoire. For example, David Hesmondhalgh notes that "nearly thirty thousand music albums are released in the U.S. each year, of which fewer than two per cent sell more than fifty thousand copies."[14] Record industry executives are well aware that most albums—98 percent by Hesmondhalgh's figures—won't achieve wide sales, and in response, they are faced with choosing among a few strategies. They could produce fewer albums and put far more resources into them or they could spread budgets widely. Likewise, each year, typically 80 percent of new television shows fail, yet every year the networks roll out a broad slate, instead of attempting to nurture just a few. Most media industries choose the latter strategy of overproduction—what Hesmondhalgh calls balancing flops against hits—because of the unpredictability of identifying which media texts will achieve commercial success.

Another practice, which has begun to erode in some sectors of the industries, is the creation of **artificial scarcity**. For decades, film viewers have accepted that they must go to a theater if they want to see the newest films, and that they'll have to wait six months to a year to rent or buy a copy of the film and even longer to have the opportunity to view it on television. Long before the advent of the VCR, residents of small and rural towns accepted that films would "open" in big cities and that they'd have to wait weeks or months for the films to reach local theaters. There is nothing natural about such practices; rather, they indicate a procedure by which the industry attempts to create scarcity in order to stretch the life of creative goods and allow **price differentiation**, or the fact that it costs about $10 to see a movie right now in the theater, but only $3 or less if you wait a few months to rent it. These efforts to create price differentiation through artificial scarcity are part of the process of distribution **windowing**, which we explore in more detail in Chapter 7.

Some of the responses to the uncertainty of knowing what consumers might like lead the industry to create particular types of texts. This is where genre and conventions come in handy. Genres and conventions are two examples of how the media industries rely heavily on **formats or formatting**—using known and successful textual forms. Formatting is clearly in evidence in the use of sequels in the film industry, but also in more general practices like using known star talent, whether actors, writers, or directors. Formatting is part of the media industry's strategy for predicting outcomes. Although "nobody knows," it is sometimes the case that formulas that have succeeded previously will do so again—at least until they become tired or overdone. Formatting may seem like grasping at straws, but it may provide the most likely prediction of success and goes a long way toward explaining why so much of what the media industries produce resembles previous products. We explore these techniques in greater detail in Chapter 6.

Finally, in addition to textual and business strategies, the media industries also employ organizational strategies for dealing with risk and uncertainty. One key practice involves taking advantage of **economies of scale.** Economies of scale operate in many industries, but they are particularly important to media industries because of high first-copy costs and the "public good" nature of their products. Economies of scale are achieved when the average cost of a commodity decreases with expansion of output. In media industries, economies of scale explain why we have a network television system. In the early days of radio, which was television's predecessor, local entities and communities developed their own stations and filled the hours with programs. The local reach limited potential sponsors to those in the local community, and developing a full day of programming for every station was costly. The reach of the broadcast signal was limited by geography, which meant hundreds of stations around the country arguably duplicated each other's efforts. The network system—in which one centralized entity creates programming that is distributed to stations throughout the country—allowed broadcasters to take advantage of economies of scale. With the ability to deliver hundreds of thousands of listeners—instead of hundreds or thousands—networks could sell advertising to national corporations and aggregate the money spread across the programming budgets of 200-some stations nationwide into one high-end production.

Here's another example that might bring home the concept of economies of scale. Universities often use this principle in lecture classes. Instead of capping classes at thirty students, lectures often enroll 100 or more students. The lecturer might deliver the exact same presentation, whether speaking to thirty students or 130, but the university is able to meet the credit needs of (and collect tuition dollars from) 100 more students. Here, too, we see the advantage from the university's perspective that can be gained by economies of scale. It is important to note that there is also a downside in both these cases. In amassing large audiences, media often have to sacrifice some of the local flavor that made content particular to where it was created, just as lecturers and students lose the intimacy of one-on-one conversations when enrollments multiply.

Conglomeration and **consolidation of ownership** are two further organizational adaptations to risk, which, some would argue, have become particularly pronounced over the last few decades. Conglomeration refers to the integration of previously distinct sectors of media industries under a single corporate umbrella. The Walt Disney Company, for example, was once merely a film studio, but it has since expanded into broadcast and cable television, magazine publishing, radio and recorded music, the Internet, and even book publishing, as well as a number of nonmedia sectors like theme parks and toy merchandising. In the past, each media industry was quite distinct and generally dominated by a small **oligopoly** of large corporations, which tended to share both hits and flops with a certain level of consistency. With the rise of new digital delivery platforms that allow us to get all of our music, voice, video, information, and data needs through a single provider such as a cable company, however, along with the continuing **segmentation** and **fragmentation** of audiences, the model of a small number of firms dominating a single sector of the media industries has begun to change.

Conglomerates are able to diversify their profit centers and spread risk by developing multifaceted corporate networks that include holdings in production and distribution, and span a broad range of media and entertainment services such as film, television, magazines, books, sports teams, and entertainment parks. In this way, conglomerates can both subsidize less successful business segments with more successful ones, and reduce overall risk by combining media ventures with less risky, nonmedia ventures.

Conglomerates can also take advantage of **cross-promoting** successful texts in one sector of the media industries throughout the other media sectors in their organization. The *Harry Potter* film series, for instance, has spawned numerous video games and CDs that are published by Warner Bros., the film's production studio. This kind of conglomerate cross-promotion, in which each new version of a text in a different medium not only makes money, but also drives sales of all other versions of the text, is known in the industry as **synergy**. The idea of synergy as a particularly effective strategy has fallen somewhat from favor since the late 1990s, as many of the media mergers never produced the combined value expected, but such synergies remain the Holy Grail for many people involved in the media industries.

Conglomeration can refer to two different organizational strategies: **vertical integration** and **horizontal integration**. Vertical integration describes the attempt to control every stage of a media text's development, from production through distribution and sales. For example, the music industry has become highly vertically integrated since the 1990s, as major music distributors have bought up record labels, which record and produce music; manufacturing companies that press CDs; and retail and online outlets from which people buy music.

Horizontal integration describes the conglomeration of various companies at the same level of the value chain. A company integrating horizontally might seek to purchase multiple production studios, for instance. Horizontal integration reduces or eliminates competition, which allows the entity to charge higher fees or control terms. The distribution of cable channels features extensive horizontal integration. Most viewers can choose only between one local cable service provider (companies such as Comcast, Cox, and Time Warner) or satellite providers DirecTV and Dish Network. While this is frustrating for consumers, those who own and develop new cable channels are also faced with few options: in order to get their channels to people they often have to accept terms dictated by these distributors.

Going back to our earlier discussion of how the media possess the possibility of operating as a democratic public sphere, you can probably see why so many people might have concerns about changes in media ownership structure. **Monopoly** power not only raises the specter of media organizations failing to fulfill their public sphere function, but perhaps more insidiously, it can mean that they maintain the *illusion* of providing a democratic public sphere while underhandedly bombarding the public with one-sided or inaccurate news. Due to these concerns, various media-reform movements have agitated—and sometimes succeeded—in both local and national politics to try to halt or reverse policies that favor media consolidation.

CONCLUSION

Because they do not sell conventional goods or services, but rather cultural expressions and ideas, the media industries have very different risk profiles than other industries, and those risks encourage several unique business practices and arrangements designed to diminish them. Most people who analyze the media industries tend to agree that much of their behavior stems from this effort to reduce risk, but the ways in which they assess the social consequences of those risk-averse behaviors differ greatly, depending upon the theoretical perspectives they adopt.

For some observers, these efforts at risk reduction have created a situation in which media owners have more and more influence, not only over the industries and their workers, but over society in general, by controlling both our access to media and its content. From this perspective, media professionals merely do the bidding of their powerful owners, at least in part because they want to keep their jobs. An important corollary to this perspective is the idea that the entertainment media do little more than distract us from the nefarious dealings of media conglomerates.

As we have suggested, we see a number of problems with this perspective, particularly its misrecognition of the political potential of entertainment media and its portrait of a work culture thoroughly dominated by the desires of conglomerate owners. We think it empirically demonstrable that, while the instances of corporate meddling in editorial decisions are numerous, at least as often journalists and media professionals operate with a fair degree of independence; in fact, few people would likely stay in the industry if they did not enjoy that independence.

A more nuanced version of the theory that large, commercial media limit diversity of opinion and expression in society begins from the starting point of dominant ideology. In this version, a wide range of cultural, professional, institutional, and personal forces come together to lead media workers—at least those who have some control over the content of texts—to share the ideological positions of corporate owners. We believe that this theoretical position has merit, even as it tends to oversimplify things. First, while all of these factors certainly do influence creators' and journalists' perceptions of what kind of media to make and how to go about making them, they can never fully determine an individual's perspectives and politics. Second, because they seek to be popular with a wide range of audiences from multiple walks of life, all commercial media content has to harness a range of aesthetic and ideological practices. Often, these practices are among the most socially volatile at the time, because controversy can be a powerful draw for consumers. Once ideologically volatile material gets encoded in popular media texts, they tend to take on a life of their own, and overwhelm the efforts of professionals and practitioners to control them.

The portrait of media professionals that we wind up with, then, is one that views them as possessing circumscribed agency to shape the texts they create and the ideologies that circulate within those texts. The Industrialization of Culture framework offers a way of studying the various social, governmental, cultural, and economic pressures that impinge on worker autonomy and the texts that get created. Cultures, mandates, conditions, and industry practices all work to restrict agency, but the drive for popularity and the conflicting and competing interests of a wide range of decision makers involved in creating an individual media text provide opportunities for agency and self-expression. The ways in which media professionals negotiate these competing pressures to make texts that speak to the interests of large numbers of people is one of the primary concerns of the chapters that follow.

QUESTIONS

1. Using the Industrialization of Culture framework, discuss some issues within a media industry you'd like to work in that you must navigate in order to get your text made. Consider, for instance, if certain conditions might affect whether you can actually create the text you have in mind. What practices might challenge your creative control of your text? How will your mandate influence how you approach your text?

2. Consider our claim that the Industrialization of Culture framework is organized vertically but not hierarchically. Why do you think this multidirectionality is an important distinction? How might the framework change the outcome of media texts if it was, in fact, hierarchically organized?

3. Think about one of your favorite media texts in relation to the Industrialization of Culture framework. Can you identify the mandate under which it was created? How might various conditions and practices have affected the content of the text? Identify a few of the text's specific features, such as a sitcom character's development or the cover of a magazine, and imagine how the text's path through the framework's metaphorical pinball machine might have led it to turn out the way it has.

4. Why do you think we emphasize culture as the background that structures industries' operations rather than emphasize it exclusively as the music, books, and other texts that are created by media industries? How does this definition change how you think about the term "culture" or how you think about the ways that media industries operate?

5. Think of a media text—song, movie, or otherwise—that you recently purchased or paid to experience. What were some of the economic risks involved in making that text? Now identify ways in which the media industry attempted to minimize those risks. Do certain risks seem like they might be harder to minimize than others?

6. Pretend you are the head of a music corporation that wants to expand through vertical integration. How would you go about doing this? Which aspects of the music industry would you want to control? Similarly, what plans would you pursue if you wanted to horizontally integrate? What are benefits to each approach to conglomeration?

7. Why is it important to understand ideologies in relation to media industries? If you wanted to investigate the ways ideologies circulate in a media industry, what questions would you ask? How would you attempt to answer them?

FURTHER READINGS

We but glance the surface of the theoretical foundations of media industry studies. More detailed and comprehensive assessments can be found in David Hesmondhalgh's *The Cultural Industries*, 2nd ed. (Thousand Oaks, Calif.: Sage, 2007). Despite its age, Joseph Turow's *Media Systems in Society: Understanding*

Industries, Strategies, and Power, 2nd ed. (New York: Longman, 1997) remains an accessible text for dealing with many of the issues covered here, and also attends in greater depth to the book publishing industry. Another framework or model for connecting the operation of media industries and their texts is the "circuit of culture" that can be found in Paul du Gay and colleagues, *Doing Cultural Studies: The Story of the Sony Walkman* (London: Sage, 1997). Julie D'Acci updates this framework in "Cultural Studies, Television Studies, and the Crisis in the Humanities," (pp. 418–446) in *Television after TV: Essays on a Medium in Transition*, edited by Lynn Spigel and Jan Olsson (Durham: Duke University Press, 2004).

The subfield of critical media industry study and production studies has grown considerably in recent years; also see John Thornton Caldwell's *Production Culture: Industrial Reflexivity and Critical Practice in Film and Television* (Durham: Duke University Press, 2008) and "Cultural Studies in Media Production: Critical Industry Practices" in *Questions of Method in Cultural Studies*, edited by Mimi White and James Schwoch (Malden, Mass.: Blackwell, 2006, pp. 109–153); *Media Industries: History, Theory, and Method*, edited by Jennifer Holt and Alisa Perren (Malden, Mass.: Wiley-Blackwell, 2009) and *Production Studies: Cultural Studies of Media Industries*, edited by Vicki Mayer, Miranda Banks, and John Caldwell (New York: Routledge, 2009) for a variety of perspectives. The authors develop their own perspective in more detail in Timothy Havens, Amanda D. Lotz, and Serra Tinic's "Critical Media Industry Studies: A Research Approach," *Communication, Culture and Critique* 2 (2009): 234–253.

We are unable to go into considerable detail or provide examples from all media industries in the pages here. Those seeking more detailed information about a particular industry might consult a number of books that offer chapters focused on the basic industrial features of various industries: *Media Economics: Theory and Practice*, 3rd ed., edited by Alison Alexander and colleagues (Malweh, N.J.: LEA, 2004); and *Who Owns the Media?: Competition and Concentration in the Mass Media Industry*, edited by Douglas Gomery and Benjamin M. Compaine (Malweh, N.J.: LEA, 2000). Also, general introductions to media often provide helpful overviews, such as Joseph Turow's *Media Today: An Introduction to Mass Media* (New York: Routledge, 2008).

Some books or scholarly articles about particular industries that we've found helpful detail include:

1. *Film*: Edward Jay Epstein, *The Hollywood Economist: The Hidden Financial Reality Behind the Movies* (New York: Melville House, 2010) and *The Big Picture: Money and Power in Hollywood* (New York: Random House, 2006); Janet Wasko, *How Hollywood Works* (Thousand Oaks, Calif.: Sage, 2003), Jason Squire, *The Movie Business Book*, 3rd ed. (New York: Fireside, 2004).

2. *Television*: Amanda D. Lotz, *The Television Will Be Revolutionized* (New York: New York University Press, 2007); Todd Gitlin, *Inside Prime Time*, rev. ed. (Berkeley: University of California Press, 2000), Bill Carter, *Desperate Networks* (New York: Broadway, 2007).

3. *Video Games*: Aphra Kerr, *The Business and Culture of Digital Games: Gamework and Gameplay* (Thousand Oaks, Calif.: Sage, 2006); Mia Consolvo, "Console Video Games and Global Corporations: Creating a Hybrid Culture," *New Media and Society*, 8, No. 1 (2006): 117–137; Nick Dyer-Witheford and Greig de Peuter, "'EA Spouse' and the Crisis of Video Game Labour: Enjoyment, Exclusion, Exploitation, Exodus," *Canadian Journal of Communication* 31 (2006): 599–617.

4. *Music*: Steve Knopper, *Appetite for Self-Destruction: The Spectacular Crash of the Record Industry in the Digital Age* (New York: Free Press, 2009); Keith Negus, *Music Genres and Corporate Cultures* (New York: Routledge, 1999).

NOTES

1. Bradley Johnson, "U.S. Media Revenue Set for Historic 2009 Decline," *Advertising Age*, 5 October 2009. Available online at http://adage.com/mediaworks/article?article_id=139445. Accessed Feb. 4, 2010.

2. Joseph Turow, *Media Systems in Society: Understanding Industries, Strategies, and Power*, 2nd ed. (White Plains, N.Y.: Longman, 1997), 26.

3. Rudyard Kipling, *The Seven Seas*, 11th ed. (London: Methuen & Co., 1907), 10.

4. When the U.S. government took significant control of that industry in 2009, it was not because of the social importance of the products it creates, but rather because of the economic importance the industry has in national and local communities.

5. Roy Morris Jr., *Fraud Of The Century. Rutherford B. Hayes, Samuel Tilden and The Stolen Election of 1876* (New York: Simon and Schuster, 2003); Jon Mecham, *American Lion: Andrew Jackson in the White House* (New York: Random House, 2008).

6. Horace Newcomb and Paul Hirsch, "Television as a Cultural Forum," *Quarterly Review of Film*, 8 (1983), 45–55.

7. The term "ideology" is both ambiguous and controversial, so we want to explain what we mean by this term, and we ask that you keep in mind that how your instructors in this or other classes use the term may differ somewhat.

8. See note 6 above.

9. Christopher Anderson, "Creating the Twenty-First Century Television Network," *NBC: America's Network*, ed. Michele Hilmes (Berkeley: University of California Press, 2007).

10. Richard E. Caves, *Creative Industries: Contracts between Art and Commerce* (Cambridge: Harvard University Press, 2008).

11. Ibid.

12. Ibid.

13. Ibid.

14. http://www.opendemocracy.net/media-globalmediaownership/article_46.jsp (accessed Aug. 31, 2010).

CHAPTER 2

—

Media Industry Mandates

For nearly a decade now, many city governments, citizens groups, and grass-roots media organizations have dreamed of creating municipal broadband networks that would provide citywide high-speed Internet to every member of the community at little or no cost. The goal is to create universal Internet service, much like efforts to ensure that everyone in the community has access to telephone service. In addition to providing networks for emergency communications and widespread access to information services, municipal broadband services promise to help bridge the **digital divide**, or the gap between those who have access to and facility with new technologies (the "information rich") and those who do not (the "information poor"). Chances are good, however, that whatever city you live in, you have only minimal community Internet access, if any at all, despite the fact that such networks have been technologically possible for years. The reason your community probably lacks municipal bandwidth is because of funding and political obstacles that have slowed, and in some cases all but killed, these initiatives. The core problem involves an ongoing debate about what mandate should govern the local broadband industry.

Finding public funding for municipal broadband requires tax money, and few city governments have shown a willingness to increase taxes or redirect tax money from other sources. This is a recurring problem facing media industries with public mandates. Most cities have contracted with private companies to provide both technological infrastructure and Internet services rather than develop their own agencies. The City of San Francisco, for instance, contracted with both Google and Earthlink to provide a Wi-Fi network throughout the city that was to provide a free, moderately fast service, as well as a faster, low-price subscription service. The deal fell apart in 2008 when Earthlink backed out of the project. This possibility that a private company might back out of a city contract, effectively ending municipal broadband, has been one of the main stumbling blocks to introducing the service. A second difficulty has been lobbying efforts on the part of large commercial providers of Internet services who see free broadband as unfair competition that might cut into their bottom lines. Such companies have spent millions of dollars trying to introduce legislation making such services illegal. Even in those instances in which the public-commercial partnership has resulted in some form of citywide broadband, controversy has sometimes erupted over the use of location monitoring for localized niche advertising, which sends highly geographically targeted ads to users. For the companies that provide the service, the capacity to locate precisely where we are accessing the network from, and deliver locally targeted ads to our browsers as pop-ups, pop-unders, or splash pages is one of the more exciting possibilities that municipal broadband offers. For users, however, unwanted advertising and location surveillance are often annoying, even worrisome, invasions of privacy.

The clash among users, commercial providers, and city governments over municipal broadband demonstrates the challenge of determining the mandate for any particular media industry, as well as the different outcomes that each mandate encourages. Should municipal wireless primarily serve citizens and civil groups seeking to collect and share information about their community, or should it serve local businesses trying to advertise their goods and services? When these goals are in harmony, the particular mandate of the network is probably unimportant, but what happens when the goals collide, as they inevitably will? For instance, when users connect to a municipal Wi-Fi network, they first encounter a "splash" page that tells them what network they're on and that gives them some information. Should this splash page be run by the city or by the commercial provider? Should it carry advertising? Should it log the location and identity of each computer that accesses it? These are important questions, and the mandate of the network will decide their answers.

The ongoing saga of municipal broadband demonstrates the difference between commercial and public mandates, as well as the strengths and weaknesses of each. Public mandates are more effective than commercial mandates at serving, well, public needs—particularly those needs that are unrelated to business activities and consumption. A free public Wi-Fi system, for instance, might allow a local bicycle co-op to promote its summer group riding schedule through its website, or a nonprofit group to announce a call for volunteers, even though neither organization may have the funds necessary to purchase Internet access and pay for a website domain. In a commercial system, by contrast, these organizations might need to place advertising on their pages in order to pay for domain registration and Internet access. Public media do cost money, however, and they need to be supported by individual or corporate taxes, which are almost always controversial. Commercial mandates, by contrast, do not require tax money, and they serve certain kinds of needs particularly well, including businesses and affluent individuals or groups. Their ability to serve the needs of other people is spottier. Mandates, then, shape the operation of media industries in many ways, including whether and how various segments of the public are served, the kinds of content that the industry produces, the organization of the industry (is it a monopoly, an oligopoly, or competitive?), and the role that the industry plays in business and civic life.

*　*　*

Those who study and discuss the media often overlook the mandate of a media industry because it's easy to take for granted. In many ways, the mandate encompasses the purpose of the media industry—its very reason for being—and, in most cases, the mandate was established so long ago that it seems unalterable. Nevertheless, as the municipal-broadband controversy reminds us, there is nothing inevitable about the mandate of any media industry, and the creation of the mandates of our established media industries often generated a similar degree of controversy. As you'll recall from Chapter 1, we delimit two categories of mandates—commercial and noncommercial, with various subcategories of noncommercial mandates such as public, community, alternative/DIY, and governmental. We divide the mandates in this way because, for the most part, those media that are relevant to a discussion of *media industries* operate with a commercial mandate in the United States. Media operating under a commercial mandate are thus emphasized throughout the book, but we want to make clear at the outset that other options exist. We often juxtapose other mandates as examples throughout the book in order to offer a reminder that what seem given and natural practices of media industries—or "just the way things are"—are a result of a deliberate determination that the media should operate with a commercial mandate. Thus, it isn't the case that "media industries just are that way," but that media are that way because their foremost goal is the cultivation of profits.

The vantage point of looking back through history allows us to better see the processes through which mandates are established. Consider the example of U.S. broadcasting. Students of radio history are often surprised to learn that when the technology we now know as radio first developed, inventors and users conceived of it as a technology akin to a mobile phone. In the first decades of the 1900s, inventors and amateurs constructed the radio sets that they used to send and receive signals across long distances. Most thought the technology, often called "wireless," was most similar to the telegraph or telephone, because it provided a wireless means to send a signal from one place to another. (At first, radio transmissions were in Morse Code, similar to telegraph messages, and the ability to transmit voice, as over the telephone, came later). In these early years, then, users perceived radio as a **point-to-point** medium that could be used to send a message from one person to another, not the **mass medium** capable of sending a message from one source to many receivers that we know it as today.

Gradually, entrepreneurs and businesses realized that radio's greater potential could be found in using it as a mass medium rather than as a wireless point-to-point form of communication; and, once this happened, the struggle to establish its mandate began. Up until World War I, the dominant use of "radio" in the United States was by young boys and other amateurs who built their own radios and used the devices to try to receive distant signals. These "DXers" would tape maps to their walls and use pushpins to record where they received signals from. During this time, and on throughout the decade, radio was also emerging as a valuable means of communication among ships. By the late 1910s, increasing incidents of interference among the use of radio for shipping communication and amateurs sending and receiving signals emerged and contributed to the sense that official policies for radio needed to be instituted. These policies became part of the establishment of the medium's mandate.

To jump to the end of this abbreviated story, there was no natural reason for the mandate that eventually resulted, and the United States and Great Britain reached very different outcomes when faced with comparable situations. In the United States, an agreement between the military and the corporate interests that had been developing radio (Westinghouse, General Electric, AT&T, United Fruit Company) led to the demise of radio as an amateur's hobby and set up radio with the commercial mandate that was established. In contrast, in Great Britain, the government took responsibility for developing and organizing radio, and there—as in most similarly industrialized countries—it took on a public mandate.

Before we further detail the various mandates, we'd like to make a few points very clear. First, *we can often identify multiple mandates for media outlets, although one is typically primary.* For example, all governments exercise some degree of control over the media systems that operate within their borders, a fact that might confuse the distinction between commercial and public mandates. In one case, Margaret Thatcher, who was the British prime minister in the 1980s, worked relentlessly to attack the perceived liberal bias of the BBC, The British Broadcasting Corporation, and to introduce commercial funding. And even in the United States, appointments to the board of PBS, the Public Broadcasting System, became highly politicized under the administration of George H. W. Bush. Both cases illustrate how government plays a role in media industries with a public or a commercial mandate.

Moreover, many critics of commercial media claim that commercial interests maintain the same kind of control over content that totalitarian regimes do over governmental media. Rupert Murdoch, chairperson and managing director of the media conglomerate News Corp., is often painted as an authoritarian capitalist who wields total control over a large percentage of the media in the West. In fact, when it comes to analyzing media system mandates in detail, *it's important to remember that each is merely a characteristic type.* Most national systems use a combination of commercial and public outlets, and it can often be difficult to distinguish between them. Many PBS imports from the United Kingdom and Canada, for instance, come from commercial production houses; and every commercial broadcast and cable television channel in the United States forewent commercial interruptions for a week after the September 11, 2001, attacks in order to air constant news. So we see that, in practice, media industries constantly blend and merge these mandates.

In addition, *certain media industries, particularly the broadcasting industries, tend to be more influenced by these mandates than others; thus, most examples of noncommercial mandates are broadcast media.* Popular music and video game industries, for example, are typically commercially funded regardless of where they are located. Still, a number of industries—including broadcasting, film, and even some kinds of music—are subsidized in whole or in part by federal governments seeking to protect their nations' cultural industries. It is now the case that, at an industry level, most countries feature broadcasting industries that blend commercial and noncommercial mandates. Other media industries are typically dominated by a commercial mandate.

WHAT ARE COMMON MANDATES?

Throughout history and around the world, media can most basically be categorized as commercial or noncommercial. The differences between these mandates emerge through considering three questions: *who pays for media, whom does it serve,* and *what determines "success."* In many ways, the last two questions are contingent upon the first, so perhaps the first question one should always ask when beginning to assess a media industry is: *who pays for it?*

Commercial Media

When asked who pays for a commercial system, many students' first impulse is to say "advertisers," and that answer is partly correct. We are often told that here in the United States we enjoy the "free" television offerings of NBC, CBS, FOX, the CW, and ABC thanks to the advertisers that pay for the commercials in the programs, just as nearly all our radio enjoyment comes to us for "free." Although we don't have to pay a specific fee to watch an episode of *Gray's Anatomy* when ABC broadcasts it over its television network, we—this time as consumers—do still pay for it. All of the marketing and advertising budgets that companies spend to buy advertising comes from consumers who pay inflated prices for goods to cover advertising expenses. So the answer to who pays in the commercial system is: you. How much money is spent on advertising? In 2008, the top 100 marketers spent $44.4 billion in the United States and $117.9 billion worldwide.[1]

Of course, advertising is just one way of funding commercial media. Most commercial media blend advertising and payment from consumers—for example, most newspapers and magazines require a small payment to receive their products, while earning the majority of their revenues from advertisers. Still other media derive almost all of their funding from consumers, as when you pay for a ticket to see a movie, buy an album or song, or purchase print or television media that have no advertising. Finally, we typically pay for media services through monthly fees, such as those you pay for your mobile phone or Internet service. We'll explore these variations in ways for charging for commercial media in Chapter 5 as one of the economic conditions shaping media industry operation. For now, it is just important to note the many ways commercial media industries earn profits from their users and audiences.

The next question in assessing mandate is: *whom does the media outlet serve?* Commercial media serve those likely to make them most profitable. Media supported by advertising are categorized as **dual product markets**. This economic concept refers to the two layers of sales that occur. As audiences, we often think of media companies designing products for our needs and "selling" us the content, but, in reality, we are the ones being sold. In the somewhat graphic language of the advertising industry, for instance, the goal of most media is to "sell eyeballs." Magazines, television networks, and newspapers design a media product and market it toward various audiences (the first market). Their economic model, however, does not rely on those audiences paying for those media (as is the case in the recording and film industries, which rely on direct pay rather than advertising). Rather, those magazines, television networks, and newspapers profit by selling the audiences they gather with their media content to advertisers. This leads these media to design content (or seek to serve) in very particular ways. On some level, they are concerned with creating good content that audiences enjoy and appreciate, but they are mostly concerned with creating content that gathers the audience that advertisers seek, and in most cases, with trying to avoid controversy. How media implement their commercial goals—or the central strategy these media use—has changed over their history. In the past, both the magazine and television industries relied on creating media products that gathered large and "broad" audiences. Both industries now seek to reach more narrowly focused audiences with products that are geared toward particular demographics or attitudes.

As a result, commercial media systems tend toward certain kinds of content and ways of portraying people and stories. Much advertiser-supported media is designed to reach a particular **demographic**—or narrow subsection of the population—because advertisers desire certain types of customers. In the television industry, this most desired demographic is described as 18- to 34-year-olds with college educations who have household incomes greater than $75,000 per year—distinctions drawn from basic Nielsen Media Research categories of income and age. Commercial media also tend to avoid content likely to disturb advertisers—which might mean avoiding news stories critical of the practices of an advertiser or member of the media company's board of directors.

It may seem cynical, but almost every facet of commercial media production comes back to a question of what those most valued consumers desire. Of course, no media company ever knows for certain what theme, story, or format will be a hit. This creates a lot of uncertainty and possibility for creativity in the production process, and it accounts for much of the variety that does exist. The various factors noted in Chapter 1 that make media industries different from many others prevent them from being able to consistently manufacture "hits" and allows some degree of artistic experimentation. In some cases, the desire to reach affluent audiences leads to high-quality media products. Consider that top journalistic outlets are motivated by commercial goals, and the desire to attract audiences that are educated and affluent can lead to rigorous and sophisticated reporting in an effort to become established as the most reputable information source.

Finally, what determines success for commercial media? For the media companies, the answer is profits. This can lead to somewhat varied strategies, depending upon the economic model of the media entity—subscription media succeed when their subscriptions increase and few people cancel subscriptions, advertising media seek to attract the most of whatever consumer their advertisers most covet, and direct-pay media such as film seek to entice as many people as possible to come out and see movies or buy pay-per-view specials.

Two more important things to remember: Even in the United States, no medium operates as a perfect free market. The government imposes some regulation on every medium, whether it is as limited as preventing monopolies and disallowing obscene speech or more nuanced regulations related to broadcast license requirements. Years of media operation have proven that some regulation of media industries is required in order to obtain various pro-social goals and expectations. And a gentle reminder: many of you reading these pages are likely young and on your way to being the educated and affluent viewers that many advertisers most desire. If this is true, it is important to remember when assessing the strengths and weaknesses of a commercial media system that you are better served than most others. Remember to account for how you would feel about a commercial media system if you weren't considered desirable by advertisers. Take a moment the next time you are talking with someone over the age of 60 about the media they use and whether they feel they see their lives and stories reflected. Ask them to note characters in film or television that they can identify with or whether the stories they find in newspapers or magazines seem relevant.

Noncommercial Media
Public Mandate Media

"Who pays" is actually a trick question, as the answer is almost always "you," regardless of the mandate. How the media industry receives that payment varies, however. You typically pay for a public media system through taxes. That is, a public system gathers funding from those who belong to a nation-state or municipality and then pools those funds to provide a media service for those citizens. The classic example of this has been the case of the BBC. In Britain, citizens are charged an annual fee for their television sets. In 2010, this fee was 149.50£ for a color television (about $225) and 49£ for a black-and-white set ($75). The government collects this money and then allocates it to the BBC, which uses that funding to develop programming for its various radio and television channels, and increasingly, its web-streaming services. In 2008, the BBC's annual budget was roughly $4.5 billion.[2]

In a public system, then, you—as a citizen of the country—pay for media service, and in return, the media system is charged with serving you, its citizenry. How does it do this, and how do we determine whether it does so successfully? A group of people may all be citizens of a country, but they likely have vastly different needs and interests, which make such a mandate challenging. Take a much smaller-scale example— imagine if your university had a media service funded through your tuition dollars (this may be the case for many of you). That campus media system is likely charged with serving the needs of the university community, but chances are that even just on your campus, there is no one student need that makes determining what should be included in that media programming easy. How should station managers decide what types of shows to develop—should they offer entertainment or "service programming" that provides news about campus? Who should the programming entertain? Should the programming focus on the needs of commuters or of campus residents?

When you consider how challenging it might be to develop a media service that adequately serves just the diverse students on your campus, it becomes easy to see how difficult it is to develop and maintain a media system that serves the needs of an entire country. One way public mandate media try to fulfill this charge is through offering a diversity of programming. Certainly, the media system cannot meet *all* the needs of *all* its citizens *all* of the time, but program directors can try to construct program schedules that meet the needs of many different groups at some point in a program day, week, or year. Take a moment and think about how you would carry out this mandate if you were the programming director for your campus radio or television station. In some cases, public media are vibrant enough that they are able to offer multiple channels, and this helps meet the needs of varied constituencies tremendously. For instance, in The Netherlands, different political and religious groups run the public service television system each of which controls its own channel or a portion of a channel's broadcast schedule. In other cases, representatives of major civil groups in the country serve on a public service oversight board that determines policy and personnel.

Assessing audience needs also provides a challenge for media with a public mandate, and programmers must weigh choices like: should they present programs with casts representative of the makeup and viewpoints of the entire country? If so, how should they go about doing this? Creating balance can be very difficult to accomplish. Should the "balance" exist in each program—such as making sure an equal number of conservative and liberal commentators and guests can be found in each show, or is it better to create separate shows or entire channels with distinctly conservative or liberal perspectives? What about representing a nation's varied ethnic, religious, class, and age diversity? Certainly it is impossible to encompass a nation's diversity within the cast of every single show, and, given that, how do you make sure you depict the various realities of people in a nation?

We noted at the outset that most countries now feature "some combination" of these mandates. Most countries around the world began their broadcasting histories with public broadcasting systems, but nearly all now have **mixed mandate systems** in which a vital public system remains, but a commercial system has developed alongside it. In many cases, public broadcasters actually run commercials and generate a good deal of their revenue from them, like the Irish broadcaster RTE, Raidió Telefís Éireann, which gets about 55 percent of its revenue from advertising. Programmers for public media in countries with mixed mandates sometimes focus their resources particularly on those underserved by the commercial media since commercial media tend to serve certain groups very well, but often provide little or no services for other groups. The question of whether public media in a mixed-mandate system should spread its resources across the population or focus more effort on those unserved or underserved by the commercial media is complicated and important. The development of media industries with mixed public and commercial components leads programmers of public systems to make different decisions about how they operate than if there were no commercial sector.

Given the diverse needs of its population, a public system typically assesses its success by trying to answer the question of whether the needs of its public are being served. This might mean continuing to schedule some shows that don't have large audiences (since public media are mostly broadcast) but that reach a particularly underserved community. In Slovenia, for instance, public radio broadcasters air programming in a variety of minority languages, including Italian and Hungarian, to serve small ethnic groups that would not otherwise have access to such programming.

Another tricky aspect of noncommercial media involves how to evaluate their success. In the United States we are so accustomed to thinking of success in terms of which media content gathers the most viewers or listeners—and therefore earns the most advertising dollars—that it can be quite difficult to conceive of an alternative measure of success, and it is easy to revert to commercial measures, such as how many people watched or listened. Rather than quantity of viewers, success might be a matter of simply making alternative content available.

Not all public mandate media are comparable. For example, U.S. students are probably most familiar with PBS. While PBS is certainly different than commercial media, it is also not nearly as robust as the public mandate media available around the world. PBS is a national entity that helps produce programming and facilitates connections among the 356 locally owned and run PBS stations around the country. Annual per capita funding of PBS in the early 2000s was $1.49, compared with public media funding of $83 in Great Britain and $28 in Canada—thus, by measures of funding alone, it is clear that the U.S. system is not at all comparable with those elsewhere. At this point, stations are largely reliant on viewer and foundation donations, though they also receive funding from a variety of other sources. Roughly 15 percent of the budget comes from the federal government, 17 percent from state and local governments, 11 percent from public and private universities, and 41 percent from private funders: 26 percent subscribers and 15 percent corporations.[3] As policy scholar Patricia Aufderheide notes, "U.S. public television is a peculiar hybrid of broadcasting systems. Neither completely a public-service system in the European tradition, nor fully supported by commercial interests as in the dominant pattern in the United States, it has elements of both."[4] Thus, we'd remind our readers with familiarity only with U.S. media that their experience with public mandate media is likely atypical compared with the rest of the world.

You may have noticed a heavy reliance on broadcasting examples throughout this section and throughout this chapter. This is because broadcast media (radio and television) are overwhelmingly the type of media that tend to operate under a public mandate. Government support of media can be found in other ways; for example, many national governments subsidize a range of cultural activities, including many, such as films and recorded music, that we would define as media. Even though there are bureaucratic institutions that decide which films get public funding, the complexity, reach, and visibility of those organizations are far less than those of a public broadcaster, and are not as extensive as what we'd consider typical of a public mandate. Most such film boards don't produce, distribute, or promote the films they fund; they simply provide financial assistance. We'll discuss the particularity of why broadcasting often uses a public mandate more in Chapter 4. Even though this is a mandate rarely found outside of broadcasting, it is crucial to understand the goals and distinctions of a public system, if for no other reason than to help us imagine alternatives to the dominance of the commercial mandate.

Although we acknowledge a range of noncommercial media that includes public, community, alternative/DIY, and governmental, the most substantial alternative to commercial media (particularly from a media industry focus) is a public mandate. We freely acknowledge that the distinctions that we make among community and alternative/DIY are fairly nuanced, and perhaps, debatable; it is difficult, however, to speak in generalizations about these other types of noncommercial mandates, because questions such as who pays and whom it serves tend to be particular to the media outlet.

Community, Alternative/DIY Mandate Media

Media with a community, alternative or DIY (do-it-yourself) mandate are arguably quite similar to public media, but they differ in scope. Still, they differ from media with a public mandate, because the public mandate can also produce some of the same problems as commercial media in their elaborate bureaucracies. While lumping these various subcategories of media together may draw criticism, they really can't be distinguished by the questions of who pays, whom they serve, and how to judge success. In all cases, the answers to these questions are specific to the case in question. Community, alternative, and DIY media are typically paid for through donations, and they might receive some governmental support. There might even be commercial support, as in the case of cable service providers offering up money for the local access stations that exist on their services. (Notably, they don't offer much money and do this only as part of the franchise agreements struck with local communities). The difference is that these types of media are meant to serve a much narrower and specific population, or they might exist only to serve the originator's desire to share a message.

Examples of community media include low-power FM (LPFM) radio stations in the United States. These stations are authorized for use as noncommercial educational stations and are authorized to operate only up to 100 watts, which allows an approximately 3.5-mile radius. Many of these are very small, even personal operations, but although the stations reach a small radius of broadcast listeners, they can reach a much larger audience by streaming live on the web. A feature on LPFM in the *New York Times* cited examples of such stations, as one in St. Paul, Minn., that focuses on the Hmong people in the city or one in Oregon focused on the issues of farm workers.[5] Other examples of community media are those shows produced for local access cable channels. The content of these channels can be all over the map—from still camera shots of city council or school board meetings to local talk shows with decent production values. Community media might exist to serve the needs of a niche population, or they might just exist because of a few people with the time and inclination to provide it.

'Zines (short for "fanzines") are often cited as an example of alternative or DIY media. These are self-published print media (similar to magazines or newsletters) with a small circulation—typically photocopied—on any imaginable topic. Most are self-financed and designed as a tool of expression contrary to the established commercial or public media. 'Zines might be considered a precursor of blogs. The ease and affordability of personal websites and aggregators such as You Tube enable the distribution of alternative and DIY media in the digital age.

The widespread availability of computerized media-production tools and broadband Internet access for distribution has led to growing popularity and awareness of media with community, alternative/DIY mandates, and also led to the development of what some observers call the **prosumer**, a compound word that incorporates both the media "producer" and "consumer."[6] In their view, consumers are increasingly involved in the production process from the beginning, and many prosumers are active producers of media texts themselves. For instance, the website TelevisionWithoutPity.com features a variety of ways for fans to interact with one another and with program producers who frequent the site, including the capacity to post scripts for entirely new episodes of current and past television series written by fans.

We would, however, qualify the perceived revolutionary nature of these developments in two ways: first, while a growing number of people are creating their own media texts and sharing them with others, this remains a small fraction of the *commercial* media activity that goes on; second, media consumers have always been able to "talk back" to media companies in various ways, and simply the ability to get involved in the production process does not undermine the economic power of large conglomerates, nor does it fundamentally change the relationship between large commercial producers and individual consumers. Going back to the TelevisionWithoutPity.com example, it has become commonplace for some producers to troll through boards in order to get feedback on plot development and to glean ideas for upcoming episodes. Because the website's owner, NBC Universal, claims rights to all submissions on the site, producers working for NBC or its partners are free to take whatever ideas they wish and use them in their shows without compensating or acknowledging the prosumer who came up with the idea. In other words, the website permits program producers and even researchers to offload some of the work involved in developing and testing new ideas. Consequently, while the ways in which ideas are generated for upcoming episodes may have changed some, the people and industries that profit from commercial television haven't changed all that much because of TelevisionWithoutPity.com.[7]

Although media with community, alternative, and DIY mandates are often very important to the people involved in them, we do not feature media with these mandates prominently in the following chapters. These media outlets indeed provide meaningful content options, and their content can sometimes bubble up into more established media outlets with public and commercial mandates, but given our focus on the operation of commercial media industries, there is less to say about community, alternative, and DIY media because they function so deliberately outside the industrial norms of a commercial mandate. It may be, as supporters of media with these mandates argue, that community, alternative, or DIY media will one day revolutionize the commercial and public media in the world. Such a revolution has not yet taken place however, and media with these mandates continue to exist largely at the fringes of the media industries—a fact that does not necessarily diminish their importance for fans.

Governmental Mandate Media

Government funding is a commonality among public and governmental media, but governmental mandate media exist primarily to serve the needs of the government in power rather than the public. Often, the societies that have media with governmental mandates also have authoritarian governments. Few purely governmental media systems remain today, and authoritarian governments often derive their power through force, so the funding for media systems may come from assets that have been seized from citizens, from taxes, or from the proceeds of goods the government sells to other countries.

Media with governmental mandates exist to serve the government. This could result in many different ends—the government could fund a diversity of viewpoints—but it more commonly has been the case that authoritarian governments use media systems to advance the singular view of those in power. The governmental media system therefore, would be considered successful when the views of the government are transmitted to the people. In other words, rather than the goal of informing or uplifting the citizenry, as is the goal of public-mandate media, or serving the desires of consumers as in the commercial model, the purpose of media outlets in a governmental system is to propagandize citizens and neutralize dissent. Historically, Nazi-era Germany serves as an example of the most egregious—and successful—governmental media system in the modern era, because of its supposedly successful efforts to spread Nazi sentiments throughout the German citizenry. In fact, the reason that many Americans remain distrustful of government-funded media systems is because of lingering memories of the Nazi and Soviet systems.

Much like public mandate media, governmental mandate systems require a good deal of capital to finance. Given the fact that most of the large economies in the world are located in nations that are, at least nominally, democratic, the challenges of funding large, modern media systems have prompted many authoritarian regimes to adopt some of the principles of commercial media systems, although the content of these commercial media operators remains tightly controlled. The film industry in Myanmar, formerly Burma, is a case in point. Though far from a cinema powerhouse, the Burmese film industry does have a long and relatively active history that dates back to the 1920s. When the present military junta took over the country in 1962, it effectively took over the film industry, but it began privatizing the industry again beginning in 1989. A single private company, Mingalar Ltd., controls the majority of the theaters in the country and plays only films approved by government censors. Moreover, independent cinema producers are required to submit scripts to censors before they begin shooting. The government even gets involved in movie casting, preventing film stars who were active in the democracy movements of the 1980s and 1990s from appearing in films, and the older films of pro-democracy directors are likewise banned.[8]

Myanmar is one of the more extreme examples of a totalitarian state, but the tendency of non-democratic governments to privatize the media while retaining control is a widespread phenomenon. Governments throughout Asia, the Middle East, Africa, and Latin America adopt similar measures. In Kuwait, government censors edit imported television programs before airing them. In China, Internet companies go to great lengths to filter search engine results and web page access in line with the desires of the Chinese government.

Quite often, the main goal of governmental media systems is the maintenance of social harmony, though the goal of maintaining harmony and eliminating dissent frequently go hand in hand. A recent incident in Thailand demonstrates how authoritarian governments exercise their power over the media system to maintain social harmony. In late 2007 and early 2008, a controversy erupted over the popular Thai soap opera *Songkram Nang Fah* (*The Air Hostess War*), which featured steamy and catty storylines about Thai Airways flight attendants. Offended by the portrayals of its members, the flight attendants' union petitioned the Thai Ministry of Culture to cancel the series. Although the series continued for a few months, it is unclear whether the Ministry did convince the series producer to tone down the more offensive elements.[9] For American audiences, such a controversy is not remarkable, as numerous groups lodge complaints about portrayals on commercial television, but the involvement of the federal government is probably surprising: after all, in a commercial media system, aggrieved groups seek to get advertisers, not the government, to put pressure on producers of controversial programs. Table 2.1 provides a quick reference for differentiating among the mandates we discuss.

Table 2.1 Mandates Chart

	COMMERCIAL	NONCOMMERCIAL	GOVERNMENTAL
Who pays for media?	You	You	You
Who does it serve?	Consumers	The people	Government
What determines "success"?	Profits	The effectiveness with which the people's needs are served	The effectiveness with which the government's views are transmitted to the people
Example	Disney, *The New York Times*, NBC	BBC, LPFM, community newspapers	Nazi-era Germany

MANDATES IN ACTION

It is important to note that these basic categorizations of mandates and quick descriptions of who pays, who is served, and how success is determined are rarely as simple or clear-cut as this suggests. In practice, there is much greater variety and complexity, but this notion of a mandate and its basic characteristics provides a starting point. As we noted in Chapter 1, we provide a framework that moves from mandates through conditions and practices in order to help make sense of what seem to be the hundreds, and maybe thousands, of factors that contribute to determining the operation of a media industry and the products it creates. These mandates offer just a first step, or deflection of the pinball, that the Industrialization of Culture framework allows. Even though we begin with mandates, we don't view them as **deterministic**. Deterministic approaches often try to explain the behavior of media industries through one aspect—typically something like a belief that the commercial mandate of a media industry to make profits will lead it to operate only in a particular way, or that the capabilities of a technology will lead it to be used only in a certain way. As you'll note, in the following discussion we explore the very different products that have been created by media industries despite a common mandate. It is impossible to provide a detailed example of all of the various forms a commercial or noncommercial media entity may take, but let's return to the opening example of how U.S. radio became established under a commercial mandate for a deeper understanding of this case.

Establishing the Mandate of U.S. Radio

The origins of commercial U.S. radio in the 1920s may seem like a history lesson with little contemporary relevance, but keep in mind that the beginning of radio is actually the beginning of broadcasting—which is a distinctive form of media because of its reliance on using a public asset for signal transmission. In fact, the negotiations that established the norms for radio created standards that shifted only slightly upon the invention of television. Some new technologies invented in the last century—particularly those that enabled the emergence of cable channels—required some adaptations in these early norms, but for the most part, the broadcast policies and practices that continue to organize U.S. radio and television can be traced to the 1920s and early 1930s. In addition, when the FCC began regulating Internet communications in the 1990s, one of the major questions it needed to face was whether the technology was similar to broadcasting, and could therefore be highly regulated, or whether it was closer to print, and therefore enjoyed greater Constitutional protections.

First, let's briefly consider the paths not chosen at the outset of U.S. broadcasting. The United States could have followed the route taken by most countries that developed radio at this time and organized radio with a public mandate. This would have meant establishing an agency charged with making radio available for the people of the country. This body would have likely organized the spectrum (the naturally occurring electromagnetic space used to transmit broadcast signals) and endeavored to create radio programming to meet the needs of all citizens. What happened in the United States was quite different. At this time, amateurs, the military, and industrial entrepreneurs all had different ideas in mind for how radio should be employed. Amateurs used broadcasting as a hobby, and most spent their time with the medium trying to receive distant signals rather than listening to programming. The military was devising uses slowly, and although it didn't prove vital to their operations, it mainly wanted to control broadcasting in case future use developed. Finally, the entrepreneurs, who we might say ultimately won out, sought to make a profit from the technology—although the system in place now was not what many initially had in mind. All these groups could have shared the spectrum; yet, in the end, the best frequencies were reserved for military and government use and others were allocated to the burgeoning broadcast business.[10]

As well as negotiating among these groups with different intentions for radio, the agency governing the establishment of radio under a public mandate would have faced challenging questions regarding whether to develop a locally or nationally based system, given the geographical breadth of the United States, and then how radio should be used to serve the public. Notably, many of these challenges faced the Public Broadcasting System that was developed in the late 1960s, and they continue to confound it today.

As we noted, Britain is one of the many countries that did choose to develop broadcasting with a public mandate at this time. Historians of the BBC have developed rich accounts of exactly how these questions and debates evolved over the decades in the British system. Some felt that broadcasting should be used as a tool for cultural uplift and focused on developing programming such as theater and opera that they believed would enrich the tastes of its citizenry. At other times during its history, some have argued that the BBC also needed to provide programming that appealed to more popular tastes, such as soap operas and comedies; in its long history, the BBC has offered all these types of programming.

Another mandate available to those establishing U.S. radio was a governmental system. While this may seem an impossible fit in a democratic system, the military was one of the main users of radio in its early years, and some felt that radio should be placed in military hands.[11] It is difficult to imagine how differently radio might have developed in this case. It may not have been made available to the general population at all, but would have been used exclusively for military communication. Or, more likely, radio might have been used as a propaganda force and featured programs with themes and messages that specifically served military or government ends.

But neither the public nor governmental mandates were long considered in the United States, and although U.S. broadcasting quickly headed down the path of a commercial mandate, it took at least a decade from the agreement that established its commercial focus until radio began to be widely available. Although a commercial mandate had been selected, some experimentation and negotiation were required to figure out how to actually finance programming and for the involved entities to profit from it. For one, there was considerable resistance to commercial messages in radio's early days. Radio did not start out with the type of commercials common today; rather, a single company paid for the costs of making a show and was announced as a show's sponsor (for example, there was a program called *Lux Radio Theater*—Lux was a brand of soap). In the early years, even discussing the attributes of a product, or hard selling, was considered unseemly, so companies sought for consumers to make inferences or to curry favor with consumers through techniques of indirect advertising. In one famous case, Cliquot Club, the manufacturer of club soda and other beverages, sponsored performances by the Cliquot Club Eskimo Orchestra—an orchestra not of actual Eskimos, but of musicians who posed for publicity photos in parkas to help indirectly communicate Cliquot's desire for consumers to associate their product with something "cool" and "refreshing."[12]

The **sponsorship model** dominated U.S. broadcasting during the radio years and into the early years of television. We'll discuss the particulars of the relationships among types of commercial funding and the production of programming in later chapters. For now, we want to leave you with the understanding that nothing happens "naturally" in the operation of a media system; there is never one right way the media should or must operate. Rather, there are many different interests, often of those in power—whether the power of government or the power that comes from controlling capital—that lead to certain outcomes eventually coming to seem natural. In the 1920s, it seemed most unnatural that a company would promote the features of its product in the midst of entertainment programming. Over years of gradually incorporating subtle advertising messages into content, that expectation of programming being free of commercial messaging eroded to allow for the hard sell of later sponsors that extolled the virtues of products during the show. Later, the pretense of sponsorship was eliminated for the inclusion of the type of commercial message we are familiar with today. Now we find our entertainment content again infiltrated with sponsored messages and **product placement** in addition to pods of commercial messages. This product placement seemed quite jarring and unnatural in the early 2000s, but by the time you read this, it, too, might seem unexceptional and quite natural.

For a somewhat different context and case of an evolving mandate, consider the development of the Internet. This project began as a governmental effort to develop an interconnected system of computers that could survive a nuclear war; commercial use was explicitly forbidden. Once access to the Internet extended beyond the government research centers, it quickly took on a new life as it became a central communication technology for both business and pleasure, as well as an interconnected marketplace that is very commercial, indeed. Given the many different uses of the Internet, we find it impossible to characterize it with a single mandate; yet it is certainly the case that the present version with which we are most familiar bears little resemblance to what its inventors and innovators imagined—as was true of radio as well.

LIMITS OF MANDATES

Although these mandates and their various mixed versions are helpful starting points for understanding characteristics of media industries, they tell only part of the story. With their particular funding norms, goals, and measures of success, mandates lead to some trends and likely outcomes; the reason we offer a framework with multiple levels, however, is because many other factors intervene and can lead to similar outcomes in systems with different mandates or different outcomes within a singular mandate.

As an example of the former, consider the case of the popular television comedy *The Office*. Many of you might be familiar with the U.S. version of this show, which chronicles the saga of Pam and Jim, the odd Dwight, and challenged office manager, Michael. *The Office*, however, first developed in Britain and was a success there for the BBC. Although the U.S. and UK versions do differ on some level, we can view this as an example of a public and a commercial system producing the same show. Understanding how this happened and why the U.S. and UK versions developed in the manner that they did cannot be explained by mandate alone, but requires that we examine the various conditions and practices that contributed to the different shows.

Or, as another example of the limitations of mandates, consider the great variety of programming produced in just one mandate. ABC's news and public affairs show *Nightline*, MTV's *My Super Sweet 16*, and HBO's *The Wire* are all products of a commercial media system, yet they are very different shows. The variation among them can be understood by examining the media industry that produced them, but we must dig deeper than the mandate of that system.

The broadcasting industry has been particularly present in this chapter as a result of the features that make public and governmental mandates more common to broadcasting than any other media industry. Even in countries such as Britain that have a long and established public broadcasting system, most other media operate under a commercial mandate. Given that many of the media industries around the world function with a commercial mandate, it is necessary to now turn to the conditions that contribute to the variation in content produced by commercial media industries.

QUESTIONS

1. Audiences are differently conceived based on the mandate of a particular medium. For instance, a cable network (commercial mandate) is designed to reach a *demographic,* whereas PBS (public mandate) serves a country's *citizenry.* What is the difference? How do these different conceptions of the audience influence the type of content in a media text? Can you think of different ways that media with a commercial mandate may appeal to a particular group of people (e.g., African Americans, gay men) than media with a public or governmental mandate?

2. Given what you have learned about public mandates, develop a programming model for PBS. What types of programming will allow it to most effectively fulfill its mandate? Will you impose quotas for types of programming (e.g., public affairs, children's shows) and how will your entertainment programming differ from that of television with a commercial mandate? What problems do you hope to address or solve with your proposals? What problems or concerns appear too difficult to fix?

3. Funding is a pressing concern for both NPR and PBS, which rely heavily on audience donations and on money from the government. But the U.S. government allocates a significantly lower amount of money to public broadcasting than governments in Britain, Germany, and Canada, among others. How do you propose that we fund NPR and PBS—taxes, pledge drives, corporate investments and co-productions, product sales, advertisements? What are the advantages and limitations of these sources of revenue? Might some of them change PBS's mandate and/or influence the content?

FURTHER READING

For more reading on establishing the commercial mandate of U.S. broadcasting, see Erik Barnouw's *Tube of Plenty: The Evolution of American Television*, 2nd rev. ed. (New York: Oxford University Press, 1990); Susan Smulyan's *Selling Radio: The Commercialization of American Broadcasting: 1920–1934* (Washington, D.C.: Smithsonian, 1994); Robert Waterman McChesney's *Telecommunications, Mass Media, and Democracy: The Battle for the Control of U.S. Broadcasting, 1928–1935* (New York: Oxford University Press, 1993); and Susan Douglas' *Inventing American Broadcasting: 1899–1922* (Baltimore: Johns Hopkins University Press, 1987).

More on U.S. public broadcasting can be found in Laurie Ouellette's *Viewers Like You?: How Public TV Failed the People* (New York: Columbia University Press, 2002) and Glenda R. Balas' *Recovering a Public Vision for Public Television* (Lanham, Md.: Rowman and Littlefield, 2003). For more on community media, see Kevin Howley's *Community Media: People, Places, and Communication Technologies* (Cambridge: Cambridge University Press, 2005); Ellie Rennie's *Community Media: A Global Introduction* (Lanham, Md.: Rowman and Littlefield, 2006); and *Understanding Community Media*, edited by Kevin Howley (Thousand Oaks, Calif.: Sage, 2009).

For books exploring media systems and their mandates outside of the United States, see Fred S. Siebert's *Four Theories of the Press: The Authoritarian, Libertarian, Social Responsibility, and Soviet Communist Concepts of What the Press Should Be and Do* (Urbana: University of Illinois Press, 1956); Daniel Clark Hallin and Paolo Mancini's *Comparing Media Systems: Three Models of Media and Politics* (Communication, society, and politics.) (Cambridge: Cambridge University Press, 2004); and Michael Tracey's *The Decline and Fall of Public Service Broadcasting* (Oxford: Oxford University Press, 1998).

NOTES

1. Laurel Wentz and Bradley Johnson, "Top 100 Global Advertisers Heap Their Spending Abroad," *Advertising Age*, Nov. 30, 2009, 1–2.

2. Steve Clarke, "Things Getting Worse for BBC," *Variety.com*, Nov. 23, 2008, http://www.variety.com/index.asp?layout=print_story&articleid=VR1117996 373&categoryid=2911 (accessed Nov. 25, 2008).

3. Patricia Aufderheide, "Public Television," in *Encyclopedia of Television*, 2nd ed., ed. Horace Newcomb (New York: Fitzroy Dearborn), 1854–1857.

4. Ibid., 1854.

5. Kirk Johnson, "From a Porch in Montana, Low-Power Radio's Voice Rises," *New York Times*, Sept. 8, 2009, http://www.nytimes.com/2009/09/08/us/08radio. html?_r=1 (accessed Feb. 24, 2010).

6. Alvin Toffler, *The Third Wave* (New York: Bantam Books, 1989).

7. Mark Andrejevic, "Watching Television Without Pity: The Productivity of Online Fans," *Television & New Media* 9 (2008), 24–46.

8. Aung Zaw, "Celluloid Disillusions," *Irrawaddy* 12, no. 3 (March 2004), http://www.irrawaddy.org/article.php?art_id=924 (accessed Feb. 12, 2010).

9. Andrew Buncombe, "Cabin Crews Protest Over Thai Massage Soap Opera," *The Independent*, Jan. 22, 2008, 24.

10. Susan J. Douglas, *Inventing American Broadcasting, 1899–1922* (Baltimore, Md.: Johns Hopkins University Press, 1989); Robert B. Horwitz, *The Irony of Regulatory Reform* (New York: Oxford University Press, 1989); Robert W. McChesney, *Telecommunications, Mass Media and Democracy* (New York: Oxford University Press, 1993).

11. Erik Barnouw, *Tube of Plenty: The Evolution of American Television*, 2nd rev. ed. (New York: Oxford University Press, 1990), 20.

12. Susan Smulyan, *Selling Radio: The Commercialization of American Broadcasting: 1920–1934* (Washington, D.C.: Smithsonian, 1994), 79.

CHAPTER 3

Technological Conditions of the
Media Industries

The nonprofit organization One Laptop per Child aims to give free, durable laptops, connected to the Internet, that run on manual power to the poorest children in the world. By 2009, nearly 1.3 million such laptops had been delivered to children in developing nations. The initiative is an effort to help disadvantaged children overcome the limitations of poor local schools by allowing them to connect to the vast educational resources of the Internet and claim responsibility for their own educations. Underlying this mission is the assumption that technology alone—absent any institutional or cultural support—can interest children in learning and improve their educational development. Becoming better-educated world citizens is not the ultimate goal, however, according to the Nicholas Negroponte, a professor at MIT and the driving force behind One Laptop per Child. Rather, the goal is to eliminate poverty. Negroponte hopes that, by using technology to help individuals, communities, and entire nations leapfrog from pre-industrial to postindustrial societies, young people in developing nations will not only be able to compete for jobs with their more privileged counterparts in the developed nations, but also that they will be able to become successful local entrepreneurs, lifting their communities out of poverty as they themselves acquire more wealth.

The science fiction writer William Gibson has much different visions of technology. In his version, large conglomerates dominate the near future, creating social and psychological alienation and using intense surveillance, all made possible by unchecked technological growth. His visions have had a strong impact on Hollywood films about the future, including such blockbusters as James Cameron's *Avatar*, the *Matrix* series, and the Tom Cruise vehicle *Minority Report*. One of Gibson's short stories, "Johnny Mnemonic," is a good illustration of these themes, and it was made into a movie that is something of a precursor to *The Matrix*. "Johnny Mnemonic" follows a futuristic "courier" who carries information stored in his cybernetic brain. After receiving some highly sensitive and deadly information, Mnemonic struggles to remove the data in order to escape an assassin and prevent an overload of information from "crashing" his brain. His search leads him into The Sprawl, a huge, postindustrial, poverty-stricken area where criminals, drug addicts, and mutants live "off the grid" in a nightmarish underworld that is almost completely isolated from the high-tech cities where Mnemonic has lived his life.

Negroponte's faith in the power of technology to create positive change in world, almost regardless of the forces that stand in the way of that change, is something that we would characterize as **technological utopianism**, an idea that dates back as far as the Enlightenment in Western societies and that sees technological innovation as bringing about an idyllic human society on earth. As we suggested back in Chapter 1, while this kind of excitement about new technology may feel very modern to us, it has, in fact, attended every new media technology since the nineteenth century. Likewise, **technological dystopianism**, like that of Gibson, may make for good reading and may raise important questions about our technological future, but such visions also intentionally tend toward hyperbole in order to make their point and evoke a response from the reader or viewer.

In contrast to these two extremes, we view media technologies and technological change as one of three powerful conditions that shape the media industries, the texts they produce, and the societies in which they are consumed, in conjunction with economic conditions and regulatory conditions. While technology is powerful, it is also powerfully shaped by these other conditions, as well as the various practices to which those technologies are put and the cultures into which they are introduced. In other words, the ultimate impact of any media technology on the industries depends on a range of factors that come from both within and beyond the technology itself.

* * *

In this chapter, we explore the technological conditions within which media industries operate. Our aim is not to give a thorough overview of current technological conditions, but rather to address some of the larger questions about the relationships between technological conditions—particularly innovation—and the media industries, as well as to account for the historical conditions that have shaped the media industries to date. We attend in detail to the role of digitization as a current force of technological change in Chapter 10. To some of you, the focus on history probably seems beside the point, given the popular impression that we live in a thoroughly different technological environment than we did even twenty years ago. If we are to truly understand how technological conditions are influencing contemporary media industries, however, we must realize that recent changes have not occurred in a vacuum. Instead, the details of those changes have a lot to do with how prior technological conditions had already shaped the industries. For instance, the ways in which cable television, Internet news, and political blogs have undermined the idea of journalistic objectivity in today's world can only be understood against the backdrop of how the earlier technology of telegraphy helped usher in the era of objectivity in journalism in the first place, as newswire services tried hard to market their products nationwide to newspapers with quite distinct—and blatant—political sensibilities.

Technological conditions generally operate independently of the other conditions we discuss in the book, but they nevertheless have a close relationship with the regulatory and economic conditions of the media industries. The television networks of the 1960s, for instance, wielded great economic and political power due to regulatory conditions that minimized competition from cable television. The technology of the time would have permitted the development of cable channels and networks, much as developed in the 1980s, but regulatory conditions, specifically, the ban against cable channels originating their own programming, prevented these developments. Beginning in the early 1970s, however, at the urging of President Richard Nixon, who had a notoriously rocky relationship with the national television networks, the FCC began loosening restrictions on cable, ushering in the beginnings of the television landscape with which we are familiar today.

Technological changes, then, can be both helped and hindered by economic and regulatory conditions. In addition, at the level of practice, media production, distribution, and exhibition processes can have profound influences on technological conditions and, of course, vice versa. As we mentioned in Chapter 3, radio broadcasting was initially an extension of the telegraph, used not for entertainment or news, but instead as a way to carry messages, much like a telephone. In fact, early radio developers promoted it as a "telephone booth of the airwaves," or a way to send personal messages to one another without wires, not unlike contemporary mobile phones.[1] Some entrepreneurs, however, in an effort to sell radio sets, began sending signals over the airwaves carrying music, which anyone with a set could access. This use of the technology came to be known as "broadcasting," a term taken from farming that refers to the practice of throwing seed widely when planting, or casting it broadly. As these production practices—that is, the creation of public messages for multiple listeners rather than private messages for a single listener—became prevalent, they squeezed out the earlier use of the technology to the point where almost no one today thinks of radio as a private communication medium. In fact, technically speaking, private messages on broadcast channels are illegal today in the United States.

THEORIES OF TECHNOLOGICAL CHANGE

The example of early radio carries two important lessons for thinking about the relationship between technology and media industries. First, the uses of new technologies are difficult to predict, even when powerful economic and regulatory forces try to shape them in particular ways. Second, technologies have inherent **technical potentialities** that make certain uses more or less possible. In the case of radio, for instance, the U.S. Navy tried hard to harness the technology for secure communication about fleet maneuvers, but despite its best efforts, the signals insisted on spreading across a wide geographic area, where enemies might intercept them. So, the very property of radio that made *broadcasting* possible initially was seen as a limitation of the technology as a **point-to-point** medium.

The idea that technologies have unique potentialities may seem an obvious one, but a good deal of debate has arisen about the degree to which those potentialities are determinant of their uses within the media industries, a theoretical perspective often referred to as **technological determinism**. In the One Laptop per Child initiative, technology is understood as dictating its own uses: it is the technologies, not the institutions that deploy them or the children who use them, that create learning. Technological determinism attributes strong, nearly omnipotent, powers to the technologies that surround us. In fact, both the technological utopian and technological dystopian perspectives discussed previously are versions of technological determinism, though one strain of thought evaluates technology positively, while the other evaluates it negatively.

A similarly weak version of the impact of technology on society also exists, known as **cultural determinism**, which argues that the cultural uses of a technology determine how that technology develops and the influences it has on industry and society. Take the example of television, which had been conceptualized as a technological possibility as early as the 1840s but did not develop as a widespread communications technology until a century later. While it is true that the earliest forms of television had images that were far inferior to those of the 1940s, it is also the case that no one could envision a useful purpose for the medium; the best application they could imagine was something akin to a fax machine. It wasn't until the development of nationwide advertising, the success of radio broadcasting, and the migration of middle-class families from the cities to the suburbs that companies and government came to see television as a potentially useful medium of information and entertainment, after which investment in the technology began in earnest. Moreover, these uses demanded a certain degree of visual and audio fidelity, as well as demands of size and design, in order to fit into the homes and routines of daily middle-class life. At its root, cultural determinism sees technology as an inert force shaped by other, far more powerful forces in a manner that disregards the meaningful role technology and other industrial and regulatory conditions may play.

As we've already said, we think any type of single determinism—whether technological, cultural, economic, or regulatory—goes too far. We believe that technologies do, in fact, have inherent potentialities that influence their uses, but also that powerful interests have a good deal of capacity to shape how technologies get used. In rare instances, the technologies may thwart the desires of these powerful interests, as was the case in early radio, but much more frequently, those in power have been intimately involved with developing the new technology, heartily embrace the changes it brings, and largely get the technology to work the way they want it to. Still, it's almost inevitable that no technology will work exactly as predicted, so new technologies do wind up changing the media industries in some unexpected ways. The television and film industries, for instance, pushed hard to integrate computer technology into editing and distribution beginning in the 1980s. New digital editing techniques saved time and money and increased the visual impact of television and film, while the development of DVD technology drove the widespread adoption of home DVD players and sparked sales and rentals of movies and television programs. The industry, however, did not anticipate how much easier **piracy** would become as a result of digitization. Suddenly, any number of people with access to the final edit of a film or television show could make a digital copy and sell it. So, a technological innovation that powerful media interests pushed wound up boomeranging and producing unintended negative consequences for them.

All technologies, then, have inherent potentialities that are sometimes only partly understood by the people and organizations involved in developing and deploying them. Typically, these technologies have minimal impact on the media industries, but in some instances, those changes can be profound and unanticipated. This is one of the reasons that large media firms tend *not* to be innovators of media technology; they prefer to leave this unpredictable and risky segment of the business to smaller upstarts. At the same time, and as we explore more thoroughly in Chapter 9, once these new media businesses do begin to turn a profit, they are often bought out by the big guys.

A Model: Circuit of Cultural Production

One model for understanding the complexity of technological change is the circuit of cultural production depicted in Figure 3.1.

This model identifies five "cultural processes" that affect cultural goods: identity, representation, production, consumption, and regulation. In their book *Doing Cultural Studies: The Story of the Walkman*, Paul du Gay and colleagues explore the introduction and early years of the Sony Walkman, tracing how these five processes interacted as 1980s societies first encountered personal, portable music. They argue that to study a technology such as "the Walkman culturally one should at least explore how it is represented, what social identities are associated with it, how

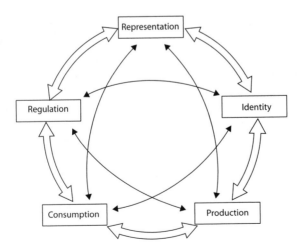

Figure 3.1 Circuit of culture graphic.

it is produced and consumed, and what mechanisms regulate its distribution and use."[2] A key aspect of this model is its emphasis on the interconnectedness of the various processes. Consequently, it counters theories of technological determinism, instead offering a framework with which to understand the significant ways that culture intersects with technological capability to influence how we come to use and understand media. Although the circuit of culture model is intended for application beyond media technologies, through the case of the Walkman, we can see how particularly helpful it is for understanding the complicated cultural processes involved in the creation and dissemination of media technologies. While the Walkman may seem dated, all of the same questions and points of analysis apply easily to newer media technologies such as the latest generation of mobile devices, DVRs, digital readers such as Amazon's Kindle, and obviously, iPods.

The cultural processes du Gay et al. consider include representation, or the attributes and characteristics that the company making the technology tries to associate with it. Illustrations of this can be found in how the company advertises and markets the technology as well as the statements about the product it offers in press releases. Representation is similar to a second process, identity, which includes the attributes, characteristics, and purposes that come to be associated with technology regardless of the manufacturer's intention. Sometimes identity and representation are closely related, but often efforts to "brand" a technology fail, and they come to take on unintended meanings. Apple's 2010 release of the iPad, a portable computing and communications device designed to replace every other portable electronic device, has been dogged by competing meanings that have frustrated the company's efforts to brand the device effectively. Is the iPad a revolution in convergence and convenience, or just another device with the same capabilities as many other portable assistants—a crass attempt to repackage the same old technology in order to get consumers to shell out a few more dollars? At the moment we are writing this, the answer to this question is uncertain, but how it is answered will certainly affect the identity of the iPad.

Production, a third cultural process, considers how processes of production, systems of organization, aspects such as how it is manufactured and where (Canada versus China), and what type of company owns it all contribute to cultural use of the technology. In the case of the Sony Walkman, the corporate culture of Sony and the fact that it was a Japanese company (during a time when the United States was feeling threatened by Japanese productivity and innovation) were both significant to perceptions and attitudes about the product. A fourth cultural process of consumption incorporates how audiences/consumers use the technology, examining questions such as who uses it and how do they use it? Often, audiences discover unintended uses or place greater priority on attributes that the manufacturer thought were secondary. This leads to adjustments in manufacturing and marketing (representation), illustrating the dynamism and interrelation the two-way arrows of the circuit of culture indicate. The final cultural process is regulation, which includes include both formal regulations enforced by a government as well as informal regulations, such as manufacturing norms agreed upon within the industry or norms of use adopted by those using the technology (like turning the ringer on your phone off during class).

TECHNOLOGY AND ECONOMIC CONDITIONS

As the Sony Walkman example makes clear, changes in technological conditions can be felt throughout the media industries and even society at large. Returning to the Industrialization of Culture framework, we often find that technological changes have a strong impact on economic conditions, because they can alter power relationships among different players in the industry, as well as bring in new competitors and ways of doing business that threaten to undermine established interests. In particular, we find that technological changes often lead to changes in industry structure and prevalent revenue models.

Technology and Industry Structure

One recurring theme in the history of the media industries is the idea that certain industries lend themselves to **natural monopolies**. According to this idea, some industries can only operate efficiently and profitably if they are controlled by a single monopoly organization. The need for a monopolistic industry structure is typically seen as a result of technological conditions, at least in the media industries. For decades, regulators treated **common carriers**, or telecommunications network operators that do not originate media content, such as the telephone industry, as natural monopolies. The quintessential example here is AT&T's decades-long monopoly over the telephone industry. In the early years of telephony, AT&T convinced the federal government of the social importance of nationwide telephone connections, arguing successfully that even the remotest parts of the country should have telephone service. The problem with providing service to remote areas, however, was that it was prohibitively expensive. In large cities, telephone providers could charge pennies per phone call because of the thousands of calls being placed daily, but in small cities, each phone call would have had to cost perhaps hundreds of dollars in order to pay for the installation and maintenance of the system! What AT&T proposed was to charge overcharge users in urban areas in order to **cross-subsidize** undercharging users in rural areas. Such a strategy could work, however, only if AT&T faced no competition in urban areas; otherwise, competitors would charge lower prices in lucrative areas without the need to cross-subsidize rural markets. Regulators agreed with this argument and granted AT&T a monopoly that lasted from 1913 to 1984.

Regulatory conditions, then, work together with media and communications technologies to create industry structures. In the AT&T case, the high costs of installing a phone system and the desirability of nationwide telephone connections resulted in a monopolistic industry structure. While regulatory and technological conditions are not the only forces that shape industry structure, they are often powerful ones. In the television industry of the 1950s, the **Federal Communications Commission** (FCC), made a series of decisions that created the oligopoly structure of the industry that lasted until Fox Broadcasting successfully began in 1987. First, the FCC decided to locate television in the VHF band of the electromagnetic spectrum, a decision that allowed for only about thirteen possible television channels, while another band of the spectrum, the UHF band, would have given many more potential television channels. In addition, in the FCC's Sixth Report and Order,[3] the Commission decided that every community would get at least one television station. While this ideal of **localism** may have been laudable, it effectively worked to further limit the number of stations on offer, as many broadcast licenses went unused in small communities that could not afford to mount a local television station. Had the Commission decided to concentrate licenses in larger communities only, they and the smaller communities surrounding them would have had far more channels to choose from. A few years later, when the Commission finally did decide to allow UHF channels, it endorsed a policy of intermixture that permitted a total of three VHF and three UHF stations in each market, despite the fact the UHF stations could not be received on most television sets and were technologically inferior to their VHF counterparts. The result of these decisions was to make it extremely difficult to form more than three national television networks. Again, the technological capacity for more channels was available, though the technology of broadcasting certainly did limit how many channels could operate without interfering with one another. Thus, the three-network oligopoly that reigned for nearly four decades in the United States was as much a product of regulation as of technology.

When Fox Broadcasting broke the network oligopoly in 1987 by creating a successful fourth network, it did so because of technological and regulatory changes, as well. With regard to regulatory conditions, a series of decisions had created a viable cable industry by the mid-1980s, particularly the Cable Act of 1984, which permitted cable franchises in every community in the country. Technologically, cable gave weak UHF stations the same quality and reach as their VHF counterparts, because the cable operator collected all broadcast signals with powerful receivers and sent them out via cables to subscribers, making UHF and VHF signals functionally the same to viewers. Fox Broadcasting, then, was able to cobble together a group of affiliates who suddenly found themselves with access to a much wider audience than they had previously.

Regulation forms an important component of both the AT&T and the network television examples, because both of these industries were highly regulated at the time. As you will read more about in the next chapter, however, other media industries are far less regulated, and, as a result, other conditions have much more influence on industry structure. We also want to note that technological conditions alter regulatory conditions as well; it is a two-way street. In fact, in each of the examples above, it was the introduction of new technological conditions that prompted changes in government regulations. These issues also remain relevant today. Some sectors of the print media industry are concerned that Google will hold a monopoly on digital access to published books as a result of its Google Books endeavor. Also, some of the problems of the digital divide are emerging because of a lack of regulation comparable to that which made AT&T subsidize rural telephony. In many cases, contemporary telecommunications providers introduce new and fast services in the most affluent communities, and rural areas, especially, have suffered from the lack of access to high-speed Internet.

Technology and Prevalent Revenue Models

Technology also affects economic conditions other than industry structure, particularly **revenue models**, or whether and how businesses actually make money off of media texts. In two examples from the print industries—changes in newspaper printing in the late nineteenth century and technological changes in industries that have come to compete with magazines in the early twenty-first century—we see how technology can create or undermine the economic viability of an entire commercial medium.

For much of the nineteenth century, newspapers in the United States served as organs of political parties. They tended to have quite small circulations, due to the costs of publishing and distribution; newspapers were printed on rags, which were expensive, heavy, and thus costly to send via mail. As a result, newspaper publishers printed only a small number of copies and generally didn't send them very far around the country. Beginning in the 1870s, however, due to increased costs and scarcity of rags, most newspapers had begun using wood pulp for newspaper, a relatively new technology that caused paper prices to plummet. By 1882, almost every newspaper in the country had begun to use wood pulp for paper. Wood-pulp paper, moreover, was lighter than rag-based paper and cost less to distribute. In the wake of this technological change, the newspaper industry took off. Between 1870 and 1880, as the newspaper industry faced significant changes in economic conditions that we detail at the beginning of Chapter 5, more newspapers were published than had been published in the previous century, and average newspaper circulation increased 240 percent between 1860 and 1880.[4]

Along with increased competition and circulation due to cheaper prices, newspapers began to change from political to commercial enterprises, in large part due to the fact that they could now serve as vehicles for national advertising. **Penny presses**, as these newspapers came to be called, not only began to reach a truly national readership, but they were also read by a wider cross-section of the population, most notably the working-class immigrants who formed the backbone of the growing national consumer society of the time. Hereafter, it became much more common for advertisers, rather than political parties, to fund newspaper publishing. In a very direct way, then, the technological development of wood pulp as a base for paper led to the development of the commercial newspaper industry. These changes also deeply influenced the target audience for newspapers, the costs of newspapers, and the content and social role of newspapers.

Fast-forwarding 130-odd years, we may be witnessing the death of another commercial print medium, the magazine, due to the development of two new technologies: cable television and the Internet. Of course, the magazine industry has survived more than a few predictions of its death, perhaps most notably the introduction of television, which undermined general-circulation magazines and destroyed some of the best-known and most influential magazines at the time. More recently, however, even longstanding, carefully tailored magazines have begun failing, and at an alarming rate.

When television was introduced in the 1950s, magazine industry executives realized that it threatened their very existence. At the time, the biggest magazines in the country distinguished themselves by reporting on news and human-interest stories with high-quality, glossy pictures. Television promised to deliver even more powerful visuals, along with similar news and human-interest stories, all for free. The magazine industry responded by focusing on certain segments of the audience, or **niches**, and creating content tailored specifically for those niches, a process we detail more thoroughly in Chapter 9. In other words, decades before the television industry, and even prior to the radio industry, the magazine industry had changed from a mass to a niche industry—to such an extent that few of us can probably even imagine magazines as a mass-appeal medium.

Beginning in the 1980s, a technological innovation known as desktop publishing rapidly changed the economic conditions of the magazine industry. Desktop publishing utilized computers and automation to make the publishing process simpler, more efficient, and cheaper. As a result, competition in the magazine industry exploded, as hundreds of new competitors flooded the market. The number of consumer magazines grew nearly 500 percent between 1981 and 2000, from 1192 to 5649. Since 2000, however, the number of new magazine launches has dropped, and the number of failures has risen. Since 2008, such long-running magazines as *Gourmet*, *Teen*, *PC Magazine*, and *Home* have shut down publication.[5] See Table 3.1 for a selection of recent magazine deaths.

The main culprit, most industry observers agree, has been the trend toward niche-focused television channels and Internet publications. Much as television channels rivaled magazines in the 1950s, niche television channels can provide the kind of tailored media experience that magazines do, with more immediate access and more engaging visuals and stories. The Internet, meanwhile, offers content equivalent to magazines that is cheap or free and more readily accessible. Like most established media industries, the magazine industry was slow to develop an online presence. When magazine websites did begin appearing, they tended to carry the same content as the print edition, delayed by a few days or weeks. More recently, some magazines have developed Internet-only content and editions in order to lure online subscribers. Still, the eventual success of these adaptations and how online advertising fits in with traditional economic models remains uncertain.[6]

The most successful adaptations to the present technological and economic conditions of the magazine industry seem to be those publications that form a central part of a successful, multimedia brand.[7] *Martha Stewart Living* offers a good example of this trend from the 1990s and early 2000s, the magazine drew readers from Martha Stewart's television series and appearances while also sending interested readers back to the television series. Both the television series and the magazine also drove consumers to the stores to buy a wide range of Martha Stewart-branded

Table 3.1   Selection of Major Magazine Titles that Ceased Publication in 2009

MAGAZINE TITLE	YEAR OF INCEPTION
I.D. Magazine	1954
National Geographic Adventure	1999
Giant Magazine	2004
Metropolitan Home	1981
Gourmet	1941
Cookie	2005
Southern Accents	1977
Vibe	1992
Nickelodeon	1993
Travel & Leisure Golf	1998
Hallmark Magazine	2006
Teen	1954
Electronic Gaming Weekly	1989
Country Home	1986
National Geographic Green Guide	1994
PC Magazine	1982
Home	1951
Playgirl	1973
Cosmo Girl	1999

SOURCE: Advertising Age, *"A Guide to Magazines That Have Ceased Publication,"* Dec. 15, 2009. Available online at http://adage.com/mediaworks/article?article_id=132779 (accessed Aug. 31, 2010).

household goods. More recently, we see an even more ambitious example of this trend with the planned launch of the Oprah Winfrey Network (OWN) on digital cable in 2011. While Oprah's magazine, *O,* and her television program, *The Oprah Winfrey Show,* never had the kind of close tie-ins with branded consumer goods that Martha Stewart's did, the proposed integration of magazine, website, and digital cable network that Oprah envisions has the capacity to become a major source of information and entertainment for young, professionally minded women.

Technological, economic, and regulatory conditions, then, are quite intimately interwoven. Most commonly, the development of new technologies that alter established conditions serves the economic interests of the most powerful media corporations, even though the technologies may lead to altered economic conditions. Similarly, regulatory changes typically serve the same interests, even though technological changes may lead to changed regulatory conditions. As we will examine much more closely in Chapter 10, however, there are times when technological conditions change somewhat more unexpectedly, when entrenched media corporations and established production and distribution practices get challenged. Although media industry players constantly encourage and prepare for technological changes, once unleashed, those changes can prove unpredictable.

TECHNOLOGICAL CONDITIONS AND MEDIA INDUSTRY PRACTICES

In the examples above, we've already hinted at the fact that technological conditions also shape media industry practices and the texts that the media industries produce. This may seem like an obvious point to some of you. Without technology, we wouldn't even have a media industry to speak of, at least not in the way we define the industry. The points to keep in mind, however, are: first, technology doesn't change media texts, but it does open up opportunities for new textual practices that certain entrepreneurs pursue; second, these new textual practices are also shaped by—but *not determined* by—economic and regulatory conditions as well as technological ones.

We primarily focus on the impact of technology on production practices and texts in this section, even though it affects distribution practices equally as profoundly, because we address the impact of technology on distribution in Chapters 7 and 10 extensively. In addition, the example above about changes in the magazine industry and how they have undermined prevalent revenue models is also a story of technology altering distribution practices. Specifically, we saw how the distribution of print media has changed from practices largely built around the physical distribution of newspapers and magazines to ones built around the electronic distribution of individual stories.

Sampling in rap music offers a good example of how technological changes lead to changes in production practices and texts. Sampling is the strategy of finding prerecorded music from a variety of different sources and combining them into a new song or musical piece. Although sampling and rap music began during the analog era, sampling really became established as a dominant feature of rap music in the late 1980s and early 1990s with the introduction of digital sampling technologies. It suddenly became quite simple and relatively cheap to take music from numerous sources, and the sounds that came to dominate rap music were closer to collage than the harmonies that one finds in rock music, R&B, and soul, the most immediate precursors of rap. The makeup of the primary creative unit in contemporary music changed as a result of sampling technology as well. DJs, at first working with vinyl albums and tape machines, could create music without other band members, basically functioning a one-person band. Given the performative nature of many rap concerts, however, other members soon joined the band, often as secondary rappers and singers, dancers, etc. Still, the centerpiece of the rap band remained the DJ, unlike rock bands, which are usually centered on a lead singer.

The story of rap music would not be complete, however, without also commenting on how regulatory conditions changed as a result of rap music production practices and how these new regulations have likewise changed texts and production practices. The era of collage that sampling ushered in quickly caught the attention of the courts and regulators, because most samples were used without the consent of—or payment to—the original artist. While short samples of prerecorded music, especially ones that are unrecognizable, had been permitted under copyright law prior to the 2000s, since that time, the courts have held that *any* use of prerecorded music without the permission of the copyright holder is illegal. Moreover, since using samples requires the payment of **royalties** to the copyright holder, the kinds of complex, sampled soundscapes that characterized rap music of the 1990s have all but disappeared today due to costs—as we discuss in the copyright section of Chapter 4. One of our colleagues, for instance, working on a documentary about sampling and rap music discovered that, if he were to use all of the sampled songs he wanted to in his hour-long video, the costs would have topped $1 million.

The example of sampling in rap music, then, offers a complex portrait of the relationships among technological conditions, regulatory conditions, production practices, and media texts. We want to emphasize again the importance of regulatory conditions in shaping the relationship between production practices and technological conditions to remind you that it is not technology alone that influences media production and texts. In addition, technological changes in one media industry can influence production practices in other industries, particularly in today's world of convergence and conglomeration in which producers in one industry are constantly aware of developments elsewhere. When the production practices and textual features of a new medium influence an older medium, we call this process **remediation**, a process we also discuss in terms of distribution practices in Chapter 7. When *USA Today* began publishing in 1982, it distinguished itself primarily through its use of arresting, full-color graphics in an effort to emulate the kinds of visuals we see on television news. In fact, the newspaper was even sold in specialized vending machines that were designed to look like TV sets. In another case, television itself has been influenced by the production practices of newer media, especially computer games. One prominent change has taken place in televised sports, particularly professional NFL football, which has begun to use camera work similar to that in computerized NFL games. This includes cameras suspended from zip wires over the head of the quarterback or at eye-level behind the field-goal kicker. Not only do these newer shots look more like computer games than earlier production practices, they also require quite different skills in operating cameras and editing the game's live feed. In both of these cases, the jobs of camera operators and editors have become more complex due to efforts to mimic computer game texts.

Technological considerations then work in concert with the conditions, practices, and mandates explored throughout this book to shape the media environment within which we live. In examining any technological innovation, we need to look at how that technology developed and interacted with these other phenomena in order to understand how that innovation changed the media industries, including their economic and regulatory conditions; prevalent production, distribution, and exhibition practices; and the texts that they produce. This approach necessarily prevents us from making arguments about how technology itself has changed media or culture, because such questions only make sense in specific historical and social situations.

INDUSTRY RESTRAINTS ON
TECHNOLOGICAL INNOVATION

We want to end this chapter with a brief overview of the ways in which media organizations, especially for-profit media organizations, stand in the way of technological progress. We do this because we often find that our students have little trouble with the idea that the federal government restrains innovation due to regulation, but few believe that normally functioning competitive markets can also hold back progress. Entrenched media companies and their interests have very good reasons to thwart technological advances; these arise from the companies' recognition that changes in technological conditions lead to changes in economic conditions. Technological changes can undermine successful business models and bring in new competitors. As a result, corporations will go a long way to try to prevent change from happening, whether we are talking about technological change, social change, political change, or other types of change.

We offer two brief examples of this tendency—one from history, one much more recent—that demonstrate the ways in which corporate interests impede technological progress. Again, let us reiterate our main point at the outset: because of their investment in maintaining prevalent economic conditions, entrenched media companies frequently thwart changes in technological conditions, often by influencing regulatory conditions.

The first example comes from 1930s radio, when the all-powerful Radio Corporation of America (RCA) successfully squashed the development of FM radio, despite the technological capacity for FM to deliver a higher-quality signal than AM radio, the dominant broadcasting standard at the time. Edwin Howard Armstrong, one of pioneers of early radio, developed FM broadcasting technology in 1935. FM was a superior technology to AM because of the fidelity of its signal. Probably, most of you know that commercial music stations typically broadcast on FM, because it has less noise and interference than AM radio. Armstrong assumed that RCA would be interested simply because the technology was better, but it rejected his technology for several reasons. First, RCA had a lucrative radio-set sales business. These sets tuned in only AM stations, and RCA did not relish the idea of re-engineering its sets to support radio stations that would compete against its own network affiliates. Now, RCA could have supported FM radio and made obsolete all of its previous sets, requiring tens of millions of Americans to buy new sets, but the company's attention at the time was diverted by television. It used profits from set sales to fund its research and development of television, and had little interest in risking those profits with redesigned sets.[8]

RCA did more than rebuff Armstrong, however; they actively lobbied the FCC to kill FM as a viable business. By the time RCA realized the amount of competition, Armstrong had already assembled a nationwide network of FM stations and manufacturers had begun selling sets with FM capability, including powerful manufacturers like GE. By 1940, FM stations existed in every major city in the

United States, and NBC had even begun experimental FM broadcasts. That same year, however, the FCC relocated the FM radio band in the electromagnetic spectrum, effectively making every FM radio station and every FM radio obsolete. It was as if you had previously been listening to your favorite FM radio station on 99.4 FM, and suddenly it had to relocate to 299.4 FM—and, your radio didn't even go above 107.9! Suddenly, every radio FM station needed to completely redesign its broadcasting equipment and every consumer—who had only recently purchased a new FM-compatible set—suddenly had to buy another new one. Needless to say, the FCC's decisions effectively killed FM radio for the time. But, most historians think that the FCC was merely doing the bidding of the most powerful radio company in the nation, RCA.[9]

Large corporations do not need regulators to squash technological innovation, and even companies that specialize in innovative technology often work to curb their inventions in order to please their larger corporate partners. DVR technology like TiVo is a good case in point. TiVo's immediate predecessor, ReplayTV, had the ability to skip commercials while recording and to share programming with other DVRs. The company was bankrupted by lawsuits before broadband Internet services became widespread, but you can imagine how broadband-enabled DVRs that can share programming among each other would undermine the revenue models of just about every television network currently in existence. The major media content producers came after ReplayTV aggressively for including these features, winning numerous lawsuits against it, and those features were eventually removed. When TiVo came along, its executives wanted to avoid the fate of ReplayTV, and the company began courting investments and guidance from established media corporations so that the technology would not damage the prevalent revenue models of established companies.[10] As a consequence, we no longer enjoy the ability to record programs without commercials or share them with friends and family. Who knows what other innovative DVR functions have been squelched because they were seen as too much of a threat to powerful business interests?

CONCLUSION

In all of the examples we have encountered in this chapter, technological conditions have not developed independently, but rather in conjunction with economic and regulatory conditions. These changes in conditions have led to changes in production, distribution, and exhibition practices. At the same time, changes in practice due to technological innovations have sometimes "filtered up" to change regulatory and economic conditions.

One of the many ironies of the media industries is that they both depend on and fear changes in technological conditions. They depend on them because technological changes drive up demand for both media hardware and software. Currently, for instance, the movie industry is betting on new 3D technology to lure viewers to into the theaters, a feat that the 3D blockbuster *Avatar* accomplished in the winter of 2009. The hope here is that such a spectacular technology will be worth the extra driving and extra price of seeing a 3D movie in the theater. Meanwhile, Panasonic and DirecTV began a partnership in 2010 to broadcast three channels of 3D television to 3D-enabled Panasonic HDTVs, with the hope of driving both consumer adoption of 3D HDTVs and DirecTV satellite services.[11] In other words, technological innovation is often commercially appealing and is built into the very fabric of the media industries.

On the other hand, established media corporations work hard to resist other forms of technological change, or at least to shape them in ways that are least harmful to their profits. They resist with lawsuits, acquisition of upstart companies, and lobbying the federal government to develop restrictive regulatory conditions. Of course, the reason for this somewhat schizophrenic approach to technological change is that powerful companies want to develop only those technologies that they see as increasing their revenues while hobbling those that seem like a threat. The wild card in this equation is the technology itself, what we called the technical potentialities of the technology. Despite their best efforts to promote only technologies that serve their interests, large corporations never know how technologies are going to be taken up and how they are going to alter the prevalent conditions and practices of their industry until those technologies have been unleashed. To sum up, then, while it is certainly bound up with the other forces we examine in this book, technology also operates as a force in its own right.

QUESTIONS

1. Recall discussions that you had or that you heard in the media or among family about the Internet as you grew up. What concerns or hopes were expressed? Was it discussed in a way that you would characterize more as technological utopianism or technological dystopianism? Can you identify ways in which ideas about technological determinism and cultural determinism factored into the fears of, and hopes for, the Internet?

2. Consider our claim that media industries both depend on and fear changes in technological conditions, for a variety of reasons. Select a specific technological development and try to imagine the reasons why a media industry would have both welcomed *and* resisted that change? What was at stake in the technological development? What could have happened that might have made the industry nervous? Did the technology end up changing the production and/or reception of particular media texts?

3. As discussed in this chapter, the magazine industry has had a difficult time figuring out how to adapt to the Internet. What are some aspects unique to the magazine industry that have made this adaption to the Internet particularly difficult, or that may affect the magazine industry more than other industries? What advantages and disadvantages are involved in a magazine being part of a multimedia brand, such as *ESPN Magazine*? Can you think of a strategy that might help magazines adapt to the Internet?

FURTHER READING

More on other models for understanding media can be found in Paul du Gay et al., *Doing Cultural Studies: The Story of the Sony Walkman* (London: Sage, 1997); Julie D'Acci, "Cultural Studies, Television Studies, and the Crisis in the Humanities," in *Television After TV: Essays on a Medium in Transition*, edited by Lynn Spigel and Jan Olsson (Durham: Duke University Press, 2004), 418–446; and Richard Johnson, "What is Cultural Studies Anyway?" *Social Text* 16, (1986–87), 38–80.

More reading on history of technological innovation and the development of contemporary technological and regulatory conditions can be found in Harmeet Sawhney, "Information Superhighway: Metaphors as Midwives," *Media Culture & Society* 18 (1996), 291–314; Ithiel de Sola Pool's *Technologies of Freedom* (Cambridge, Mass.: Belknap Press, 1983); Robert Britt Horwitz's *The Irony of Regulatory Reform: The Deregulation of American Telecommunications* (Oxford and New York: Oxford University Press, 1989); Ken Burns' *Empire of the Air: The Men Who Made Radio* (Washington, D.C.: Florentine Films and WETA Television, 1991. Original broadcast date: Jan. 29, 1992); and Leslie Cauley, *End of the Line: The Rise and Fall of AT&T* (New York: Free Press, 2005).

NOTES

1. Harmeet Sawhney, "Information Superhighway: Metaphors as Midwives," *Media Culture and Society,* 18 (1996), 291–314.
2. Paul du Gay et al., *Doing Cultural Studies: The Story of the Sony Walkman* (London: Sage, 1997), 3.
3. Federal Communications Commission (1952) "Television Assignments: Sixth Report and Order" 41 FCC 148.
4. Ithiel de Sola Pool. *Technologies of Freedom* (Cambridge, Mass: Belknap Press, 1983); David C. Smith, "Wood Pulp and Newspapers, 1867–1900," *The Business History Review*, 38 (1964), 328–345.
5. Samir Husni and Emily Main. "Life after Death in the Magazine Industry," *Publishing Research Quarterly* 18 2 (2002), 3–11; Advertising Age, "A Guide to Magazines That Have Ceased Publication," Dec. 15, 2009. Available online at http://adage.com/mediaworks/article?article_id=132779 (accessed Aug. 31, 2010).
6. Lisa M. Guidone, "The Magazine at the Millennium: Integrating the Internet," *Publishing Research Quarterly,* 16 (2000) 14–33; Samir Husni and Emily Main, "Life after Death in the Magazine Industry," *Publishing Research Quarterly,* 18 (2002), 3–11.
7. Guidone, "The Magazine at the Millennium: Integrating the Internet," 3–11.
8. Robert Britt Horwitz, *The Irony of Regulatory Reform: The Deregulation of American Telecommunications* (Oxford and New York: Oxford University Press, 1989); Ken Burns, *Empire of the Air: The Men Who Made Radio.* (Washington, D.C.: Florentine Films and WETA Television, 1991) Original broadcast date: Jan. 29, 1992.

9. Horwitz, *The Irony of Regulatory Reform.*

10. Matt Carlson, "Tapping into TiVo: Digital Video Recorders and the Transition from Schedules to Surveillance in Television," *New Media Society* 8 (2006), 97–115.

11. Mayumi Negishi, "Panasonic Envisions 3D TV Sales Surge," *Reuters*, Jan. 8, 2010, http://www.reuters.com/article/idUSTRE6080AE20100109 (accessed Jan. 12, 2010).

CHAPTER 4

—

Regulation of the Media Industries

When studying the history of the U.S. film industry, one crucial event fundamentally altered what was a thriving and vital media business and forced a transformation of nearly all of its standard industrial practices. What emerged after this event was a film industry that again became thriving and vital, although many of its creative, distribution, and economic norms changed. This event is commonly known as the **Paramount Decree,** and we begin with it here as an illustration of the enormous implications that regulatory conditions can have on the operation of media industries.

The Paramount Decree refers to the outcome of *United States v. Paramount Pictures, Inc.,* a 1948 anti-trust case decided by the Supreme Court. Although only Paramount is mentioned, all of what were then known as the "Big Eight" film studios had their businesses at stake in this case. In short, before the Paramount Decree, eight studios dominated the film industry and controlled all aspects of film creation, distribution, and exhibition—perhaps offering the most extreme version of **vertical integration** ever achieved in a media industry. This meant that a studio created films (using directors, writers, and actors who were all on staff or contracted to the studio) and then distributed the films to theaters that the studios also owned. The studios didn't own all theaters, but they enforced challenging terms for the independently owned theaters through a practice known as **block booking**. In order for an independent theater to get the big new studio film with top talent, it also had to agree to take another block of films selected by the studio that were much less desirable. This was a brilliant arrangement for the studios as it allowed them to control competition by determining when films were screened, in what location, and for how long, enabling the creation of **artificial scarcity** (see Chapter 1).

This degree of control over the film industry came under scrutiny as an unfair trade practice, however, and legal proceedings against the studios began in 1938. The studios managed to draw out the battle for a decade, but after losing in the Supreme Court and being found in violation of the Sherman Anti-Trust Act, the studios divested themselves of their theaters.

As a result of this regulatory action—in this case, a judicial decision—the film industry experienced a complete overhaul and had to adjust many of its practices in response to the new competitive environment. The creative output of the industry also changed as a result, as the studios could no longer rely on forcing mediocre films on theaters. Quite accidentally, the 1948 decision coincided with the launch of television in the United States, which also required the film industry to adapt its norms. This new technology threatened to draw away audiences, as those who could afford to purchase sets now had a new in-home entertainment option. The loss of guaranteed exhibition through self-owned theaters led the film studios to create fewer, higher-quality movies, as there were few takers for the lower-quality works that had flourished because of block booking. This regulatory change also required substantial adjustments in the economic norms and conventional financial practices of the industry.

The film industry has adapted to many other changes since 1948. Over the long term, the studios gradually reduced their reliance on income generated from the first domestic theatrical screening of films and produced more and more revenue from international distribution, the home rental market, licensing of films to television networks, and other distribution windows—a process we describe more fully in Chapter 7. The film industry of 2010 bears little resemblance to the film industry of sixty years earlier, even though the major studios again have become part of massive conglomerated media entities. The Paramount Decree is but one event in a long industry history, but it is one that nevertheless indicates how regulatory conditions can alter the content of media even when content is not being directly regulated. This single regulatory action contributed to a complete reinvention of the economics, studio operation, and nature of film art.

*   *   *

This chapter focuses on **regulation**, or the laws, guidelines, and policies that govern how media industries produce, distribute, and exhibit their products. These regulations are commonly imposed by the nation in which the media operate, but they also can be transnational—as is the case with international treaty agreements. For our purposes, regulation encompasses the creation of laws and rules governing the operation of media industries and the enforcement of those laws, which often requires the creation of specific regulatory bodies. Like technology, regulations determine a playing field of options for media industries, or rather, often remove some ideas and ways of creating them from the realm of possibility. Thus, regulations operate as one of the conditions of media industries in the Industrialization of Culture framework.

Regardless of mandate, the norms of operation and possibilities for all media systems are further determined by various structural conditions—for example, in the case of the film industry noted above, the industry operated with a commercial mandate both before and after the Paramount Decree. Structural conditions such as regulation are broad forces—typically larger than any one company—that organize how media systems and industries can operate. In our look at these conditions, we focus on technology, regulation, and economics. As in the case of mandates, none of these conditions are natural or inevitable, despite how obvious they may seem, but have developed for complicated reasons that may no longer even be relevant. As we saw in the previous chapter, the various conditions within which the media industries operate do not exist in isolation: new technologies require the development of new regulations, while existing economic practices and regulations lead inventors to manufacture technologies that do some things and not others. Arguably, the adjustments in the film industry developed both because of the technological invention of a new competitor (television) as well as the adjustment in practice forced by the regulatory outcome of the anti-trust action.

We can begin to understand regulation by exploring three interconnected questions:

1. *Who regulates?*
2. *What is regulated?*
3. *How do regulations have consequences on the products media industries create?*

In brief, one of the most common regulators is the "state," or government. In most cases, the government does not directly regulate media, but rather it sets up a particular body to manage certain media or enact policy initiatives. Some regulations established nearly a century ago remain in place today, while others have been eliminated or adjusted over time. Some media industries—particularly broadcasting—face regulations that are specific to some aspect of their operation. Almost all media industries, though, face two types of formal regulation: either **content regulations** or regulations on **industry structure**. In addition, technological regulations are important in certain industries, such as telecommunications and broadcasting, but we do not attend to those substantially in this chapter. We did address some of the technological dimensions of regulation in the previous chapter when we addressed FCC decisions that led to the failure of FM radio and the three-network **oligopoly** that dominated television for forty years. The vast majority of technological regulations, however, cover technical minutia that few people in the industry, with the exception of engineers, even understand. Arguably, another category of regulation is becoming more relevant because of the transition to digital media and the way they are delivered. We also discuss regulations governing **access** to media as an increasingly crucial component of media policy. Access regulations and policy are not new, but historically they have been more relevant to point-to-point technology such as telephony. The growing importance of the web as a mass medium for sharing information has led to the need to reassess regulations regarding access to media.

Traditionally, media industry textbooks such as ours have primarily focused on formal regulations enforced by official bodies. While we too, consider these in fair depth, we want to stress from the outset the need for a broader conceptualization of regulation. Often, forms of self-regulation, both conscious and unconscious, most stringently regulate media industries. Many of these are addressed in Chapter 6's discussion of creative practices, in which we explore how individuals impose informal, yet consequential, limitations based on their internalized belief systems and norms and their routines of organizational operation.

The variation in regulatory structures in different countries—and even among different types of media within a single nation—makes the regulation of media industries and their products an expansive topic, and we can only begin to address some of the commonest or most important types of regulation. We must first note that in the United States, the **First Amendment** is a necessary starting place for considering the regulation of most media. The guarantee that "Congress shall make no law … abridging the freedom of speech, or of the press …" provides most media with substantial protection regarding the content they produce. Consequently, many issues regarding the regulation of content come back to issues of constitutionality and key provisions handed down by the Supreme Court regarding matters of indecency, obscenity, and "clear and present danger." As a result of First Amendment protections, many media industries (film, magazines, newspapers, music) are not regulated more heavily by the government than most nonmedia industries. The key exception here is broadcasting, and we explain the specificity of broadcast regulation in the next section.

Although media industries may not face substantial formal regulation, they are still very much regulated by an array of assumptions and perceptions about the nature of their products. This is particularly true of media operating with a commercial mandate. In this case, a broad range of beliefs—about what audiences want, what might worry advertisers, and what might succeed (by commercial measures)—impose strict regulation on the possible range of media products created.

WHY IS BROADCASTING DIFFERENT?

Broadcasting—encompassing aspects of both the radio and the television industries—is the most heavily regulated form of media in the United States and most other countries. It is also the most likely to operate outside of a commercial mandate. As we noted in Chapter 1, this extra regulation results from some of the inherent features of broadcasting. Whether we mean the transmission of voice only, as in the case of radio, or voice and video, as in the case of television, or even newer efforts to broadcast voice, video, and data, broadcasting involves using the radio waves of the electromagnetic spectrum to transmit the signal (Figure 4.1).

Radio waves are a naturally occurring resource, and as inventors identified their uses, it quickly became clear that some sort of organization of the spectrum and set of rules governing who could transmit where would be needed in order for anyone to receive the benefits of using it. An oft told, and perhaps embellished, tale recounts how the chaos of the unorganized radio spectrum led to confusing and contradictory reports about the Titanic disaster.[1] Supposedly, many amateur operators reported receiving signals that gave false accounts of survivors, and others in official capacities claimed that they were impeded from communicating important information because of the amateurs' interference. This situation

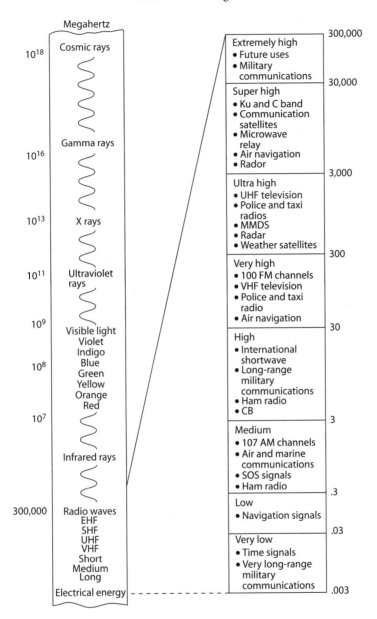

Figure 4.1 The electromagnetic spectrum.

resulted from the lack of regulation at the time about what part of the spectrum an operator could use and the absence of a regulatory body to enforce the few rules that did exist. The result was chaos: without assigned locations on the spectrum, signal interference was inevitable and could make deliberate communication impossible. As the commercial norm of broadcasting was established and the

Federal Radio Commission (**FRC**, the precursor to the Federal Communications Commission or FCC) was created, only licensed broadcasters could use the airwaves, and in being licensed, they were situated on a specific part of the spectrum, to prevent interference. This is still the case today. If the radio station you listen to is 107.1 FM, those numbers identify the position of the radio spectrum that the station uses (107.1) and the sector of the spectrum (FM).

The question of why broadcasting is different, then, comes back to the spectrum. In the United States, policymakers identified the spectrum as a national good that belongs to the people; without some oversight, however, no one would get any benefit from this good because we might all be transmitting overlapping signals. Or, more likely, because most of us don't have the time or inclination to use our spectrum, we are better served by the government organizing the spectrum for us and leasing it out to other parties, which are then charged with serving the public interest. This is the exchange involved (in theory at least) in obtaining a broadcast license in the United States: A station (radio or television) applies to the FCC (which represents the public) for a license, and if the necessary conditions are met, the FCC allows the station to use the airwaves so long as it operates in the **public interest, convenience, and necessity**. The station does not have to pay to use the spectrum frequency. In being licensed by the FCC, it effectively "borrows" the spectrum that belongs to the public in exchange for agreeing to supply a service that benefits the public.

Radio and television stations have been among some of the most profitable industries in the United States. Station owners are able to make great profits through their use of the publicly owned spectrum without having to pay fees or share any percentage of their profits. Consider the difference in the case of a cable system owner. In this case, wires, instead of the airwaves, transmit the television signals. The government did not lay the miles and miles of cable that now connect much of the country; rather, that expense was paid for by the cable company out of its net revenues or was taken on as debt to be repaid once the service gained subscribers, began to operate, and achieved profitability. Similarly, in the cases of satellite radio and television, companies such as XM, Sirius, DirecTV, and Dish Network paid for the satellite links and spectrum necessary to transmit their signals to those who receive their service. Broadcasters do face costs of building the transmission towers that send the signal out, but they use something that belongs to the public to get that signal from the tower into homes. This difference in how we access media has supported the different regulation of the broadcast and cable industries to date.

Since we can't see the spectrum, it is often difficult to understand its value or how it might belong to the public. To make spectrum seem more tangible, think of it as akin to a national park: the land belongs to the public, but without someone managing the space, there would likely be such chaos that no one would get any use out of it. We can perhaps more easily conceive of how this land has value than how the spectrum does. Certainly, if the parkland was sold to developers who would build houses or commercial properties, great sums of money could be gained. The spectrum functions quite similarly. The government allows broadcasters to borrow certain parts of the spectrum in exchange for serving the public. Other parts of the spectrum have been sold off—at this point chiefly to wireless communication providers and satellite companies. These companies paid billions of dollars to effectively own certain parts of the spectrum. Since they bought their spectrum, they are not mandated with the same requirements of serving the public.

There is one more important point for understanding the regulation of broadcasting. Even though we often think of broadcasters—particularly in the case of television—in terms of national networks such as NBC, ABC, Fox, or CBS, the FCC has no direct jurisdiction over these networks. Rather, the FCC has regulatory power over the individual stations that make up the network, or its **affiliates**. This is because the FCC gains its regulatory power by managing the licenses that each broadcast station must apply for and maintain. For example, when you hear about the FCC levying a fine, it is against individual stations in particular markets, not against the network itself. The FCC also only fines stations if a listener or viewer in the station's market (the geographical area reached by the station) complains, and it finds the complaint appropriate. Consequently, it is usually the case that stations in a few cities may be fined, but many others go without penalty for airing the exact same content. Ideally, this allows for variance in community standards around the country. These fines do affect the network, because the network typically owns its largest and most profitable stations, such as those in markets including New York, Los Angeles, Chicago, Philadelphia, and Dallas. These stations, known as **owned and operated stations, or O&Os** in the business, guarantee a steady stream of revenue for national networks, whose business is more volatile. It is essential to remember, however, that the FCC directly regulates only broadcast stations, not the networks.

Perhaps we have belabored the distinction of broadcasting, but this distinction is a crucial and often overlooked part of media policy. For as long as we have been teaching about media industries, there has always been some policy issue that comes back to this distinction. In recent years, considerable attention has been devoted to questions of "indecency" on television—whether sexual content, vulgar language, or violent portrayals. Even though many of us now simply think of television—not of broadcast networks as distinct from cable channels—broadcasting is very different from a regulatory perspective. In recent debates, legislators have threatened to apply the same rules regarding content that govern broadcasters to cable channels. While the legislators are certainly within their rights to make such rules, it would be highly inconsistent with existing precedent and policy for any court to uphold such rules for cable.

Additionally, we mustn't forget that broadcasters still make millions of dollars in profits using something that belongs to "us." It is through the use of the people's airwaves that much of the regulation regarding both content and industry structure has been justified. This is also why we should reasonably expect more from broadcasters; we should never think of them as simply "businesses" like any others because they are businesses that we underwrite by allowing them free use of spectrum.

We will spend much more time attending to broadcast examples in this chapter because of the more significant influence that government-enforced regulation has for these media. We also, however, attend to laws and regulations regarding copyright, industry structure, and First Amendment protections that structure the behavior of media such as newspapers, films, and magazines, as well as regulations imposed internally by self-regulating bodies (such as the Motion Picture Association of America's rating system).

WHO REGULATES?

Just as the governance structure of every country is a bit different, so, too, is there wide variety in who regulates media industries. Some countries spread powers over a broad range of commissions and bodies, while others try to centralize them in just a few. Certainly, in media with a public mandate, there is a significant amount of decision-making power concentrated in the body that oversees the operation of the national broadcasting system.

In the United States, the FCC oversees many media regulations and is the governmental agency charged with managing telecommunication policy. It particularly has oversight of broadcasting (radio and television) and telephony (wired and wireless). Over the years it has also taken on considerable regulation of the cable industry. **The Federal Trade Commission (FTC)** regulates many aspects of the Internet and the advertising industry. Media companies are also subject to the regulations faced by any other industry. The FTC and Department of Justice (DOJ), for example, oversee the practices of all industries and ensure that companies do not develop unchecked or monopoly power.

Agencies such as the FCC and FTC carry out the policies enacted by the legislative and executive branches (for example, major policies such as the Telecommunications Act of 1996), but also derive considerable power through their ability to make rules and selectively enforce them. The FCC comprises four commissioners and a chairperson, all appointed by the president and confirmed by the Senate. The FCC can develop and enact policies, but these can be "checked" by both the legislature and the judiciary. For example, the courts have stayed (prevented the implementation) and the legislature has overturned some of the FCC's recent policies regarding ownership regulation.[2]

Although the *making* of policies and regulations may be limited to Congress and the FCC, many other groups can *influence* policy. Perhaps those with the strongest influence are the **lobbyists** that represent the telecommunications industries. Most sectors of the media industry—particularly broadcasting and telephony—have industry associations that represent their interests to the FCC and Congress. Groups such as the National Association of Broadcasters (NAB), National Cable and Telecommunications Association (NCTA), Motion Picture Association of America (MPAA), and Recording Industry Association of America (RIAA) have deep pockets filled by the dues of their members. They use these funds to lobby the FCC and legislature to make sure new policies help rather than hinder their businesses. The watchdog group the Center for Public Integrity reported that the communications industry spent $764 million lobbying Congress and regulators from 1998 through the first half of 2004. Even a single industry can spend significantly; the RIAA reported that it spent nearly $2.1 million lobbying Congress for tougher copyright laws in 2007.[3] Such industry organizations also influence policy by testifying before Congress.

Certainly, we, too, as voters and as consumers of media products, play a role. The FCC regularly invites "public comment," and legislative representatives often receive letters from constituents regarding policies. Unfortunately, the public is rarely organized, nor does it have the extensive funding of industry lobbyists. Not-for-profit groups such as the Consumers' Union and Free Press have developed considerable clout in recent years and do their best to represent the interests of the average citizen and to make sure changes in policy don't happen without public awareness. The media reform movement has grown more vibrant in recent years, but it often remains no match for the media industries' resources. Even though telecommunication policy affects all of us every day—from regulations regarding the bills we pay for services to content different media outlets offer us—we rarely get involved in these issues or even form a position on a policy in the same way we might have a personal position on the death penalty or Social Security policy.

Although we, the public, are often at a disadvantage in affecting media regulation because we lack the millions of dollars to spend on lobbyists and are often too busy with the demands of day-to-day life to organize and make our opinions known, even small acts can make a big difference. In 2002, the FCC prepared to change a number of ownership rules that would make it possible for an already consolidated television industry to become even more so, and to allow greater ownership conglomeration across the television, radio, and newspaper industries at the local level. Consumer and citizen-based interest groups managed to make the policy change news and people around the country came to understand the issue and rally against the proposed change. The FCC received millions of letters, postcards, and calls from citizens complaining about media conglomeration. In the end, the public outcry derailed the FCC policy as many legislators began pressuring the FCC to rethink its plans.

Well-organized citizens were largely responsible for the FCC's recent stringent application of "indecency" rules in the early and mid 2000s. The FCC has no power to censor a television or radio network in advance, nor does anyone at the FCC watch or listen to all programming to make sure no rules are violated. The FCC only acts on content questions when it receives complaints from citizens and viewers. The Parents Television Council (PTC), a conservative interest group, successfully organized its members in the early 2000s through the Internet, and members bombarded the FCC with complaints about sexual content and explicit language on broadcast stations. Regulating "indecency" on television became a major piece of the legislative agenda as the FCC asserted that it had received many complaints. Then-FCC Chair Michael Powell told Congress that the FCC had received 14,000 complaints in 2002 and 240,000 in 2003, after receiving only 350 in each 2000 and 2001. Although many legislators rallied behind the call for stricter regulation—as this is almost always a winning political position—it was later revealed that 99.8 percent of the complaints in 2002 and 2003 came from members of the PTC rather than a spontaneous outpouring of public sentiment.[4]

The lesson to take here is that the public can play a crucial role in the regulation of media industries and there are many points in the decision-making process where we can have a voice. It is also the case, however, that the deck is considerably stacked against us, as the companies that are regulated can devote much more time and money than can the public-at-large to making sure the policies advantage them.

Additionally, a variety of transnational regulatory organizations have been created because national regulations are often inadequate when media circulate across national borders. For example, in 1998, ICANN, the International Corporation for Assigned Names and Numbers, was established as a nonprofit entity that coordinates the unique naming on the Internet that allows worldwide coordination. In another case, the World Trade Organization is an international agency that deals with trade among nations. It has been active in developing international copyright policies and settling disputes. Similarly, the World Intellectual Property Organization, a specialized agency within the United Nations, works to harmonize intellectual property laws across nations and mediates disputes.

Finally, we close this discussion of who regulates with the concept of self-regulation, which is arguably the most substantive regulating mechanism for a commercial media industry with free-speech protection. The "regulations" that are most responsible for producing the media content we are familiar with emerge from **informal self-regulation** that leads industry workers to perceive certain types of content as more or less commercially viable. In addition to this self-regulation based on what media creators perceive as commercially viable (which many would probably not think of as a regulation), they also engage in **formal self-regulation** through the creation of self-imposed rules limiting or categorizing content. For example, there is not an external governmental body that requires films or video games to be rated or that requires album manufacturers to note explicit lyrics. These are all practices of self-regulation that the industries developed and maintain themselves. For example, the Entertainment Software Association—the trade group for game developers—created the Entertainment Software Rating Board (ESRB) to assign content ratings to video and computer games and to maintain agreed-upon standards regarding advertising. The MPAA and its film ratings system function similarly. In both cases, these groups assign ratings rather than mandate certain kinds of content as permissible or impermissible—as was the case from the 1930s to the 1960s in the film industry, when the so-called Hays Code provided strict (yet self-imposed) rules regarding what content could be included in a film.

In many cases, media industries use formal self-regulation as a defensive move in order to head off any legislative regulation, which almost always will be more stringent than what the media companies might enact on their own. One example of this can be found in the Family Hour regulation of television in the 1970s. In response to mounting cultural discussion about the content on television, the three networks agreed to broadcast only programs that might be suitable for the entire family during the first hour of primetime, 8:00–9:00 PM. There was no body set up to make sure that all the networks followed this agreement, and it gradually faded from practice after the threat of formal regulation dissipated.

All sorts of self-regulation could be seen in the mid-2000s as the television networks attempted to figure out the boundaries of what the FCC felt was a finable offense. The immediate precipitating event was Janet Jackson's infamous "wardrobe malfunction" during the 2004 Super Bowl halftime show, when fellow pop star Justin Timberlake tore at her blouse, briefly exposing her breast. In the wake of this event, the Parents Television Council stepped up its pressure on networks and congress people to reign in indecency on television, and many networks toned down the sexual and violent content of series because they were uncertain what would be considered acceptable. A number of affiliates also chose not to air programming offered by their network. In one of the most profound cases, several ABC affiliates chose not to air the film *Saving Private Ryan* in 2004 (scheduled in honor of Veterans' Day) out of concern that the violence and explicit language might lead to fines from the FCC—despite the fact that the film had aired previously without penalty.

An interesting counterpoint to self-regulation in the broadcasting industries comes from the magazine industry, in which cases of self-regulation have been based around operating principles due to the different ways that the industry is regulated. In the late 1990s, a few states' attorneys general announced they were seeking to ban magazine sweepstakes, a promotional practice whereby publishers seek to gain new subscribers through direct mailings that both publicize magazines and offer opportunities to win prizes. The attorneys general claimed the sweepstakes were deceptive, as the mailings suggested purchases were necessary in order to win. The Magazine Publishers Association responded by setting its own new set of ethical guidelines, which included conspicuous "no purchase necessary" disclaimers, in hopes of preventing an outright sweepstakes ban.

As some of these cases indicate, merely the threat of regulation can be enough to change media-industry content, and self-regulation can be very real and significant. In another case, some media critics posited that one of the reasons that many of the networks accepted the increasingly stringent FCC policy on indecency in the mid-2000s was because they wanted the FCC to adopt more liberal ownership policies. Of course, it is impossible to know, but this points to the kinds of interconnections between structural conditions and industry practices that the Industrialization of Culture framework highlights.

WHAT IS REGULATED?

Content Regulations

These days, it is difficult not to be aware of debates over content regulations of the media. It seems that this policy issue has been in the news almost constantly since the Janet Jackson incident. While this incident may have been a particularly notable event, given the size of the audience, **social panics**—or widespread outcries of hysteria related to fears about media content and their social and psychological effects—have existed since the beginnings of the media. Most commonly, these panics raise concerns about the consequences of sexual and violent content and the effects this content might have on children. Such social panics occasionally arise about films (concern about juvenile delinquency in the 1950s), music (explicit rap lyrics in the early 1990s), or video games (violence in first-person shooter games); because of broadcasting's use of public airwaves, however, regulators have been able to impose more formal regulations on broadcast content, while these concerns have more commonly been addressed in the film, music, and video game industries through formal and informal self-regulation.

Content regulation by any body—government appointed or otherwise—in the United States is difficult because of the First Amendment guarantee of free speech. Most policies that attempt any prior censorship of the media typically run afoul of the right to free speech, with a few significant exceptions. By rulings of the Supreme Court, content can be prevented from circulating—called **prior restraint**—if it is **obscene**, a type of speech that is not protected by the First Amendment. The Supreme Court provided the current working definition of obscenity in the 1973 case *Miller v. California*. This ruling emphasized the idea that different communities are likely to have varying definitions of obscenity—so what might be considered obscene is not the same everywhere. Obscene works are those "which, taken as a whole, appeal to the prurient interest in sex, which portray sexual conduct in a patently offensive way, and which, taken as a whole, do not have serious literary, artistic, political, or scientific value." As you can see, this definition isn't exceptionally clear, and because most media content is designed to circulate in many communities, most content created by the media industries steers well clear of the distinction of obscenity.

A second type of speech, that which is **indecent**, is also prohibited on the airwaves at certain times, but it is not subject to prior restraint. In a 1992 policy statement, the FCC defined indecency as "language or material that, in context, depicts or describes, in terms patently offensive as measured by contemporary community standards for the broadcast medium, sexual or excretory activities or organs"—a definition derived from the Supreme Court's finding in *FCC v. Pacifica Foundation* (1978). After extensive negotiation among the FCC, legislature, and the courts, the court of appeals upheld the FCC practice of establishing the hours of 10:00 p.m.–6:00 a.m. as a **safe harbor** in which indecent content is allowed because broadcasters can reasonably assume children will not be in the audience. Although statements by recent FCC chairmen have led broadcasters to wonder, it is generally the case that broadcasters need not fear fines for airing content deemed indecent, so long as it airs during the safe-harbor time frame.

Despite the broad protections of the First Amendment, there is considerable content regulation that develops as a part of a commercial system that is unrelated to formal regulatory mechanisms enforced by the government. Commercial media determine their success by their profitability, and consequently, commercial media industries are highly aware of general sentiment regarding the lines of acceptable content, because it will affect whether consumers are willing to purchase media directly (in the case of the film or music industries, for example) or advertisers are willing to be associated with certain types of content (related to the feedback they get from their consumers). Particularly in the era of mass media, the need to draw the largest possible audience led media outlets to develop content as inoffensive to as many as possible. The television networks sought to create programs that could be watched by the whole family—from grandparents to the young children who were still likely to be in the audience during early-evening hours. Much of the "wholesomeness" of earlier periods of television came less from any kind of formal regulation than from more stringent social standards and from self-regulation based on commercial interest at the time.

Content standards have certainly loosened in the past few decades, and much of this can be traced to changes in the business of many of these industries, particularly the kinds of large economic changes that have swept the world economies since the 1980s, which we discuss in Chapter 9. Consider television: as new cable channels and broadcast networks such as Fox, MTV, and ESPN began competing with the "Big Three" (ABC, CBS, NBC) for audiences, most achieved success by targeting narrow and specific audiences—such as teens and young adults in the case of Fox and MTV. These audiences always had watched television, but they were not specifically targeted by the Big Three, who had an economic mandate to simultaneously reach older adults as well. New networks and channels didn't try to capture the broadest audience; instead, they offered programming that might not be considered acceptable to all audiences (as those who might remember rules about what shows or channels parents wouldn't let them watch can recall). Increasingly, risqué language and controversial stories uncommon in television's past have begun to appear more frequently. Rather than a shift in regulation, adjustments in economic conditions and business practices account for much of this change. The steady addition of many more narrowly targeted broadcast and cable channels created outlets for programming that attends to the more mature tastes of some audiences. In many cases, these new networks drew away the audience members who were most attractive to advertisers: the young and affluent. In order to compete to maintain these viewers, the Big Three then had to also broaden their definitions of acceptable content in order to stay competitive.

Even though we might think of content norms as regulated by formal rules, in a commercial system, it is arguably the case that the system of commerce also provides a stringent, and perhaps even dominant, form of content regulation—that informal self-regulation mentioned a few pages ago. Media producers are wary of including content that will not attract a profitable audience, and in the case of advertiser-financed media, they are also concerned about maintaining content standards that will be acceptable to advertisers. Every advertiser has a slightly different threshold of concern regarding the content it advertises in and its willingness to be associated with controversy. Some advertisers are highly risk-averse and back out of programming with even a whiff of controversy because they fear boycott from consumers or the tarnishing of their "family-friendly" brand (this, for example, has been reputation of consumer health care products manufacturer Johnson & Johnson). Other advertisers might have a product less likely to be negatively affected by a boycott; they may particularly seek the lower advertising rates they might receive as a result of other advertiser boycotts and willingly buy up advertising in boycotted material. Film studios, for example, are rarely boycotted as a whole because of the advertising of a single film. Still others seek the audiences likely to consume media that garner controversy and find boundary-defying content particularly valuable—as is the case of "alcopop" and liquor manufacturers who mainly advertise on cable. As a result, this form of commerce-based self-regulation operates inconsistently.

Copyright

We often think of content regulations in terms of what the government or business conditions will or will not allow the media industries to create, and, as you've seen, the First Amendment tends to allow very few restrictions of this nature. A much more limiting type of content restriction that affects both the operation of the media industries and the behavior of media consumers are limits resulting from **copyright** laws.

Copyright law is crucial to the media industries because it ensures the ongoing economic value of their products. Copyright protects the creators of music, poetry, books, and all sorts of video creations from those who might access a copy and distribute this work as their own for profit. The need for and specificity of copyright law in some ways relates to those distinctive attributes of media we discussed in Chapter 1. The "public good" status of media makes them particularly susceptible to being stolen in a manner very different from private goods with a physical form. This susceptibility has only grown in recent years with the introduction of **digital reproduction**, which allows users to generate exact copies of original media files, and **digital distribution** through **peer-to-peer networks**, which allows consumers to share media files broadly. In these examples, changes in technological conditions and distribution practices have led to revised regulatory conditions for the media industries.

Many of our students enter our classes vaguely familiar with copyright laws as a result of stern warnings that they've received from their parents and universities about illegal downloading and piracy. We'll talk about the ways that digital distribution has complicated copyright law and led to some new thinking about intellectual property later in this section, but it is first important to understand that copyright is a very old legal concept and without it, it is likely the media industries would never have emerged as they have. Some scholars trace the origins of copyright to the advent of the printing press in the 1600s, and this concept has been part of legal thinking in the United States virtually since the founding of the country, as the copyright clause was added to the U.S. Constitution in 1787. Article I, Section 8, Clause 8 explains, "To promote the Progress of Science and useful Arts, by securing for limited Times to Authors and Inventors the exclusive Right to their respective Writings and Discoveries." Copyright law then protects "all works of authorship fixed in a tangible medium of expression" and gives to the author or owner of the copyright the "sole and exclusive right to reproduce the work in any form for any reason."[5] No one else may reproduce the work without prior consent. Copyright thus prevents others from using or profiting from expressive or artistic creations.

Duration of copyright has been an issue of ongoing contention for regulators. Copyright law was revised in 1976 to generally allow for copyright to last for the life of the author plus fifty years, or, in the case of corporate authorship, seventy-five years. In 1998, The Copyright Term Extension Act extended the copyright period to life of the author plus seventy years, and for corporate authors to 120 years after creation or ninety-five years after publication, whichever endpoint is earlier. The relevance of copyright law to media industries is evident in the degree to which they lobbied heavily for the extension. Copyright law creates valuable markets in which media industries license their products to viewers, readers, or listeners. Without copyright protection, consumers would be free to use creative products in any way they desire. Or, of more concern to media industries, once copyright expires, media products fall into the **public domain**. This means that rights no longer need to be paid to the originator.

One important exception to copyright law is the **fair use** provision. Fair use allows for limited copying or use of a product that is protected by copyright as long as it is in accord with a few key provisions. The 1976 Copyright Act allows that, "The fair use of a copyrighted work…for purposes such as criticism, comment, news reporting, teaching (including multiple copies for classroom use), scholarship or research is not an infringement of copyright."[6] Fair use is of great importance to your teachers, who otherwise would have to license every clip shown in class, and would prohibit class resources such as making readings available on electronic reserves.

There is also ongoing legislative debate about what counts as "personal use" for media consumers in general—in reference to what kinds of personal uses consumers are entitled to after purchasing media. For example, when you buy a CD of music or pay to download a song, what rights do you have? A series of decisions growing out of the Audio Home Recording Act of 1992 and the Digital Millennium Copyright Act of 1998 have been enacted to set clear parameters on what consumers can do with the media they purchase and authorizing consumer electronics industries to create technological barriers to some actions. The recording industry was particularly keen to have these regulations enacted before consumer electronics companies introduced technologies that would allow digital recording, out of fear that consumers would then be able to make "perfect" copies that they would then distribute illegally—an action termed **piracy**. The recording industry was reasonably concerned that the ability to make recordings would lead to widespread piracy and depress sales, as consumers made copies of music for friends. Similar regulatory actions have followed that allow for the DVD zone system (which enables film studios to maintain artificial scarcity around the globe in DVD release schedules), the **broadcast flag**, which prevents digital recording from television, or mechanisms that prevent us from freely moving purchased audio files among devices or recording them to a physical medium.

The technological enforcement of copyright is commonly referred to as **digital rights management** or **DRM**. DRM can control your use of media in many different ways, such as allowing only a certain number of viewings, allowing digital files to work for certain periods of time, allowing only specified movement of files (loading to so many computers or players), and preventing printing or saving of files. Considerable debate and uncertainty about the stringency of DRM remains, as some argue that many aspects of DRM violate fair use provisions. Much of the legal support for DRM can be found in the Digital Millennium Copyright Act of 1998. These provisions remain controversial; many of the provisions have been subject to court rulings that have sometimes tightened, and at other times loosened, the Act's original provisions.

As you may have guessed by the repeated use of the word "digital" in the last few paragraphs, the digital media are ushering in new challenges for the media industries in their efforts to maintain and enforce copyright protections—challenges that might force them to fundamentally redefine their operations. The ability to easily create "perfect" copies of media texts has heightened many of the concerns about piracy or illegal file sharing. To a considerable extent, it is the actions of a few or even just the technological possibility of violating copyright that has led to disabling personal use of media through DRM. Nevertheless, these threats remain very real for media industries, as widespread adoption of such behavior threatens to undermine their economic models. Another challenging aspect of contemporary copyright policing results from the easy circulation of digital files over international boundaries. In many cases, international copyright is supported through a series of treaties, but adjudicating violations becomes much more challenging when dealing with different systems of law and justice.

Chances are many of you wouldn't dream of selling "bootleg" copies of media (we hope), yet some of what might seem basic media activities that you engage in daily may still violate copyright laws. Have you ever made a video and used a popular song in the background? Have you ever reproduced the lyrics of a poem or a song on a blog? These activities may also violate copyright unless you license the song or lyrics from the copyright holder (and in the case of poems and song lyrics, just a few lines are often held as violations).

Others who create media works may sample from licensed works or subtly alter an existing work in order to create a parody. To date, the Supreme Court has upheld the use of copyrighted works in parodies that add new perspective to the work, critique it, or encourage audiences to see it in a new way—although meeting these grounds is a fairly subjective judgment. Sampling, once a staple of hip-hop music, has diminished considerably in response to rising costs of licensing and more stringent interpretations of copyright law. In 2008, the average base cost of "clearing" a sample (establishing a legal agreement that allows the use of the sample and sets a payment for its use) was $10,000, and much higher in many cases. Samples must be cleared with both the owners of the master recording (typically the recording label) and the owner of the publishing rights (typically the songwriter). Legal action against unauthorized sampling has been much more expensive. In 2006, Bridgeport Music and Westbound Records won $4.2 million in damages because of unauthorized samples on Notorious B.I.G.'s *Ready to Die* album.[7] While this has curbed the use of sampling by those within the commercial music industry, sampling remains curiously central among alternative and underground DJs. One notable case is a musician who performs under the name Girl Talk who has released a number of albums made up of mashups and sampling. To date, Girl Talk has never been sued despite the clear violation of copyright in his work. Such situations point to the complexity of media industry operation, as the major labels whose work he uses are certainly aware of his violations, but allow him to continue. Chapter 7 begins with more on the issue of sampling and distribution.

One response to the dangers and promises of the digital age—for both sharing and producing media—has been the **Creative Commons** movement. Those who establish a Creative Commons (cc) license for their work waive some of their rights in order to more easily allow others to share and build upon their work while still maintaining some of the rights of copyright. There are six different Creative Commons licenses; the most restrictive only allows redistribution with attribution, the least restrictive allows redistribution as well as changing and adjusting the work, even for commercial ends, as long as the original author is credited. Creative Commons founder Lawrence Lessig is a central thinker involved in exploring new models for the circulation of ideas and creative products, particularly on the Internet. Without a doubt, there remain many unresolved and unclear aspects of how copyright law will be enforced in the digital age and what rights users will maintain in their personal use of media.

Structural and Operational Regulations

As a media consumer, you probably have more familiarity with content regulations than with this second type of regulation, which we categorize as structural and operational regulations. These regulations are related to the business practices and functioning of media companies. Rules regarding who can own media companies and how many media entities an individual or company can own, either in a particular location or across the country, are prime illustrations of structural regulations. Regulations on ownership are quite extensive and varied in comparison with non-media industries; this increased attention to ownership mainly evolves from those factors we discussed in Chapter 1 that make media industries unlike others. We also include economic regulation of the media industries as a type of structural regulation. Such regulations include rate controls and policies that provide subsidies to the media industries. Structural regulations vary by industry and some industries, such as broadcasting, face much more extensive structural regulations than others.

Ownership Regulations

Perhaps the most extensive form of regulation governing the media industries can be found in the varied ownership regulations of both specific industries and across industries. Some ownership regulations particularly target broadcasters; other media, however, also are subject to some regulations regarding ownership scale and concentration that distinguish media industries from the regulation of ownership common in other industries.

In the case of television, although we might associate a station in our home city with a network, it is likely that the network doesn't actually own that station. Most stations were once stand-alone businesses owned by "mom and pop" operations around the country. Now, stations are typically owned by a **station group**—that is, an entity that owns stations affiliated with various networks located in cities around the country—or are network-owned and -operated (O&O) stations. In the past, fairly significant limitations on the number of stations an individual entity could own nationwide existed. This number increased until the FCC shifted to the current "percent reach" standard. Now, instead of limiting the *number* of stations a single entity can own, the regulation specifies a *percentage* of the population that any station owner may reach, which is 39 percent as of this writing (although some exceptions were granted that allow a few companies to minimally exceed this limit as a result of mergers).

In the radio industry, the **Telecommunications Act of 1996** lifted the limit on national ownership, and a massive consolidation of the industry quickly followed. Companies such as Clear Channel quickly amassed enormous station holdings, at one point owning more than 1,200 stations nationwide. This act also increased the possibilities for television-station ownership and set up a structure of regular review of rules with the possibility of continued loosening of the restrictions. The example of radio proved a cautionary tale, however, and efforts to continue to expand the ownership limits of television have been met with protest and resulted in keeping close to the guidelines set out by the Telecomm Act. Ownership rules have also limited the number of stations (radio and television) that can be owned in a specific market.

The FCC has devoted much of its policymaking work since the Telecomm Act of 1996 to ownership, particularly during Michael Powell's tenure as FCC chair. Why is ownership such a significant policy area? All industries face some ownership regulation—ultimately this is how we might categorize regulations against monopolies. More stringent regulations for media industries exist because of the undeniable social and cultural role of media and the perceived value of preserving a diversity of voices and particularly those of the local community. Ownership is a central site through which regulators can prevent the control of media outlets by too few entities and make them responsive to the communities in which they are located.

Another set of media ownership regulations deals with **cross-ownership**—or the ownership of companies in multiple media industries. Ownership of a newspaper and a broadcast station in the same market was prohibited until 2007 (now there are a complicated array of situations in which that is allowable), and cross-ownership of a cable system and a broadcast station in the same market was forbidden until 2003, yet limits on owning television and radio stations within the same market in cities of a certain size remain. These regulations have been in place because of the particularly local nature of media in the past and the value associated with local media. For example, if most of your news comes from the local radio station, television station, and newspaper, then it is desirable to prevent one company from dominating all of those outlets in order to maintain a diversity of voices—even if that media company also owns other media entities outside of the city. Ownership regulations, then, are typically structured to address the desire to maintain both a **diversity of voices** and **localism** in media industries.

Ownership remains one of the most contested sites of media regulation and policy. Many in the media industries desire continued deregulation to be free of the limits that prevent them from further expanding their businesses. From the perspective of the media industries, the advantage of expansion involves increasing the **economies of scale** of their businesses. This is a term we'll come back to in discussing the economic conditions that act upon media industries in the next chapter. For now, think of economies of scale as the economic advantage companies may gain by consolidating their operations. For example, many stations desire to develop **duopolies** (owning two stations in one city) so that many of the "backroom" costs can be consolidated—such as combining the sales forces of these stations and eliminating many of the positions, since a single sales staffer can efficiently service two stations when making a sales call. Or, perhaps in traveling around the country you've noticed radio stations that sound practically the same or television stations using identical graphics. This is because station groups combine as many of their needs as possible within one facility. For example, NBC has a production facility in Fort Worth, Texas, that produces many of the graphics and design features for all of the NBC-owned-and -operated stations around the country.

Consolidating work such as graphic design and sales may not seem to threaten the diversity of voices in a community, but the efforts at cost saving do not stop there. Clear Channel drew considerable criticism in 2003 when reports emerged that "voice-tracking" had become an increasingly common part of its operations. Voice-tracking takes another job out of the community and uses talent outside of the market; for example, a DJ based in San Francisco may voice the morning show in San Francisco but have an afternoon show in Dallas that is produced from San Francisco with no suggestion to the Dallas audience that the show is not local. In another disconcerting case that many media activists have pointed to as illustrative of the real dangers of lifting ownership limits, some stations operate with few or no live personnel, instead having their content piped in by satellite. This allowed for a dangerous situation in the town of Minot, North Dakota in 2002.[8] A freight train carrying a dangerous substance—anhydrous ammonia—derailed, and a cloud of gas threatened the town. The city's emergency alert system failed, so police called the town radio stations—six of which were owned by Clear Channel. Police were unable to reach anyone at Clear Channel-owned KCJB, the designated emergency broadcaster, because the station did not keep anyone at the station, since the programming originated elsewhere.

A desire for cost savings and efforts to make news media more profitable have led to increased reliance on news services such as the Associated Press and have led to fewer jobs for journalists. It was once the case that each of the television networks had news correspondents based around the world and that large newspapers maintained their own reporters in Washington and other cities with important regular events. As media have consolidated, many of these jobs have been eliminated, with just one reporter providing the same story for most of the country. Sometimes there may be valuable efficiencies here, but many of the local aspects of national and international stories get lost when a journalist is charged with writing a story as relevant to the residents of Albuquerque as of Ann Arbor.

Economic Regulations: Rate Control and Subsidies

Another way media industries are regulated is through rate control. In the United States, this typically has been applied in industries that are allowed to function as monopolies. Some media have argued that they are **natural monopolies**, monopolies that develop because it is so inefficient for there to be competition. This was, first, the case of the telegraph. Connecting the country by wire required an enormous initial investment, and Western Union argued that it should be allowed to exist as a monopoly because it was so wasteful for a competitor to duplicate its effort in stringing wire. The outcome was for the government to allow Western Union to remain without competition as long as the government was granted more extensive regulatory powers. This same logic then followed with the telephone and cable television industries.

These days, we are probably most aware of rate regulation in cable television. As cable was deployed around the country, cable providers entered into contracts with cities and municipalities. These agreements established the cable provider as the sole cable service for the community, and to win these **franchises**, cable providers guaranteed a specific package of services—often the availability of a certain number of public access channels and some funding to support production for them. These franchise agreements set up a monopoly for service in each community. The agreements are renegotiated periodically (roughly every fifteen years), but they allow individual cable subscribers little recourse if rates rise precipitously or they receive poor service (other than dropping the service entirely). Cable rates nationwide rose so significantly in the 1980s (three times the rate of inflation in some cases) that Congress stepped in with re-regulation of cable at the same time it took a deregulatory approach to other media. Since satellite television began competing with cable, and the Telecommunications Act of 1996 allowed phone companies to offer "cable" service as well, the market force of competition has led to somewhat greater accountability by the cable industry. It also has tried to use the growing number of satellite subscribers as a justification for the end of rate regulation.

Certain kinds of taxes and requirements to fund various initiatives also function as a type of rate-related regulation. If you've ever taken the time to go through your phone or cable bill, you'll find a number of small fees that you pay each month for things such as the "universal service" fund and 911 fees, among others. In some cases, Congress has determined that access to certain media may be necessary for basic functioning in society. This is the case with the universal service fund, which was established to help subsidize the cost of basic phone service for those who cannot afford it. Additionally, access to emergency services, as provided by dialing 911, is thought to be a service fundamental to the public good. Legislation requires its availability, and phone companies pass the costs of maintaining it to their customers.

These regulations do not always require fees; sometimes they have to do with mandating certain services. For example, the cable industry is mandated to provide a basic service package (that it does not advertise) that provides truly basic service for $10–$15 per month. This service, sometimes called "lifeline," typically includes no more than the local broadcast networks, public access channels, and the local Public Broadcasting Station. In recent years, the legislature has threatened to require cable systems to offer a greater array of packages for subscription, such as a "family tier" or even **a la carte** channels, meaning that subscribers could pick whichever channels they want and pay a fee per channel, rather than being forced to select from packages determined by cable providers. Although a la carte channel selection sounds like a great idea, it would force a significant adjustment in cable economics and might lead to costlier service than the current, bundled plans. It is also possible that much of the diversity of cable offerings would not be commercially feasible in an a la carte system, which illustrates the interconnections among regulatory and economic conditions.

Governments also offer provisions that aid the operation of media industries in the form of subsidies to various industries. For example, United States corporate tax code allows corporations to deduct their spending on advertising from their profits to reduce their tax payment. In another case, many countries (not the United States) provide subsidies to their domestic film industries in order to help increase indigenous production and to help smaller national cinemas compete with the output of media capitals such as Hollywood, Bombay, or Hong Kong. These subsidies often come in the form of tax breaks or outright grants. In the United States, various states and municipalities have been developing similar programs in recent years in hopes of bringing productions (that would spend considerably in the local economy) to their regions.

Licenses and License Renewal

Licensing is a structural regulation that affects only broadcasters. The FCC grants licenses. In the past, stations were required to file for renewal every five years, but recent deregulation has decreased that frequency to every eight years. Typically, renewal is the only time the FCC really checks to see if a station is making an acceptable effort toward serving its public interest obligations, and even this review is cursory. Citizens are invited to submit letters regarding the performance of the station, and if the FCC has received complaints since the last renewal or has levied fines against the broadcaster, these are also likely to be part of the renewal consideration. All that said, it has been very uncommon for a station to lose its license; the FCC renews more than 98 percent of licenses.[9] One of these rare and oft-cited times involved the television station WLBT in Jackson, Mississippi. Complaints against this station, which was accused of blatantly discriminating against blacks in the community—a group that comprised 45 percent of its audience—began in 1955, but the station's license was not canceled until 1969, when the FCC was ordered to do so by an appeals court.[10] The drawn-out hearings and legal decisions from this case are what led the FCC to recognize that citizens have legal standing in license renewal cases, rather than just considering whether there is signal interference or economic injury to another broadcaster, which had been the previous standards. Despite this, regular license renewal has not served as a significant form of regulating the behavior of stations so much as it has been a periodic bureaucratic exercise.

Recently, some activists concerned about media policy have attempted to use license renewal as an opportunity to hold broadcasters accountable. Organized efforts to contest the renewal of stations developed in 2006, with community advocates arguing that the stations had not served their public-interest obligations, particularly because they had afforded limited attention to local politics. To date, none of these efforts has resulted in the loss of a license; it may be the case, however, that the organized threat led stations to pay greater attention to serving the public good. Such a situation could be considered an example of self-regulation—illustrating how media industries often police themselves in order to avoid the incursion of formal regulation.

Monopoly and Anti-Trust Restrictions

Monopoly and **anti-trust regulations** prevent too much industry consolidation—and can be very significant to media industry operation, as our opening anecdote about the Paramount Decree illustrated. In the United States, the Department of Justice commonly handles these policies along with the FTC, which is also responsible for rules regarding truth in advertising and consumer complaints against companies. The nature of the media industries perhaps leads to more potentially monopolistic arrangements than others. For example, the creation of a monopoly has been proposed recently in the satellite television and radio businesses. When these industries began, the FCC auctioned off a limited number of licenses for the necessary spectrum to operate these technologies, and in both cases two competitors emerged (television: DirecTV and EchoStar; radio: Sirius and XM). Also in both cases, after roughly a decade of competition, the companies proposed to merge. The television merger was turned down by the FCC in 2002, but talks of a merger re-emerged five years later, after News Corp. purchased and again sold DirecTV. The satellite companies argued that their merger would not really create a monopoly, because satellite has cable as a competitor (at least in the case of television). One of the most persuasive arguments against the satellite television merger, however, was what might have happened to many rural households that live far enough from major cities where cable is not available. These homes would face just one provider if a satellite monopoly were allowed.

In what seemed almost a case of déjà vu, the two satellite radio companies also proposed a merger in 2007. The Department of Justice and the FCC both had to approve this merger, and they imposed some conditions before ultimately approving it. Significantly, the FCC required the merged companies to provide a la carte pricing so that consumers could purchase only stations of interest, that 4 percent of channels be reserved for pubic service or minority programming, and that the company allow any manufacturer to make sets capable of receiving the service.

OTHER REGULATORY CONDITIONS

Regulations Governing Distribution

The question about whether to allow satellite monopolies highlights the increasing importance of regulating the distribution of media goods. The regulation of distribution involves rules about how media distributors use their technologies to help or hinder the messages that pass along their systems. This wasn't a big issue in the past because media service providers weren't really technologically capable of providing differential service. This is quickly emerging as a major policy concern as digital broadband networks become the central media infrastructure of society.

The words most commonly associated with this area of media policy are **network (or net) neutrality**. Net neutrality is the principle that Internet service providers not discriminate among messages or users, that they pass along all messages at equal speeds, and that users be able to access all webpages regardless of their service provider. Concerns about establishing regulations ensuring net neutrality developed in response to suspicions that Internet service providers might try to be more profitable by selling premium speeds of delivery service and that some providers were not operating with neutrality by slowing peer-to-peer file sharing.

As we write, the broadband industry remains in relative infancy, and the history of other communication technologies has illustrated that these industries often evolve significantly from the industrial models that undergird their first decades. In just a decade, we have witnessed a transition from a pay-per-minute model of dial-up access to the all-you-can use subscription model now common with broadband, and some providers have suggested a transition back to a use-based fee schedule. While these are economic matters—that are more the provenance of the next chapter—we seek to point out the degree to which the Internet industry, such that there is one, lacks much certainty in these operating conditions. Although it is difficult to say much about existing Internet regulation, it is certainly the case that this will be a primary area of debate about media regulation in coming years.

An Emerging Area: Broadband Policy

Just as regulators, citizens, and commercial interests struggled to develop the regulatory structure for broadcast technology in the first part of the twentieth century, the early twenty-first century requires the establishment of policies governing the broadband devices that will only continue to grow in importance. Although we are very familiar with broadband technologies, and would perhaps be lost without them, it is the case that many countries have only limited formal broadband policies (the United States lags particularly behind here). Many of the existing rules and ideas about how broadband services should be regulated are adapted from the precedents of broadcast and telephony policy. Just now, as we write in late 2010, the United States is beginning to embark on a coherent and systematic approach to broadband policy. The chances are good that much of this policy determination will remain ongoing as this book finds its way to readers.

While there are far fewer rules, policies, and certainly limited judicial review of broadband regulation at this point, much of the history of broadcast policy may indeed provide a conceptual starting point for thinking about how broadband can and should be regulated. Imagine the likely policy difference if legislators determine the infrastructure of the Internet to be a public good in the same manner as the electromagnetic spectrum used for broadcasting. This would lead to a model of regulation very different than if they continue to leave most decisions about "regulating" broadband to the commercial marketplace. Or imagine how different broadband access and opportunities might look if legislators advance policies that make universal service a goal, in the same manner as was done in the case of telephony.

Pro-Social Regulation

Content regulation can take on additional dimensions beyond those mentioned previously. In addition to *restricting* the kinds of content that the media industries produce, in some cases, regulations actively *encourage* the creation of particular kinds of content. Media scholars David Croteau and William Hoynes describe efforts to encourage the production of certain types of media as a **cultural interventionist** approach to media regulation[11]; such policies are most often found in the case of media with a public mandate. Cultural interventionist policies seek to encourage voices other than those of commercially motivated media and can take the form of content and structural regulations. Often in public media systems, the state is viewed as a legitimate intervener in cultural policy. Unlike the norm in a commercial system, in which the mantra is often "let the market decide," cultural interventionist policies encourage the production of media believed to have some sort of pro-social effect.

A historical example of this can be found in the early development of the BBC. Under the management of Lord John Reith as Director-General, the BBC particularly developed programming believed to "uplift" the population—the sort of "high art" content that is often caricatured as the only content produced by a public system. In these early years of broadcasting, some argued that the medium could be used to bring art and cultural forms that had been available only to the upper classes to the mass population. Consequently, production budgets favored the broadcasting of operas, symphony performances, and the staging of "great works" of theater in order to "advance" the tastes of mass culture.

Perhaps a more recognizable example of cultural interventionist policies can be found here in the United States: government support of the Children's Television Workshop and the production of shows such as *Sesame Street*. In addition to giving some financial support to programming designed to help children learn in an environment free of commercial messages, children's commercial television is also more highly regulated than other forms. For example, broadcasters are mandated to air a certain number of hours of children's programming per week, and specific regulations dictate how many commercial minutes can be included in that content.

Another regulation of content common outside of the United States, although not necessarily particular to public media systems, are regulations on the national origin of content. Such regulations—often described as production quotas—were created to help support the development of indigenous media content after years of heavy reliance on imports, particularly from the United States. The Audiovisual Without Frontiers directive, for instance, requires that European broadcasters air a majority of programming produced in the European Union. In addition, most countries, with the exception of the United States, have what are known as **co-production** treaties with other nations, which permit television programs and films created by an international production team to count as domestically produced content in both signatories' markets. Many of these culturally protectionist regulations are taken up in more detail in Chapter 11.

Technological Standards: The Case of the Digital Television Transition

Sometimes the government steps in with major regulations. While we've discussed some aspects of the Telecommunications Act of 1996 already, perhaps the regulation most directly affecting many of our readers was to require a change in spectrum use by television broadcasters in mandating the shift from analog to digital television signal transmission. Since television's origins in the late 1940s, stations were licensed to use 6 megahertz (mhz) of spectrum, over which they broadcast an analog television signal. The analog signal is made up of two carrier waves, one each for video and audio information, in which the content of a television program is reproduced and transmitted by variation in the signal. Both television and radio broadcasters used analog transmissions for most of their history in the United States.

In the 1990s, as the legislature prepared a significant overhaul of some tele-communication policy, it reconsidered spectrum use and organization. Mobile telephone technologies were just becoming widely used, and industry forecast-ers identified a growing demand for spectrum by these technologies. The many reasons for the transition to digital television in the United States are too compli-cated to recount here—although the story provides an excellent case for exploring the intricacies of media industry operation.[12] Suffice it to say that for a variety of reasons (mostly related to lobbying by various industries), Congress decided to require all of the nation's television broadcasters to switch from transmitting an analog signal to transmitting a digital one.

As you may well be aware, digital technologies speak a language of ones and zeros. In the case of television signal transmission, this means that instead of audio and video being reproduced in the analog signal, they are translated into codes of ones and zeros that are then transmitted. The digital transition required consider-able changes for both broadcasters and television viewers. Television stations had to purchase new equipment and transmitters, which cost billions of dollars, and to access these signals, viewers without cable or satellite service had to purchase sets with digital receivers. Despite this downside, the same digital signal required less spectrum, meaning that after the switchover, more room was available for new services, such as wireless broadband, expanding local television channels, and high-definition television (HDTV). In theory, some benefits for the viewer included greater selection of channels and new features such as on-screen listings, interactivity, and audio description and subtitling for people with visual and audio impairments. Originally mandated in 1996, the digital transition was first sched-uled to be complete by December 31, 2006. Delays led Congress to rethink this deadline, and the transition dragged on as deadlines were proposed and missed, until Congress set a "final" deadline of February 17, 2009, which was shifted to June 12, 2009, just weeks before the planned February cut-off. When the transition began, Congress authorized broadcast stations to use two parts of the spectrum, both 6 mhz, one for each the analog and digital signal. On the deadline date, the stations stopped operating the analog signal, and the government reclaimed that spectrum space to auction off to wireless providers.

The question of the deadline was of such significance because televisions that were manufactured with only an analog receiver were no longer able to receive broadcast signals once the stations switched to only the digital signal. In other words, the government created a regulation that rendered many television sets useless; but there are some other important factors to keep in mind. Roughly 85 percent of television households subscribed to cable or satellite at this time. These services could translate the signal, so even sets with only an analog receiver con-tinued to work as long as they were connected to cable or satellite services that provided digital conversion. Viewers could also purchase devices called converter boxes that translated the over-the-air signal so their televisions would still work.

The digital transition may seem to be quite a big hassle, so the question you might have now is "why," and there are many reasons. At the time Congress was considering the legislation, the consumer electronics industry was poised to intro-duce **high-definition television**. Instead of the 480 scan lines of standard defini-tion sets, high-definition sets can receive either 720 or 1,080 lines, creating a much crisper and superior image. The amount of data needed to transmit a high-defini-tion signal (at least back in the mid-1990s), however, could not be compressed into the 6 mhz analog signal. Therefore, the perception was that in order to make high-definition television possible, it was necessary to switch to a digital signal that was capable of carrying more information. This transition was of great interest to the consumer electronics industry as an opportunity to sell more and higher priced sets. It was also the case that U.S. standard definition is of poorer quality than the norms adopted in much of the rest of the world, so there was some technological logic behind this decision, as well.

The stronger explanation of "why the transition?" is probably the financial windfall Congress expected upon auctioning off the spectrum after broadcasters returned their analog space. Estimates placed profits in the range of $80 billion—which is also an important reminder of the value of what broadcasters are given to use for free (and justifies why we really should expect more from them).

The mandate to switch to digital transmission is an example of massive gov-ernment regulatory involvement and should be regarded as fairly uncommon. Typically, such structuring regulations are established early in the life of a medium, and then they become too entrenched to alter. The United States is not alone in undergoing this transition. Countries as wide-ranging as Australia, Brazil, Kenya, Malaysia, and many others also have plans to transition from analog to digital in place, if they have not already switched.

CONCLUSION

As in the cases of the mandates and other conditions discussed in this sec-tion, it isn't that specific regulations have clear or specific consequences for media industries. Rather, factors such as the nature of existing regulations; the current cultural, political, and economic environment; particular mandates; technologies; economic norms; and the practices of individuals working in media industries channel the range of possibilities. In the examples we've noted throughout this chapter, it has often been the case that factors that comprise the broader cultural and economic contexts in which media operate are as sig-nificant in shaping what the media industries create as are regulations (or their absence). Concerns about government involvement led the networks to create the Family Hour and tamed the first hour of prime time, at least for a little while. Competition from niche channels, fragmentation of the audience, and the erosion of family viewing necessitated that broadcasters loosen some of their content standards—suggesting that a shift in the competitive environment can produce changes as substantial as a regulation. The desire for greater dereg-ulation of ownership caps can lead content creators to self-regulate content to curry government favor.

A truly contentious issue within the study of media industries in recent years involves the question of how the ownership structure and factors such as conglomeration might be seen to produce consequences on the content of media. The dominant perspective has been that conglomeration and consolidation of media industries narrow the range of content produced, or, in a simple shorthand, that conglomeration produces homogenization in cultural products. While proponents of this perspective can often list some anecdotes and examples in which this seems the case, the evidence of this *always* being the case, in a manner that would more definitely suggest causation, has been lacking. Most of the attention to consequences of conglomerated ownership on content has also been focused on the news media, used questionable measures of diversity in assessing content, and paid little attention to the varied and difficult-to-quantify aspects of creative texts. While we are not suggesting that ownership configurations and the regulations that enable or disable them do not produce consequences on media content, we do not find explanations of consistent consequences compelling, nor do we find ownership structure alone nearly as determinant as other thinkers on this topic, as we explore more in the next chapter. Rather, we find that there is much empirical work to be done that considers the conditions and practices within conglomerated media companies to understand their operations. It is also the case that the new digital technologies remaking the media industries—and the Internet in particular—require entirely new approaches to regulating media.

QUESTIONS

1. Select a media text that you have consumed or interacted with today, thinking about it in terms of the three interconnected questions listed in this chapter. Can you identify who regulates the industry that created that text? What, exactly, is being regulated? Finally, think about a specific regulation in that industry. Can you explain the consequences it had on the text you have chosen?

2. As noted in this chapter's discussion of broadcasting, the FCC allows stations to use the publicly owned airwaves as long as they operate in the "public interest, convenience, and necessity." Do you think this is a fair deal and, more important, do you think that broadcasters are currently holding up their end of the deal? What types of content and services do you think would fulfill that requirement?

3. We have discussed the importance of the ways in which industries formally *self-regulate*. (Informal self-regulation is discussed more thoroughly in Chapter 6.) Identify an instance of formal self-regulation in a particular industry, or think more thoroughly about one of the examples we provided. How did this self-regulation help secure the survival or profitability of the industry? How did it, in turn, affect the sort of media text that was produced—if at all? Can you make a case that it either limited or expanded the possible types of media texts available to us?

FURTHER READING

Books on issues of content regulation can be found about nearly every media industry. See Eric Nuzum's *Parental Advisory: Music Censorship in America* (New York: Harper Paperbacks, 2001); Stephen Tropiano's *Obscene, Indecent, Immoral and Offensive: 100+ Years of Censored, Banned, and Controversial Films* (New York: Limelight Editions, 2009); and Heather Hendershot's *Saturday Morning Censors: Television Regulation Before the V-Chip* (Durham: Duke University Press, 1999). For more on the issues surrounding intellectual property and copyright, see Kembrew McLeod's *Freedom of Expression: Resistance and Repression in the Age of Intellectual Property* (Minneapolis: University of Minnesota Press, 2007) and Lawrence Lessig's *Free Culture: The Nature and Future of Creativity* (New York: Penguin, 2005).

There are many much more detailed works on media policy and regulation. See Patricia A. Aufderheide's *Communications Policy and the Public Interest: The Telecommunications Act of 1996* (New York: Guildford Press, 1999); Robert McChesney's *The Problem of the Media: U.S. Communication Politics in the Twenty-First Century* (New York: Monthly Review Press, 2004); Mara Einstein's *Media Diversity: Economics, Ownership, and the FCC* (New York: Routledge, 2004); and Des Freedman's *The Politics of Media Policy* (Cambridge: Polity, 2008). For a historical view, see William Boddy's *Fifties Television: The Industry and Its Critics* (Urbana: University of Illinois Press, 1990).

A detailed account of the forces behind the U.S. digital transition can be found in Joel Brinkley's *Defining Vision: The Battle for the Future of Television* (San Diego: Harcourt Brace, 1997).

NOTES

1. See Susan J. Douglas, *Inventing American Broadcasting 1899–1922* (Baltimore: Johns Hopkins University Press, 1987).
2. See http://www.lasarletter.net/drupal/node/10 for a timeline of the controversy over media ownership rules from 1996–2006 (accessed 16 Sep. 2010).
3. Becky Lentz, "Regulation is Boring," *Flow*, 11, no. 1 (2009), http://www.flowtv.org?p=4479 (accessed 16 Sep. 2010); E. Bangeman, "RIAA Spent $2 Million Lobbying for Tougher IP Laws in 2007," *ArsTechnica.com*, April 21, 2008, http://arstechnica.com/news.ars/post/20080421-riaa-spent-2-million-lobbying-for-tougher-ip-laws-in-2007.html (accessed Nov. 5, 2008).
4. Todd Shields, "Activists Dominate Content Complaints," *Mediaweek*, Dec. 6, 2004; UPI, "Most Complaints Come from Single Group," Dec. 7, 2004.
5. Donald R. Pember, *Mass Media Law* (Boston: McGraw-Hill College, 1999), 459.
6. Ibid., 459, 469.
7. Matthew Newton, "Is Sampling Dying?" *Spin*, December 2008, 31–34.
8. See Ben H. Bagdikian, *The New Media Monopoly* (Boston: Beacon Press, 2004), 1.
9. Sydney W. Head, Thomas D. Spann and Michael A. McGregor, *Broadcasting in America: A Survey of Electronic Media* (9th ed) (Boston: Allyn & Bacon, 2000).

10. Ibid.

11. David Croteau and William Hoynes, *The Business of Media: Corporate Media and the Public Interest*, 2nd Ed. (Thousand Oaks, CA: Pine Forge Press, 2006).

12. See Joel Brinkley, *Defining Vision: The Battle for the Future of Television* (San Diego: Harcourt Brace, 1997).

CHAPTER 5

—

Economic Conditions in
Media Production

In the early 1800s, U.S. newspapers were more comparable to some sort of contemporary magazine, although even that isn't a great comparison. Many newspapers were allied with political parties and published long treatises debating the issues of the day, rather than the short, objective digests of the news of the day we are accustomed to now. Most Americans did not read the papers, due largely to the level of illiteracy and the high cost of papers. Joseph Turow notes the costs and conditions of the time necessitated that publishers charge $6–$10 per year, in advance, for a subscription to the paper.[1] (Today that rate would be the equivalent of paying approximately $100–$180 for an annual magazine subscription). As available technology changed, so, too, did the economic model supporting the newspaper industry, and with a new economic model, the content also changed radically.

In the early 1830s, entrepreneurs began imagining a newspaper that would circulate much more widely. To reach a broad audience, the paper would have to be much more affordable—just a few pennies—and in order to entice readership, it would have to attract the interest of readers. Soon the political treatises were gone, replaced, as Turow describes, "with stories of crime and love, humor and human interest."[2] Here, the transition from a fairly expensive advance subscription as the means for financing the paper to a blend of advertising and direct payment from consumers led to a considerable shift in the very nature of the medium. In addition, as we explained in Chapter 3, the shift from rag-based to wood-pulp-based paper made newspapers far cheaper to produce and lighter, which made them cheaper to distribute, and that helped drive down prices.

Much has been said in recent years about the "death" of the contemporary newspaper industry as the immediacy and ease of access provided by the web have led to changes in various aspects of production, how people read, and their willingness to pay for newspapers. As was the case in the early 1800s, it is not the case that newspapers are dying, but, rather, that the economic norms of the industry are in a state of adjustment. The history of media industries is filled with many such stories, because how media are financed and how audiences pay for their products can have significant implications for media texts.

* * *

The final condition we consider encompasses how economic conditions lead media industries to function in particular ways. Like technological and regulatory conditions in the Industrialization of Culture framework, economic considerations, ranging from who owns media to how media creation is funded to how media are paid for, produce a range of consequences. As with the other conditions and practices we study, it is difficult to speak in generalities when it comes to the impact of economic conditions on texts and other dimensions of media industry operations, because how media are financed leads to wide-ranging variations.

French media theorist Bernard Miege attempted a rough organization of the media industries in three different models that distinguish among the dominant operation of various media industries: publishing, flow, and written press.[3] Media such as books, music, films, and video games generally operate under his **publishing** model. Such media are characterized by their production of "isolated individual works" that are purchased by individuals. Particularly key here are that 1) audiences purchase distinct works (unlike in the written press model we'll explore next), and 2) these media tend to be mainly financed through direct pay by audiences, rather than primarily advertiser supported. The **written press** model is similar to publishing, except in this case—of media such as magazines and newspapers—the media produce a "series of commodities, purchased regularly." This difference is important, because the constant product of written press industries means that they are financed differently because they just keep making the same thing—thus they aren't organized around a series of discrete products. Finally, in the **flow** model, radio, television, and what Miege identified as "new media" in 1989 produce "a continuous flow requiring daily contact and the development of audience loyalty." In some ways, flow industries blend features of the publishing and the written press models. They must produce many goods constantly in a way that leads to similarities with the written press. Even in the somewhat less complicated media context of the late 1980s, such distinctions were rough and generalized, yet Miege's articulation of the three models offers language to distinguish among the economics of various media that otherwise might seem the same (such as operating under a commercial mandate and being supported by advertisers).

In this chapter, we first examine the broad and structuring role of ownership and conglomeration on the media industries. This is an issue that has drawn considerable attention in the past two decades due to the steady increase in the scale of the companies involved in media production into multimedia behemoths with global reach. We then explore the costs involved in making many media products and consider how the practices media producers use to finance these costs lead to particular consequences for the products they create. Finally, we close by bringing these money matters home by considering the various ways media products are commonly paid for and how this also affects the content of media. To some degree, this chapter assumes that we are dealing with media industries that operate under a commercial mandate. This focus allows us to address the great majority of media industry operation, as even nations with broadcasting systems dominated by a public mandate feature commercial media in sectors such as film, music, and publishing, and those with public broadcasting also tend to have a commercial broadcasting sector. It is also the case that the costs of media creation are similar regardless of mandate. While this chapter cannot cover all of the ways that economic matters contribute to the production of media products in the situation of all mandates, it does offer a broad sketch of key considerations that might be applied to a variety of instances.

WHO OWNS MEDIA: UNDERSTANDING OWNERSHIP AND CONGLOMERATION

Without doubt, the dominant concern among those who have studied media industries over the last decade is a worry about the consequences of conglomeration and consolidation of media ownership. Although concern has been acute recently, questions of ownership always have been central to studying media industries. Most basically, **conglomeration** refers to the increased dominance of companies involved with many different products or services. The alternative to conglomeration would be an industry organization in which many different firms participate in only one aspect of production. An illustration of conglomeration is evident in tracing the growth of a company such as Warner Communications. Warner began in the 1970s as the parent company of Warner Bros. Pictures and Warner Music group, along with other, non-media businesses. (See Table 5.1.)

Throughout the 1970s and 1980s, it acquired enough music labels to rank as one of the world's five largest music companies, and then it diversified with acquisitions of DC Comics and the electronic-game maker Atari. It also launched a satellite company that began the cable networks Nickelodeon and MTV to provide programming for the cable systems it owned. Warner then merged with Time, Inc. in 1989, which brought a vast publishing empire into the stable of media holdings, and then in 1996 it purchased Ted Turner's expansive Turner Broadcasting system, which encompassed cable channels, including CNN, TBS, and TNT. Finally, the conglomerate attempted to jump into the new media era when AOL purchased it in 2000, becoming AOL-Time Warner. By 2003, it became clear that the older media holdings would actually prove the more valuable, and the company returned to its identity as Time Warner. Although its holdings are constantly evolving through acquisitions and sales, Time Warner grew to be a media conglomerate possessing film and television studios, a broadcast network, music labels, cable channels (both in the United States and internationally), a cable service provider, more than 150 magazine titles, professional sports teams and arenas, and amusement parks. (See Table 5.2.)

While the exact composition of their holdings may vary, this ownership structure characterizes the development of other global media conglomerates—such as News Corp., The Walt Disney Company, and Viacom—as well.

Conglomeration involves not only a company expanding into other aspects of media production, but also its diversifying existing non-media industry operations to compete in media industries. An illustration of such conglomeration can

Table 5.1 Growth of a Media Conglomerate

WARNER COMMUNICATIONS SELECTED GROWTH	
1972	**Warner Communications, Inc. established** • **Warner Bros. Pictures** • Warner Music (Fleetwood Mac) • DC Comics, *MAD* magazine • Garden State National Bank Acquired Elektra, Atlantic, and Asylum Records (The Eagles, The Doors)
1975	Expands with Warner-Amex Satellite Entertainment • Nickelodeon, MTV
1976	Purchases Atari
1978	Purchased Sire Records (Madonna, Ramones, Ice-T)
1980	Purchases the Franklin Mint • Eastern Mountain Sports (outdoor apparel & retail)
1983	Purchases the Pittsburgh Pirates
1989	Purchases Lorimar-Telepictures
1989	**Becomes Time Warner, Inc.** • Time, Inc. (*Time, Sports Illustrated, Entertainment Weekly*) • HBO, Cinemax • IPC Media (*Marie Claire, NME*) • Little, Brown and Company (*Twilight*, David Sedaris)
1993	Purchases Six Flags Theme Parks
1996	Purchases Turner Broadcasting Systems, Inc. • CNN, TBS, TNT, TCM, Cartoon Network, Adult Swim, Court TV • New Line Cinema, Castle Rock Entertainment • Atlanta Braves • World Championship Wrestling • Hanna-Barbera Productions
2000	**Becomes AOL Time Warner, Inc.** • AOL, Inc.
2006	Creates the CW Television Network with CBS Corporation

be seen in General Electric's purchase of NBC. GE encompasses many seemingly unrelated industries, such as manufacturing health care technologies, offering financial services, and operating a variety of media companies, including NBC, Universal Studios, Telemundo, and several cable channels. By the mid 2000s, involvement in the media industries was decreasingly valuable to GE, leading to the sale of its controlling interest in these assets in 2009.

Vertical integration, discussed in Chapter 1, is a competitive strategy related to conglomeration that involves owning companies that allow the conglomerate to control each stage of the production process. In media industries such as film and television, this is most often achieved by conglomerates attempting to own the means to produce and distribute their media products—as in the case of a conglomerate that owns a broadcast network and also owns a studio that produces the programs for that network. As an illustration of the extent of such conglomeration, independent production studios (those unaffiliated or not owned by a company that also owns a network or film studio) have all but disappeared from the business of narrative television production. In the 1980s, considerable competition existed,

Table 5.2 Time Warner assets

TIME WARNER U.S. ASSETS				
A SAMPLE INCLUDING SUBSIDIARIES OF WARNER BROS. ENTERTAINMENT, TIME INC., TURNER BROADCASTING SYSTEM, AND HOME BOX OFFICE				
FILM	PRINT	TV & CABLE	INTERNET	FORMER ASSETS
Warner Bros. Pictures	DC Comics	CNN	TMZ.com	AOL
New Line Cinema	*MAD*	Headline News	NASCAR. com	Time Warner Cable
Castle Rock Entertainment includes movies such as	*Cooking Light*	HBO	PGA.com	Time Warner Cable Arena
	Entertainment Weekly	Cinemax		Atlanta Braves
	Essence	The CW (jointly with CBS)		Comedy Central
	Fortune	TBS		Six Flags theme parks
Harry Potter series	*Golf Magazine*	TNT		Little, Brown and Company
Matrix trilogy	*Health*	Turner Classic Movies		Warner Bros. Records
Lord of the Rings trilogy	*InStyle*	Cartoon Network		Atlantic Records
	Money	Adult Swim		World Championship Wrestling
	People	ER		Mapquest.com
	People en Español	*Gossip Girl*		MovieFone.com
	Real Simple	*Big Bang Theory*		Netscape
	Sports Illustrated	*Ellen DeGeneres Show*		
	Teen People	Looney Tunes cartoons		
	Time U.S.	Hanna-Barbera cartoons		

thanks largely to the **Financial Interest and Syndication** rules, which prevented networks from producing much of their own programming. During the years in which these rules were in effect (1970–1995), the networks were prohibited from owning a stake in their prime-time programming. In 1995, the networks had already regained ownership of an average of 40 percent of their schedules, and by 2000, three of the networks had a stake in more than 75 percent of their schedules.[4] Similar illustrations can be identified throughout the media industries—such as in the film industry before and after the **Paramount Decree**, which we discussed in the opening of the last chapter.

The magazine industry, like book publishing, is not a vertically integrated media industry, as magazines are generally not distributed by stores and stands owned by the same conglomerate that creates them—although magazines are an important component of many media conglomerates. Yet, still, large magazine companies such as Hearst and Condé Nast have started to exert control over different aspects of the production process. For instance, Condé Nast (which publishes *Vogue* and *The New Yorker*, among many other titles) has set up an in-house advertising agency to work with clients in creating ads that will run in the companies' magazines, and many magazine publishers own their own presses. Situations

such as these allow publishers even greater control over the content in their magazines, as they can create ads that they think will best fit into their particular titles
and also control the expenses of production. They also help publishers to sell
advertising pages while generating new revenues, as clients would otherwise pay
outside agencies to create ads.

Concentration, or **consolidation of ownership**, is another industry strategy that is often noted in concert with conglomeration. According to David
Hesmondhalgh, concentration of ownership "refers to the extent to which a
market or industry is dominated by the largest businesses."[5] For example, in the
above case of television production since the end of the Financial Interest and
Syndication Rules, the production of scripted television series in the United States
has become a much more consolidated industry (meaning fewer competitors),
as well as a conglomerated one (because the same companies that air the shows
on their networks also produce the shows in their studios). Although the terms
"conglomeration" and "consolidation" are often conflated, much of the concern
about shifts in ownership patterns in recent years centers more on consolidation
than conglomeration. Consolidation more precisely describes the concentration
of many media industry operations into the hands of just a few companies.

We often think of consolidation as a recent development, and that is the case
for some media industries, but similar sizable shifts in ownership occurred in
the newspaper industry at the beginning of the twentieth century. Between 1910
and 1930, the number of cities with competing local papers fell from 689 to 288.
By 2006, that number was just 38. Consolidation of the newspaper industry was
already apparent by 1933, when the six most powerful chains controlled about
one-quarter of the daily circulation in the United States.[6]

So, have the media industries generally become more conglomerated and
consolidated, and, if so, why? Ben Bagdikian begins his 2004, revised edition of
The New Media Monopoly with some stunning descriptions of the level of conglomeration and consolidation of the media industries. For instance, he notes that
by 2003, five men controlled the range of media that had been run by fifty men
just twenty years earlier.[7] In their expansive and detailed third edition of *Who
Owns the Media*, published in 2000, Benjamin M. Compaine and Douglas Gomery
note that the top five firms in the recorded music industry account for 80 percent
of the market, and that in theatrical film, six studios account for 90 percent of
the box office receipts.[8] By 2005, two of the five music firms had merged, resulting in the "big four" controlling all but 18 percent of the global music market.
Similarly, Hollywood studios continued to control 90 percent of the market in
2009.[9] Radio ownership has consolidated considerably since the passage of the
Telecommunications Act of 1996, which eliminated limits on how many stations could be owned nationwide. The anti-conglomeration activist group Free
Press reports that before 1996, no company owned more than 65 radio stations
nationwide, but after the Act's passage, Clear Channel corporation expanded to
own nearly 1,200.[10] Or in television, Free Press reports that "between 1995 and
2003, ten of the largest TV-station owners went from owning 104 stations with

$5.9 billion in revenue to owning 299 stations with $11.8 billion in revenue."[11] And the situation is little different in print. According to Free Press, "Since 1975, two-thirds of independent newspaper owners have disappeared. Today less than 275 of the nation's 1,500 daily newspapers remain independently owned, and more than half of all U.S. markets are dominated by one paper."[12] Even in newer media industries, such as gaming, the gaming console industry operates as an oligopoly among three main companies (Sony, Microsoft, and Nintendo), while the publication of games is also highly consolidated among a few companies, with the added hurdle that game designers need to license their games with the various console companies.[13]

As you can see, a fair amount of evidence exists that media industries have become more conglomerated and consolidated. What remains much less certain, however, is what this means for the operation of media industries and our understanding of them. There are generally two schools of thought on this issue. One position might be loosely described as "conglomeration equals homogenization." Scholars and media critics including Robert McChesney and Ben Bagdikian have extensively chronicled the numerical illustrations of conglomeration and consolidation that we note above and often tie in examples indicating the dangers inherent in these ownership configurations. Importantly, it is not simply a matter of what these conglomerates own directly; rather, conglomeration is also relevant when you consider the complex, interconnected webs that consolidate power such as connections among corporate boards of directors, conglomerate owners of media (particularly those with holdings outside of media), and the commercial mandate of news entities that requires them to placate advertisers and sponsors leads to significant compromises in the provision of news.

The other school of thought on the consequences of conglomeration and consolidation on the operation of media industries is not directly opposed to thinkers such as McChesney and Bagdikian, rather, they would suggest (and your authors fall into this category) that we do not yet know enough to make decisive statements about the internal operations of these conglomerates, do not have enough case studies beyond news production, or have a way to explain the pro-social outcomes that conglomerated media industries sometimes enable. Many in the conglomeration-equals-homogenization camp tend to rely on frameworks of media industry operation that place much more emphasis on ownership as the deciding factor of what industries do than the Industrialization of Culture framework. In their thinking, the routines and cultures of companies and agency of individuals that we allow for in our exploration of "practices" are unimportant, because they believe that workers consistently serve the needs and will of the conglomerate only. Based largely on a range of anecdotes, because little in-depth or exhaustive research on the internal operation of media conglomerates really exists, we have found that conglomerates are too vast to operate in the single-minded and concerted manner proposed.

Although it makes sense that conglomerates would operate with extensive self-interest, their scale is often simply too great for such coordination to occur.

Conglomerates are organized into units and divisions and the individuals who work in them are much more concerned about the needs of their unit or division, rather than beholden to the broader conglomerate as a result of how reward and evaluation are structured. For example, performance is typically measured at the level of a single division (e.g., did the home video division make its sales goals, etc.), which means that workers tend to place the performance of their division above that of the conglomerate. This has tended to prevent the conglomerations from achieving **synergies** that the purchases or mergers that led to the conglomeration were claimed to create. Synergy was a big buzzword of the mid 1990s through early 2000s that described the efficiencies and advantages that could be achieved through conglomeration—basically the idea that the combination of two entities was greater than the simple sum of their parts. In a few cases, synergies could be found in successful cross-promotional efforts, but more often, one division wasn't willing to do something for another if there was nothing to be gained for the complying division. One story we heard from someone working for Time Warner (which we can't officially verify) is that when the Internet service arm of Time Warner sought to use the Road Runner character from the Warner Bros. Looney Tunes franchise as its name, the Warner licensing division initially allowed it only with an exponential licensing fee. While this was eventually worked out (as Road Runner is the trademarked name of the Time Warner Internet service), the notion of synergy suggests that such divisional self-interest as levying a license fee on another arm of the conglomerate would not exist.

Or, consider the example of HBO's international operations. HBO not only produces its own programs that it sells abroad, it also owns HBO-branded channels in more than 50 countries. We might, then, expect the company to engage in a variety of anti-competitive practices in an effort decrease costs across a variety of operations. These practices might include selling original programming cheaply to its foreign channels, giving those channels privileged access to HBO programming, and forcing HBO's foreign subsidiaries to air original programming in order to spread production costs as widely as possible. However, because the distribution division operates independently of the foreign channels, which also operate independently of one another, these practices are rare. Instead, HBO channels must bid against other competitors in their markets for the rights to original HBO programming. And local channels have control over what they do and don't buy from HBO's international distribution division. The reason for such independence is simple: from the perspective of the channels, the most important economic concern is whether subscribers are willing to plunk down their monthly fees, and serving merely as a pipeline for HBO's original programming is rarely the best way to convince them to do so. By contrast, the distribution division is charged with maximizing profits on HBO's expensive original programming, and its revenues would be sorely diminished if it sold to anyone except the highest bidder.

Of course, HBO's status as a subscription channel may also help explain the arms-length relationship among its divisions (although all these divisions are part of the Time Warner conglomerate). In other media industries and instances, anticompetitive behaviors certainly do arise. The major Hollywood movie studios, for instance, own theatres around the world, and often give their own and other Hollywood films privileged access to their screens. The point, then, is that the kinds of ownership consolidation that we've seen in the media industries over the past couple of decades has certainly enabled different arms of the conglomerate to operate in anticompetitive ways. The analysis of whether, how, and how frequently these things happen, however, requires a more nuanced assessment of particular industries, organizations, and instances.

The end of the first decade of the twenty-first century is a difficult moment in which to assess the state of conglomeration and consolidation in media industries. Although the evidence mounted by the conglomeration-equals-homogenization camp remains valid, there is also growing evidence that conglomeration has failed to be effective as a business strategy and that a trend toward disaggregation may be developing. For one, no company has emerged with a success story of the synergies that conglomeration was heralded to bring. In fact, many of the high-profile mergers—much like AOL and Time Warner—are now regarded as poor decisions. Furthermore, some companies have disaggregated and broken apart or sold off some of the assets once thought to be central evidence of conglomeration. The split at the end of 2005 of Viacom back into the separate entities of Viacom (holding the basic cable properties) and CBS Corp. (encompassing the broadcast, premium cable, radio, and outdoor advertising divisions) or Time Warner's 2009 sale of its Time Warner cable system division are primary illustrations of this reversal in strategy.

In recent years, the key trend in media ownership has not involved continued acquisition or growth among conglomerates so much as it has involved a tension between publicly and privately held media companies. **Publicly held** companies are those that anyone can buy stock in and consequently have a responsibility to stockholders to protect their investment. They are also subject to a variety of government regulations that require disclosure of financial details and particular accounting. **Privately held** media companies are typically managed by a family and are not subject to the same disclosure rules. Analysts of the business performance of media companies have noted a number of cases of private media companies thriving in the uncertain times of the last decade and suggested that the daily assessment of public company performance via fluctuations in stock prices has prevented publicly held companies from developing strategies likely to innovate over the long-term. The trend—most recently—has been for companies to buy back publicly held stock or to seek to take publicly traded companies private, rather than the reverse. At this point, perhaps this is more rhetorical business strategy than true trend, as in the last five years ample business reporting has announced the ambitions of Sinclair, the *New York Times*, Cablevision, Playboy Enterprises, Trans World (music retail chain), and Clear Channel Communications to go private, although Univision (Spanish language broadcasting), Cossette (advertising), Ion Media Group (broadcasting), and Cumulus Media (radio) have done so.[14] Media scholars have not yet thoroughly investigated this trend, but it does appear to be a development of some consequence that is now on the horizon. If so, it might mark the next stage in the evolution of dominant trends in media ownership. Media industries were first most commonly local family businesses before developing into broad, publicly traded global media conglomerates. Certainly, these trends do not characterize the ownership of all companies, but the questions of who owns a media company and whether it fits the dominant ownership trend of its industry at the time are important considerations in applying the Industrialization of Culture framework.

Given the range of thinking among media scholars on the subject of media ownership and consolidation, you may be wondering what to make of this situation or what knowledge you can take away. It is clear that who owns what can be very important to the operation of media industries. What remains contested is how important ownership is. For some scholars and approaches to the study of media industries, ownership is a crucial and primary indicator of how an entity will operate. It is the position of the authors and the Industrialization of Culture framework that ownership is meaningful, but it is only one of many factors that figure into how media industries operate and what they are likely to create. Returning to our pinball metaphor in Chapter 1, ownership may be one bumper that sends the ball forcefully in one direction, but despite the potential of that forceful push, the ball could deflect in a number of directions when it hits the next obstacle, or it may be the case that the ball only glances the bumper, and the bumper has little effect on the text. As the remainder of this chapter explores, however, economics alone encompasses much more than just ownership and financial control.

THE CREATIVE AND CULTURAL
IMPLICATIONS OF COST STRUCTURES
AND FINANCING MECHANISMS

When you think about financing media, the first thing that may come to mind is how you pay for the media you consume. While this may be the most pressing concern for us as media consumers, as you might imagine, many significant financing and economic decisions take place well before a media text reaches us. Because of some of the characteristics specific to media industries that we discussed in Chapter 1, particularly high first-copy costs, variations in the financing of the products they create can have significant implications for what gets created. Some media industries have extraordinarily high production costs (television and film), while in others, new technologies have made it increasingly possible for amateurs to produce high-quality media as well ('zines, music, and increasingly video). Many of the traditional financing practices that we'll talk about below are starting to experience changes introduced by new forms of distribution and digital media, which we address in Chapter 10. When examining current industry issues such as piracy or the availability of music, video, or print via new media, it is important to recognize the economic issues related to production costs that contribute significantly to industry behavior. The costs of media for users (whether through advertising or direct pay) are linked to the costs of production and how they are financed.

There are countless different sites at which we can examine how matters of economics affect media industry operation and production. In the remainder of the chapter, we explore some of the broadest factors. First, we explore the economics of making media and the costs and financing practices that producers negotiate in making media. The subsequent section then examines the audience as an economic entity and the different ways that audiences pay for media products. While there are many concepts and terms included below, the key point of the chapter is to encourage you to think through how the various costs involved in media products and the different ways audiences might pay for them lead to the production of certain kinds of content. This chapter primarily uses media with a commercial mandate as its focus. We draw comparisons with media created with a public mandate where possible.

The Costs of Making Media

What costs are involved in producing media? Certainly there are obvious costs, such as those related to **talent**—the cost of hiring performers (journalists, actors, musicians), securing the raw media good (scripts, lyrics), and the basic costs of production (sound stage, cameras, news service, recording studio). These costs only scratch the surface, however. As we address many times throughout the book, one of the key characteristics of media industries for at least the past half-century has been the organization of the activities involved in making media products into highly specialized and distinct roles. A central consequence of this is that the creation of media products requires vast staffs of people, since their skill sets are not interchangeable. We really cannot stress enough how many workers play some role in the media products you encounter every day.

In order to try to make the broad array of costs more comprehensible, we organize them into four categories: overhead, planning, production, and marketing and distribution. There are certainly many costs that don't fit any of these categories or that fit into more than one, as well as a fair amount of variation based on whether a media industry operates with a publishing, flow, or written press model—but these categories offer a general framework.

Overhead costs include those required to maintain media institutions, and this concept is particularly relevant to media organized under the Miege's publishing model. These costs are not isolated to a particular product, but are required to maintain the infrastructure used by film studios, record labels, and game and book publishers. For many media in today's conglomerated industrial organization, these are the costs of the conglomerate or its subcomponents. For example, the Sony film studio employed 7,000 full-time employees in 2003, illustrating how a film or television studio maintains a staff of thousands year after-year who work in varying capacities—including as executives, lawyers, bookkeepers, publicists, and clerical staff—that provide support for the different projects produced by the studio.[15] In addition to substantial salaries, overhead costs include the considerable real estate costs of studios and their back lots or office high rises. Indeed, given the premium value of land in the greater Los Angeles area and in Manhattan, one of the biggest assets of the media conglomerates results from their land holdings and real estate.

Overhead is arguably the best subcategory for many of the costs of media industries in the written press model. The regularity of these industries—they produce the same product every day or every month—is clearly different than most industries working in the publishing model: film studios produce a vast range of films or a record label creates different albums. This regularity leads us categorize many of the costs of the print industry as overhead as well. Also, these industries incur nearly all their costs in making their product and have much less tied up in distribution and marketing expenses.

Another key category of overhead costs result from the materials needed to run media industries, including everything from the computers and cubicles used by executives and studio employees to the cameras and technical equipment found on set. The significant expansion of overhead costs is a central consequence of the organization of media production today. However, even though this organizational structure predominates in many media industries, it is not the only way media can be made. "Independent" media makers largely exist outside of this structure and may instead rent or subcontract many of the goods and services included in the overhead of conglomerates.

After separating overhead costs that transcend any particular media product, costs might be classified based on when they are incurred during the production process. The first set of costs then are those sustained during **planning**. Planning costs can include the costs of acquiring creative goods—for example, the fee a studio pays to secure a script, a book publisher pays for a manuscript, or a game developer sustains to develop a prototype to try to sell to a game publisher. Planning costs are often risky expenditures, as they often involve monetary or time commitments that are never repaid because many media goods aren't ultimately created. In his research on the operation of the film industry, Edward Jay Epstein learned that only one out of ten scripts that studios buy is ever developed into a film.[16] This is also the case in television, where planning costs include scripts and also the production costs—over a million dollars each—for **pilot episodes** of shows that are never seen by more than a handful of executives.

Media workers invest their time following a variety of models. Many times scriptwriters and journalists work on a "freelance" basis, meaning that they are paid a fee in exchange for the rights to a specific creative work. In other cases though, creators might have a contract with a studio, newspaper, or magazine and receive a regular salary. The structure of these deals vary considerably, particularly in visual media: some creators may be under contract to create a certain number of shows or films; sometimes the studio is only guaranteed a "first-look" and the creator can then take a project elsewhere; sometimes the creator may be called upon to develop a particular project or might be contractually prevented from taking an idea to another network if the studio he or she is contracted to is uninterested.

Such practices are uncommon for freelance journalists. In the music industry, a record label hires A&R (Artist and Repertoire) representatives to seek out new artists that may be offered recording contracts that require them to create a set number of CDs for the label to sell. The label provides money up front, known as an "advance," to cover costs of living as well as expenses related to the making of the music. These contracts give the label rights to the CDs whether they choose to release the music or not. Record labels also offer publishing contracts to songwriters, who receive a salary while writing songs that are offered to various artists on the label's roster. As you can see, there is no single model within an industry, or even among media operating within a particular model, as evident in the variation among publishing media noted here.

While the terms that govern the working conditions of media workers can take many different forms, we are less concerned with relaying all of these nuances than with encouraging you to think about how the conditions of planning—even something seemingly as small as whether creative writers or journalists work on freelance or salary basis—might produce consequences for the projects they develop. If you were a journalist, how might the content of the articles you develop differ if you were guaranteed a weekly paycheck versus whether you had to sell a magazine on an idea in order to get paid? Or from a different vantage point, why might a studio or magazine prefer to keep workers on a freelance-only basis? What consequences would this likely have for the creative products they make?

Costs multiply as production begins. Production costs include all those salaries and costs involved in the actual making of a media product. Again, media working within the written press economic model are somewhat exceptional in that they maintain a steadier labor base for each issue, making production costs more similar to overhead costs. The salaries or fees of those who work on a project (movie, show, game, album) consume a large percentage of production costs and the costs of the goods (costumes, sets, insurance) needed to produce it. In the case of film, Epstein notes that the start of production brings initial payments to talent agencies for the actors, directors, and other workers who must be paid in full as soon as the project begins. Another set of expenses, including the salaries of many of the technicians as well as costs as tangential as catering, are incurred on a day-to-day basis throughout production. A wide range of independent vendors who provide computer graphics, digital effects, titles, and trailers must also be paid.[17] Additionally, work such as editing, sound synchronizing, mixing the various sound tracks, balancing the color, and cutting the negative are also part of making the product. To consider production costs in another industry, we might look at the costs involved in recording an album. The cost of recording the sound tracks, mixing them, and preparing the master for reproduction typically can run to as much as $50,000.[18]

Marketing and distribution costs include the cost of having films printed and shipped to theaters and the cost of having records, tapes, and CDs made and shipped to stores. Just making copies of a film to have enough prints to open in theaters across the county can cost $6 million.[19] Likewise, print industries incur

marketing and distribution costs of printing newspapers and magazines, and the
music industry has the costs of pressing CDs. Media industries that sell their products through retailers face costs related to getting their goods (albums, magazines,
newspapers, games) to those retailers and sometimes added costs for desirable display. Significantly, some of these distribution costs have been diminished or eliminated as a result of new digital means of distribution that reduce the need to create
and transport physical copies of media—such as when you purchase a download
of a song instead of a CD. We'll discuss the consequences of digital distribution on
media industry economics in greater detail in Chapter 10.

Marketing and distribution also include the costs of promoting a text, which
often can be as considerable as the cost of making it for media operating under
a publishing model. Consider, for example, the expansive television advertisement buys common for big studio films that blanket the airwaves just before a
film opens. In 2003, the studios spent an average of $34.8 million per film for
advertising—although this is only an average.[20] Those films intended to be
international blockbusters require much more. The 2007 international debut of
Spiderman 3 cost $100 million in advertising.[21]

Further marketing and distribution costs might include those required to distribute the media product in additional markets—for example, the costs related
to editing a film to prepare it for distribution on television or to produce and distribute DVD copies for rental or sale. Epstein reports that creating the DVD and
adding features can cost $30,000–$50,000 per film and require marketing costs of
$4–$5 per copy sold.[22]

How Are the Costs of Creating Media Products Funded?

If you remember back to some of the key economic characteristics of media industries explained in Chapter 1, you'll recall that media industries require considerable sunk costs or high first-copy costs. The overhead, planning, production,
and marketing and distribution costs illustrate this concept, as pretty much all
of these expenses must be paid before a single dollar of revenue can be earned,
while once the media product is created, producing additional units has minimal cost. The fact that such considerable costs are incurred before producing any
revenue requires that media industries pursue a range of funding mechanisms in
order to finance these costs. The funding options vary, based on whether media
are operating under a publishing, flow, or written press economic model. Written
press industries and, to a large degree, flow industries as well, sustain themselves
with daily products and consistent sales, so they don't incur the massive promotion expenses for each new good faced by those in publishing industries. Those
using the publishing model typically rely on the "publisher" to finance new productions based on the profits earned from previous projects. An alternative, in a
media space dominated by large corporations, is that of the independent. What
it means to be independent varies by industry, but for the most part, independents either self-finance the creation of their products or solicit investors to pay
for production.

Fans of the television show *Entourage*—a show about a film star and his group of friends—might remember the depiction of the guys securing funding for their independent passion project, *Medellien*. Vince, the emerging film star, wanted to develop a reputation for more complicated roles and fell in love with a script about a Colombian cocaine dealer. Despite Vince's emerging star reputation, he and his friends couldn't convince a studio to make the film (perhaps because the role disguised Vince's movie-star looks and was in Spanish) so they purchased the script themselves, sought out a financier, and struggled to make the film on the budget that allowed. Rather than taking advantage of infrastructure paid for in overhead, independent productions have to contract for all the materials and goods they need and produce their work with no guarantee that any money will be recouped (but, also, with no interference from a studio). The guys and their financier hoped to make their money back by finding a distributor who would buy the film. In some cases, independents simply hope to find a distributor so that people see their work, while investors often hope their financing proves profitable.

The viability of creating media "independently" varies considerably by medium. A feature-length film is much more expensive to produce than a music album or 'zine. Furthermore, different media industries have mechanisms for distribution that make independent distribution easier in some industries. Independent music distribution has been made exponentially easier in the digital era, as has basic "print" publishing. Blogs are really just self-published independent newspapers/magazines that eliminate the costs of printing and distribution by publishing online. The film industry has also long had mechanisms in place for the exhibition and distribution of independent films. Film festivals often provide the necessary showcase for films to find distributors, while small art house theaters have provided exhibition. In contrast, the control of distribution in television by just a few broadcast networks during the network era prevented any kind of substantial independent television production from existing. There have been independent studios—or, those not associated with the major film studios—but even these "independents" were limited in creating for established networks and channels. The age of digital distribution of video online may finally change that, as venues such as YouTube, FunnyOrDie, and AskaNinja, or experiments such as *quarterlife*, a serial drama that started as **webisodes** and briefly migrated to primetime on NBC in 2008, arguably provide illustrations of independent television distribution.

In contrast to the independent route, most media are created by large conglomerates able to rely on past successes or other sectors of the company to finance the sunk costs. The profits a project eventually returns then go to finance subsequent projects. Next, we detail the process of funding video games and television in the United States to offer more specific case illustrations of corporate media funding strategies. Although the specific mechanisms vary somewhat in other industries, the general structures for taking on debt, earning outrageous profits from a few products, and using those profits to develop new products can be found in many media industries.

Case One: Financing a Publishing Medium: Game Software[23]

The creation of videogames is largely controlled by a handful of publishers, companies such as Electronic Arts, Nintendo, UbiSoft, Infogrames/Atari and Take 2. Game software is typically classified one of three ways: first-party developers, which are internal teams that are part of the publishing company; second-party developers, which are contracted to create a game based on a concept originating with a publisher; or third-party developers, which are typically independent of publishers and develop their own projects that they then try to sell to publishers. Industry estimates suggest that first-party development dominates the industry, with nearly two-thirds of game production done this way.

Regardless of type of developer, the dominance of the game industry by three hardware manufacturers (Sony, Nintendo, and Microsoft) and the fact these console/handheld manufacturers use closed hardware systems that are proprietary and not interoperable structure the economics of gaming software in other ways. The closed-system hardware means that game developers must get licenses to produce games for each machine. The license fee, collected per game sold, is typically about 20 percent of the cost of the game. Thus, the sale of games is extremely lucrative for the hardware developers and accounts for most of the revenue in their profit model (the hardware systems operate as a **loss leader**). In some cases, platform manufacturers demand exclusivity so that a game will be available only for their platform. In addition to being integral to most game development, the big publishers also own roughly 80 percent of the distribution channels. Games primarily sell from retailers independent from the publishers, large chains such as Wal-Mart and Best Buy, which are estimated to gross 35–40 percent on the full price of a game.

Other economic distinctions among games can be found as well. Notable differences exist between the console and PC game industries. Games playable on PCs have open, nonproprietary systems, which makes them cheaper to develop (and cheaper to consumers) but also leads to much more competition, as access to this market isn't regulated by platform companies that can control the number and type of games available for their systems. Massively multiplayer online games (MMOGs) require ongoing support costs after development, typically monthly subscription fees. We'll discuss the consequences of payment structures in the last section of the chapter, but, for now, note that most console and PC games have a one-time purchase price, although many other revenue models—such as pay per download, pay per play, and advertising—also can be found in some sectors of the game industry.

As is common in media industries, many development costs come early in the creation of gaming software. In the case of third-party development, the planning necessary to develop a proposal and design a prototype to shop to publishers typically costs about $1.5 million. To finance these expenses, developers seek venture capital funding and other private sources. The cost of developing a console game is typically around $7.5 million, although licensing known sport or entertainment properties can increase costs significantly, and MMOGs require double the expense. Third-party developers use their prototypes to secure a contract and advance funding from a publisher. The advance funding is used to develop the games. Profits for the developer then are only achieved once a game goes to market and the publisher earns back the advance payment. The developer then earns a percentage on subsequent sales. Many new developers are forced to sign over the intellectual property of the game to the publisher in order to get a contract, which can be a significant issue if the game proves successful and the publisher seeks a sequel. Developers with established track records or those who already possess the license for creative properties perceived as valuable have a stronger position for negotiating contract terms. In contrast, first-party developers face fewer initial hurdles, as the publisher has already determined that it needs a game of specific genre targeted at a specified audience, eliminating many of the business-plan aspects that can be onerous for third-party developers.

Funding is not the only thing a third-party developer receives from a publisher. The developer must also negotiate the dynamics of working with a much larger corporate entity, and all developers must negotiate with the platform manufacturers.

Many of these features of financing creative goods can be found across publishing industries—simply replace the term "developer/publisher" with "director" or "producer/studio" for the film industry, "author/publisher" for the book industry, and "artist/label" for the recording industry. Similar variations on the dynamic of first-party versus third-party development also exist in different industries. In some ways, the written press industry bears some likeness to the operation of first-party funding, since individual creative goods do not need to be sold to a publisher as much as the publisher recognizes a need and then has them created by an existing staff.

Case Two: Financing a Flow Medium—Television

The dominant process for financing most U.S. prime-time television programming is one that always seems to surprise students. The profits and costs of television aren't where many would expect, and some aspects of the business seem downright insane. Let's begin with a key practice: **deficit financing**. Deficit financing describes the process whereby production studios lose money in making series during the first few years, even if their show is a hit. This is how the process typically goes: A producer will pitch a show idea to a network, and if the network likes it, the network will give the producer some money to write a script. If the network likes the script, then it will give the producer money to shoot a "pilot"—typically the first episode of the series. A pilot is an expensive proposition; it requires building sets and developing a full cast, and most pilots (as many as 80 percent) are never developed into series and are typically never seen by anyone except the network executives. (Remember that practice of intentional overproduction).

If a network does like the pilot episode, and it has a good place for the show on its schedule, it will license the show. The license fee the network pays typically covers about 80 percent of production costs. A typical drama in the early 2000s cost a studio around $1.5 million per episode to produce. The network license fee, which gives the network the right to air the episode a couple times (typically a first and rerun episode), would probably be around $1.2 million. It doesn't take strong math skills to recognize that the studio is going to lose money making this show—about $300,000 per episode, or about $6.6 million over a standard twenty-two episode season. This doesn't look like a very smart arrangement for the studio, which covers the deficit not paid by the license (hence, deficit financing), but because the studio still owns the show, it maintains a possibility of other revenue streams. After the studio makes enough episodes (historically about 100 episodes or three to five seasons), the studio then sells the episodes again in **secondary markets** (also called **syndication**) to entities such as local stations to air during the hours the network doesn't provide programming, to independent stations and cable channels, and by releasing DVDs of series. The studios often also sell episodes to networks in other countries from the beginning of the show's production.

Selling the show in all of these secondary markets gradually helps the studio recoup its deficit and provides the profits for the show. So, even though a brand-new show might be a huge hit, chances are good that the studio making it is losing money on its production, at least in the short term. See Table 5.3 for a general sketch of this process.

What we've presented here, though, is a best-case scenario. Most shows don't become hits. Most shows don't survive to make a second season of episodes; actually, most don't even make it through a first. So even though a studio might make millions, even billions, of dollars on a successful show (as was the case for shows such as *Friends* and *Seinfeld*), far more frequently they never recover the deficit. Consequently, they rely on the profits from successful attempts (and in the past we are talking some pretty extraordinary profits) to cover the deficits of shows that fail.

This system of deficit financing leads to certain other industry practices and affects the creative content likely to be produced. First, because studios initially lose money, it effectively requires them to redistribute their shows in secondary markets. As a result, when they think about concepts for shows, producers think

Table 5.3 Primary and secondary markets for television

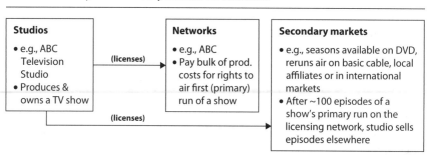

not only about what creative components might be likely to get their show on the network in the first place, but also about what features might make their show likely to succeed in other markets. As the international marketplace becomes more and more important to profits, concern about themes and stories with international appeal leads producers away from some concepts and toward others. This system of finance also contributes to the similarity of so much entertainment fare, as we'll explore in the next chapter, in the discussion of formatting. Shows similar to those that have succeeded in the past offer a sense of being a known commodity—even though they also often fail—and hits, likewise, can come in unexpected forms.

To give you a sense of how this works, the CBS series *How I Met Your Mother* was sold in various second-run markets in the fall of 2008. The cable channel Lifetime paid about $750,000 per episode (110 episodes were sold). In addition to this cash payment, Twentieth TV, the studio distributing the show, also received three thirty-second commercials in each episode that it could then sell to national advertisers, and these were expected to be worth another $200,000 per episode over the four years of the deal.[24] In addition to the sale to Lifetime, Twentieth TV also negotiated with station groups owning local stations from which the series was expected to earn another $350 million.[25] Sales in these markets alone (as international sales are not included here) total nearly half a billion dollars.

There are other ways to finance media. A model that has been common in the public mandate sector of the British television industry is called the **cost plus** system. In this case, a producer brings an idea to a network, and, if the network wants to develop the idea, the network pays the cost of production plus a fee or profit to the producer, perhaps 10 percent. The cost plus system greatly reduces the risk for the studio producing the show, as it does not take on deficit expenses and is guaranteed a certain amount of profit. In this arrangement, however, the studio effectively sells the show to the network, so any value to come from selling the show in another market would benefit the network rather than the studio. In exchange for the reduction of risk, then, the studio gives up the opportunity for exceptional reward.

Although this need to distribute television shows through multiple markets has long been a part of the television industry, increasingly the film industry is also becoming defined by revenue from other markets. At the close of the studio system in 1947, the film studios earned more than 95 percent of their revenues from theatrical exhibition, but now the studios routinely lose money on the theatrical release.[26] By 2003, the studios earned five times as much from home video as from theaters, and were increasingly reliant on licensing their films for all manner of home viewing.[27] Put another way, Epstein found that now eight-five percent of studio revenues come from viewing movies on DVD or television or from other licensed adaptations such as games.[28] Or, in the music industry, most of the money earned by artists comes through touring and the merchandise they sell, rather than from music sales.

The involvement of large corporations in the media industries—those capable of taking on the considerable debt of production costs—must be understood to have profound effects on the creation of media texts. These consequences aren't simple to define or uniform, but they lead strongly to certain tendencies. Many of the norms tilt the playing field in favor of the conglomerates, and in many cases it is difficult to work in media without working with the conglomerates. Most creative workers have very little leverage in negotiating contracts, unless a bidding war develops among multiple studios, publishers, or labels, as they need them to create and distribute the project. Most creators work on a freelance basis and enter into contracts that may provide a share of net profits; yet in the film industry, the norm of "**Hollywood accounting**" prevents that from ever amounting to much, if anything. Hollywood accounting is the casual term used to describe a manner of accounting for the costs of production (mainly through overhead charges) that reduces the net profits of a media text to a loss in order to avoid payment of royalties or percentages of net profits. The studios closely guard the details of their budgets, and detailed accounting is often only available in legal documents in cases of payment disputes. To be sure, studios and conglomerates do take a considerable risk in financing media products, but they are also handsomely rewarded in the case of success. The conglomerate control of media industries has also contributed significantly to the level of unionization in the industry, as the unions serve as a key mechanism to help workers negotiate for a fair share.

The Economics of Audiences: Ways of Paying for Media Products

The audience, or consumer, is a crucial component of the economics of media industries, and the first thing to understand is that there are two versions of the audience. The first audience is the **"real" audience**—the actual people who show up for a film, subscribe to a newspaper, or buy a new album or song. The problem with the real audience is that it doesn't enter into the equation until after the product has been created and all those costs have been sunk. While real audiences can be more meaningful in some of the financing structures discussed below, for the most part, the more important version of the audience is the **"constructed" audience**.

The constructed audience is the audience—its characteristics, likes, and dislikes—imagined by creators and those throughout the industry while making media; the audience that Angela McRobbie describes as a "useful fiction."[29] The constructed audience comprises knowledge about how real audiences have behaved in the past, but mostly perceptions and extrapolations. The constructed audience is so important because it is the entity held in mind when hundreds of daily decisions are made in the process of making a media product: Is the end of the movie too depressing? Is this an issue the community cares about? Does that song go on too long? Although the audience doesn't appear explicitly in any of these questions, it is the constructed audience—decision makers' perceptions of how they think the audience will answer—that will render the final verdict. In seeking to design media products that will be attractive to an audience, creators develop constructions of the audience in their minds whom they seek to serve. The constructed audience consequently drives the creation of media products.

The financial underpinnings of how media content is made and paid for affects it in many different ways. In discussing mandates, we explored the differences in commercial and noncommercial mandates, while noting that there are many variations in the practices of commercial media that affect the content of media produced under this mandate and how it is produced. This is because different structures for commercial media lead to different business strategies. The primary options for funding commercial media are through advertising or various forms of direct payment, although, as you'll see below, there is also a range of ways of using each of these payment methods.

Characteristics of Advertising-Supported Media

We often perceive advertising-supported media to be "free," but it is important to remember that old adage you may have heard in an economics class, that there is no such thing as a free lunch. Indeed, even if we don't pay a particular fee for advertiser-supported media such as broadcast television, we do pay for it—at least the people who buy the products that advertise in the shows do, because the costs of advertising are added to the cost of the goods. Setting that aside for now, advertiser funding sets up certain conditions that affect how media industries operate. Pure advertiser support is common in the economic model of flow media industries; thus, we focus on broadcasting here, although advertiser support is crucial to media that blend advertiser and audience payment.

Most important, introducing advertisers is what makes many media **dual product markets**. This is because there are effectively two things being sold. The main commodity is the audience: a radio station is selling an audience of listeners to an advertiser. Most, however, never consider this, and it seems the station is also "selling" a schedule of programming to us. Too often, we focus on the part of this equation that is likely most of interest—what songs the station is offering and whether we like them. Instead, it is important to remember that the programming is just the bait the stations use to draw us together so that we hear the content of real importance (in an economic sense at least), which is the advertising message. We don't mean to suggest that it is not also important to examine the content of advertiser-supported media; even as stations and networks gather us to sell us to advertisers, the content they offer still does significant cultural work, but we are focusing on economic matters here.

Because the advertisers, rather than the audience, are paying networks and radio stations, the advertisers gain a significant role in the creative process. In the early days of radio and television, the company doing the advertising was often responsible for developing programming—or at least that was the responsibility of the advertising agency that it hired. The agency would then bring the programming to the network, which had little involvement in developing the programming at all. This was the case as long as **single sponsorship** was the norm. In the case of single sponsorship, there is typically only one advertiser—or sponsor—associated with a program, and that sponsor pays all of the costs of production as well as fees to the network and the advertising agency. The lower production costs of radio made this system more feasible for that medium. The costs of video production, as well as a variety of other industrial factors, made sponsorship less practical for television. In addition to television production being too costly for most single advertisers to finance on a weekly basis, the networks desired to take greater control of their schedules and programming as audiences moved from radio to television.

If you were an advertiser, think about how your expectations and concerns might differ if you sponsored a program, in comparison with just paying for one of a handful of advertisements in the show. If you were sponsoring, chances are that a huge percentage of your advertising budget would go to financing just one weekly show. Having so much of your advertising budget concentrated in one place and having your product so closely associated with that program—for example, the name of your product would likely be part of the title of the show, as in the *Texaco Star Theater*—would probably lead you to be very concerned with every aspect of the content of the program. Everything about the show would reflect on your product, and you might want to use the show to try to create some type of association between how viewers regard the show and how they regard your product. Unlike the advertising we are accustomed to now, when single sponsorship dominated, many companies sought to use advertising to advance **corporate image** rather than to focus on the attributes of the product. Sponsorship, and the amount of control over content that came with it, was particularly ideal for this advertising strategy.

As television developed, however, single sponsorship faded as the dominant advertising strategy. What is often called **magazine-format advertising**, because magazines had long featured advertisements from multiple companies, soon became the norm on television. Instead of paying the production costs of an entire program, advertisers purchased thirty-second spots in the manner we are accustomed to today. Competition from television led to radio's transition from radio programs to the music and talk formats familiar today. These formats also lent themselves to an array of advertisers.

For the television industry, this switch in strategy had a number of consequences. This practice allowed the networks greater control as they became responsible for developing programming and deciding how to schedule it. Advertisers now had their budgets spread across spots in multiple shows, which decreased their association with any one show. Advertising could attend more to selling attributes of the product because it became unnecessary to integrate the good into the program in some way, as viewers quickly came to understand the commercials as separate from the content of the shows.

Given this history, perhaps it is somewhat surprising to witness the return to older strategies with the increasing prevalence of **product placement** and integration in the last decade. In the case of television, the addition of this commercial strategy—while maintaining traditional commercial pods as well—has developed from the new technological abilities viewers have that enable them to readily skip the commercial pods. Placement brings yet other concerns and issues for media industries. Many in the advertising industry believe that product placement must be "organic" (seem natural or fit well) if it is to succeed. This, then, leads certain types of content to be more likely to receive product placement advertising dollars, which, in the long term, might curtail other types of programming.

Advertisers still worry about the content surrounding their commercials, but they offer less direct day-to-day influence over the process than was once the case. Advertiser influence is now more indirect and often a matter of perception; similar to the constructed audience, decision makers often have a "constructed advertiser" in mind. Advertisers do see the shows that their commercial will air in before they are broadcast (or, rather, the advertising agency responsible for buying the spot typically manages this work), but it is rare for them to pull an advertisement. If they do, it is typically not because of major ideological conflicts with the show, but because of concern about correlations viewers might draw. For example, a car company might pull an advertisement set to air in the midst of storyline about a grizzly car crash on a hospital show. It is not that the company wants to keep stories about car crashes from being told, it is just that they don't want to promote their brand in the midst of that story and risk viewers associating their product with the crash.

Despite the rarity of such direct advertiser influence, the perception of what advertisers might and might not like certainly governs much of the thinking of media creators throughout the process. Media workers have internalized many of the concerns various advertisers have had in the past, and they are likely to steer content in certain directions even if they aren't given specific directions. In the case of television, the experience of "getting notes" from the network also influences creative staffs. While every creator may react to these situations differently, over the course of working in the industry, writers and producers quickly learn what types of content networks and advertisers prefer and what types of stories will require fights with the network. Even if the influence of advertisers isn't direct—as in the case of an advertiser refusing to run their commercial in a particular show or magazine—the indirect influence is very real and powerful.

In selecting and developing content that will be supported by advertisers, media creators must negotiate a fine balance with both viewers and advertisers. Creators must try to figure out what content will attract audiences as well as be acceptable to advertisers. Given the unpredictability of audiences when it comes to their tastes for cultural products, this is no small feat. The final subsection discusses media that rely on advertising as well as some form of audience payment, which is characteristic of most media using the written press model. All of the things we've discussed for advertising-only industries are true for those that rely on multiple strategies, but they are made more complex by the need to entice audiences as well as advertisers to spend on their goods.

Characteristics of Media Not Supported by Advertising

Media that are not advertiser supported are paid for by audiences or consumers, typically either through **subscription** or **direct pay**. In this case, the viewer, reader, or listener is the only source of revenue for the media outlet. Subscription television channels such as HBO and Showtime operate with this model, as do the film, music, and most of the gaming industries, and even a few specialized print media (*Ms. Magazine* and *Consumer Reports*, for example). In some ways, the tasks of these media are easier, since they don't have the extra layer of advertisers in their process. This also means that we might expect them to operate in much different ways.

Subscription. The consequences of subscription payment vary by media industry. No content-based media industry dominantly uses subscription (as opposed to media services such as Internet, mobile telephony, or cable service), so the particularity of entities that do use subscription-only is largely significant, as it leads them to differ from the norm of their industry. In the case of television, even though subscription channels are just as much "television" as the broadcast networks and basic cable channels, relying solely on subscription payments allows channels such as HBO and Showtime to operate much differently. Most people assume the biggest differences have to do with the greater content freedom that comes from not having advertisers who might worry about offending part of the audience and because they are regulated differently. While these factors are important, the bigger consequence comes from the way that focusing on keeping viewers happy enough to maintain a monthly subscription allows them to worry less about each and every program scheduled at each hour of the day.

Subscription networks don't care how many or which shows on their network you watch. All that really matters is that you find enough of value to maintain that monthly subscription fee. This allows them to approach programming much differently than an advertiser-supported channel. In some ways, the most viable strategy is to maintain just a little programming that meets the needs of vastly different audience groups and particularly program content those audiences can't get anywhere else. HBO provided a good example of this strategy in the early 2000s. Chances are that the channel's sports programming, such as boxing and *Inside the NFL,* reached a different audience than might have tuned in for *Sex and the City.* What HBO hoped, however, was that the young, single women who loved *Sex and the City* would want to watch that show so badly, and maybe a movie every now and then, that they would maintain their subscriptions, while young men would want to be able to see the big boxing matches badly enough that they, too, would maintain their subscriptions, even if they watched little else on the channel. (Of course, men also watched *Sex and the City*—a fine example of the broad generalizations characteristic of the constructed audience.) In contrast, the advertiser-supported network has to gather a big audience to sell to advertisers throughout every day. Just having a few specific programs won't be enough for them to succeed.

The question of how an industry is financed is of crucial importance to the way it develops. When *The Sopranos* appeared on HBO in the late 1990s, it led many to reassess the storytelling potential of television. Certainly, some aspects of *The Sopranos*— its exceptional violence, use of profanity, and incorporation of sexual content—would be impossible for broadcasters because of their different regulatory conditions. Much of the storytelling sophistication, however, such as concentrating on an ambiguous hero and the use of actors who did not conform to conventional looks, were aspects that could work in other forms of television—and the FX cable channel in particular quickly made a name for itself by developing shows such as *The Shield*, *Rescue Me*, and *Sons of Anarchy* that reproduced various aspects of *The Sopranos* template. These examples should indicate just how different media industry operations can be when financed by viewers/readers/listeners rather than by advertisers.

In the case of the few magazines funded solely through subscription, this financing is meant as an indicator of independence and of a particular editorial mission. For example, the reputation of *Consumer Reports* largely depends on consumers knowing the magazine's editorial staff operates independently of the products that they review and that there is no chance of bias toward an advertiser. *Ms. Magazine* started out with advertising, but reconciling the magazine's feminist mission proved too challenging to support with advertising messages the editors found acceptable. Sometimes the reason for relying on subscribers is more vague. *Cooks Illustrated* magazine does do some of the product reviews typical of *Consumer Reports*, but for the most part, it is just a cooking magazine absent advertising. Other media have used subscriptions to offer audiences a service rather than in connection with the creation of original content that has come to characterize subscription television channels. NetFlix, for example, operates on a subscription model, as do some digital music providers such as Rhapsody. In both of these cases, the subscription service works as a distributor of others' content. Disney took a slightly different approach in 2009, when it began offering monthly and annual subscriptions to digital versions of its children's books.

Direct Pay. Many media that use a publishing economic model rely on direct payment from audiences for their revenue. The direct pay of film admissions, movie rentals, and music sales are similar. In all of these cases, media industries need to convince their audiences that their products are worth paying for. And unlike in the case of subscription payment, these industries have to marshal audience interest for each and every product, which leads to marketing costs that often rival the costs required to produce the goods. Certainly the fact that audiences develop some attributes—for example, that the movie going audience tends to be young— leads these industries to operate in specific ways.

Characteristics of Media with Dual Revenue Streams
To complicate economic conditions in commercial media industries further, it is increasingly the case that many media rely on some blend of advertiser support

and subscription or direct payment by the media user. This is the case with most print media and basic cable television. These media are often discussed as having **dual revenue streams,** as they receive funding from both advertisers and viewers/readers.

Dual revenue streams enable these industries to operate in ways that have particular consequences for their creative content. These media must be more to their audiences than free media, because they require the viewer or reader to pay some amount for their product—so there is a cost for use that is not the case for fully advertiser-supported media. Most media with a dual revenue stream depend most heavily on advertisers, however. For instance, advertising generally accounts for 50–60 percent of a magazine's revenue, although that figure may be closer to 80 percent depending on the magazine type, with the rest of the revenue coming from subscriptions and newsstand sales. Consequently, keeping advertisers happy remains as essential for dual revenue as for media supported by advertising alone.

Like media supported only through advertising, those operating with a dual revenue stream have significant pressure for their content to appeal to a sizable audience. The dual revenue media need subscribers to derive enough value that they keep paying their subscriptions or making direct payments, but they also want to keep that vast audience base, because that is part of what they are selling to advertisers. Losing a viewer/reader hurts in two ways then: one fewer subscription fee and one fewer audience member to sell to advertisers. This explains why you sometimes might receive offers for magazines discounted so considerably that you wonder how they can make any money off of your subscription (they don't). In this case, the title is probably seeking to increase its advertising rates by showing growth in its subscription base.

The dual streams also explain some of the differential pricing evident in some media industries. For example, *Wired* magazine editor Chris Anderson notes that readers might face three different costs when accessing the content in magazines.[30] Readers can find articles free online, although typically with less design and fewer photographs; they can buy an issue for $4.95 on the newsstand; or they can subscribe and receive a year's worth of issues for as little as $10. The economics of each is a bit different, as you might guess. The web price is supported through advertising only—which Anderson notes amounts to between $5 and $20 per thousand views, or between one and four cents per person. Publishers amortize the cost of creating the content over the entire audience (print and online), which means it costs the magazine less than a cent to make that content available.

The revenue from the newsstand version is split with the retailer (retailer typically gets a bit less than half). The magazine typically earns $1 or $2 of profit after the printing and distribution costs are factored in; more than half the copies of most magazines printed for retail, however, don't sell. These are returned and pulped, cutting into the profits of those that do sell. Anderson explains that most magazines lose money on newsstand sales, but that this is a good promotional strategy to get new subscribers and they do earn advertising revenues on the copies that sell.

Finally, the actual cost of printing and mailing twelve issues is about $15 (and more like $30 if you include the costs of acquiring subscribers). Yet magazines routinely charge as little as $10, which provides some direct revenue while the advertising makes up the difference. Interestingly, Anderson notes that most magazines earn enough from advertising that they could be made available for free. The minimal $10 charge is psychologically important, however, because it suggests that the reader values the magazine (unlike, say, junk mail), which makes advertisers willing to pay as much as five times more for that reader.

As this magazine example illustrates, the combination of revenue streams offers some flexibility in how dual revenue media target audiences. Notably, despite the dual revenue, in most cases, the more lucrative funding stream comes from advertisers. Thus, when seeking to understand dual revenue media, it is important keep in mind all of the factors addressed in the advertiser-supported media section.

CONCLUSION

As this chapter illustrates, economic conditions can influence the operation of media industries in many different ways. Considerations as varied as the ownership of the media entity, the methods used to finance production, and the range of ways audiences pay for media all combine to push content in various directions. As the Industrialization of Culture framework points out, these economic considerations combine with a set of possibilities made feasible by the technology of the time and parameters set by regulations. In the next chapter, we begin our consideration of the various practices that influence operation.

While we have tried to address the broad range of factors that contribute to media economics, we've only scratched the surface and emphasized media industries with established histories. The economics of media industries are in the midst of considerable change—some more than others—as a result of the many ways that digitization is reconfiguring the costs of production and distribution, as well as how and how much audiences pay for media.

As is often the case, the "new media" industries (and newer applications of "old" ones) are drawing heavily from the models of the past, and it is still too early to know what aspects of old media economics will best transfer to today's conditions. Although advertising is now rapidly migrating to support media distributed online, online advertising is in many ways very different from its offline equivalent. Online advertising holds the promise of more accurate targeting and the ability to charge companies only when users "click through" on an ad. Moreover, the valuation of advertising is still being worked out. As one media executive famously explained, advertisers are paying media companies pennies in the digital world for what they paid dollars for offline. This forces companies that create content to adjust their budgets and processes (and likely the texts they produce as well). As advertisers come to better understand the opportunities of advertising in online media, they may also come to be willing to pay more for exposure to fewer eyeballs because of the specific targeting online advertising allows and the ability to better gauge advertising effectiveness.

The economic model of every media industry established before digital distribution is in some sort of crisis as we write. Such moments provide exceptional opportunities to radically reconfigure businesses; but in the midst of that change there is also considerable uncertainty. We imagine this chapter might look very different if we revise it ten years from now. We've emphasized the known and tried-and-true components of media economics throughout the chapter, though we by no means forecast these as likely to dominate the future. Nevertheless, as a conceptual framework, it remains helpful to begin by thinking about how a media organization can finance the creation of its texts and how it will then recoup those costs as new uses and forms of media develop. We offer the reminder to be wary of the Underpants Gnomes discussed in Chapter 1. Some of the new media that currently have the most "buzz" lack that middle step of earning profit. While they seem dizzyingly cool to users, revenue models have proven frustratingly difficult to incorporate in many cases, at least to an extent that captures that level of audience interest and engagement. The online world makes a great many things possible, but, in commercial media industries, those things must also have a profit model to recoup costs if they are to be sustained.

In conclusion, we note some of the in-process economic experiments. While the dual product market of advertiser support allowed for some "free" media in the past, Chris Anderson imagines a range of ways media industries might profit despite allowing free distribution of their content.[31] One strategy involves subscriptions for premium access to content. In this model, media companies give away access to some features—perhaps the ability to stream, to play certain levels of games, or to read recent newspaper or magazine coverage, but they also charge audiences to download songs, access additional game levels, or search and access archived stories.

Shifting the profit center of media industries is another strategy. At this point, this is best seen in the music industry, in which musicians have given away access to their music or experimented with pricing as in the oft-cited case of Radiohead's 2007 *In Rainbows* release in which the band allowed fans to select how much to pay for the album, in order to reach a larger audience that then pays to go to concerts and buys concert merchandise. In this case, the free content works as a way to promote a larger range of texts or media experiences. Certainly, this type of loss-leader or cross-subsidy economics was in use throughout the media industries even before the digital era. Game companies have discounted the cost of game hardware and made up the costs in the charges for the software of games, and mobile phone providers often discount phones considerably in exchange for a service commitment. Some of these strategies may be more applicable to some media industries than others, and the degree of experiment evident is largely correlated with the level of crisis. Nonetheless, such experiments may offer the foundation of economic conditions in the future.

QUESTIONS

1. Select a media text that you purchased or experienced this week and list all of the expenses involved in its creation that you can think of in the four categories (overhead, planning, production, and marketing and distribution). Which categories seem the most and least excessive—and why?

2. Consider the growth of Warner Communications. What were some advantages to its variety of holdings? Using the chart in this chapter, can you think up a plan to effectively utilize synergy among its holdings? What concerns might people raise about Warner Communications' growth as a conglomerate since the early 1970s, and what might Warner have said in response?

3. We have noted that the dominant perspective in media studies has been that conglomeration and consolidation of media industries narrow the range of content produced. Can you point to examples in which conglomeration has produced homogenization in cultural products? Can you point to examples in which this has *not* occurred?

4. If you were a journalist, how might the content of the articles you develop differ if you were guaranteed a weekly paycheck versus whether you had to sell a magazine on an idea in order to get paid? Or, from a different vantage point, why might a studio or magazine prefer to keep workers on a freelance-only basis? What consequences would this likely have for the creative products they make?

5. Imagine that you are a television producer. How might selling a show in the deficit financing and the cost plus system lead you to behave differently? What type of show would you think is likelier to succeed in one versus the other? Or, how might you develop the same show differently in each system? Thinking through these questions should give you some sense of how the method of financing a show contributes to determining the creative forms likely to circulate in a culture.

6. Think about the media you subscribe to. What do you expect from them to maintain your subscription? Also, think about the nature of your experience with other media you pay for. Many of our students buy much of the music they listen to through single-song transactions on iTunes. How might your music listening and purchasing differ if you could buy a "subscription" allowing access to any song you want as long as you pay a monthly fee? Or, can you remember when Internet access was commonly purchased in packages of minutes? How did your Internet use change once you had unlimited access?

7. Can you imagine how films might be different if they were advertiser supported? How about the music industry?

FURTHER READING

More detailed accounts from an economics perspective can be found in Richard E. Caves, *Switching Channels: Organization and Change in TV Broadcasting*

(Cambridge: Harvard University Press, 2005) and *Creative Industries: Contracts between Art and Commerce* (Cambridge: Harvard University Press, 2002), and Colin Hoskins, Stuart M. McFadden, and Adam Finn, *Media Economics: Applying Economics to New and Traditional Media* (Thousand Oaks, Calif.: Sage, 2004). For matters of media economics with attention to culture, see Bernard Miege, *The Capitalization of Cultural Production* (New York: International General, 1989) and David Hesmondhalgh, *The Cultural Industries*, 2nd ed. (London: Sage, 2007).

Various accounts of concerns related to ownership structure and conglomeration can be found in Ben H. Bagdikian, *The New Media Monopoly* (Boston: Beacon Press, 2004); Benjamin M. Compaine and Douglas Gomery, *Who Owns the Media: Competition and Concentration in the Mass Media Industry*, 3rd ed. (Mahwah, N.J.: Lawrence Erlbaum Associates, 2000), and almost anything by Robert McChesney. An interesting contrast can be found in the cases explored in Michael Curtin's "Feminine Desire in the Age of Satellite Television," *Journal of Communication* 49 (1999): 55–70 and Christopher Anderson's "Creating the Twenty-first Century Television Network: NBC in the Age of Media Conglomeration," in *NBC: America's Network*, edited by Michele Hilmes (Berkeley: University of California Press, 2007), 275–290.

Also, see further readings suggested at the end of Chapter 1 for readings that deal with the particular operations of various industries.

NOTES

1. Joseph Turow, *Media Today* (New York: Routledge, 2008), 301.
2. Ibid., 305.
3. Bernard Miege, *The Capitalization of Cultural Production* (New York: International General, 1989).
4. Jennifer Holt, "Vertical Vision: Deregulation, Industrial Economy and Prime-time Design," in *Quality Popular Television: Cult TV, the Industry and Fans*, ed. Mark Jancovich and James Lyons (eds.), 11–31 (London: British Film Institute, 2003), 14–17.
5. David Hesmondhalgh, *The Cultural Industries*, 2nd ed. (London: Sage, 2007), 309.
6. Joseph Turow, *Media Today* (New York: Routledge, 2008), 309, 312.
7. Ben H. Bagdikian, *The New Media Monopoly* (Boston: Beacon Press, 2004), 27.
8. Benjamin M. Compaine and Douglas Gomery, *Who Owns the Media: Competition and Concentration in the Mass Media Industry*, 3rd ed. (Mahwah, N.J.: Lawrence Erlbaum Associates, 2000), 485.
9. Leo Cendrowicz, "Sony, BMG Pursue Merger on Two Fronts," *Billboard* (Oct. 28, 2006), (accessed Dec. 27, 2009 via Lexis Nexis); "2009 Market Share and Box Office Results by Movie Studio." *Boxofficemojo.com*, http://www.boxofficemojo.com/studio/?view=company&view2=yearly&yr=2009&p=.htm (accessed Dec. 27, 2009).

10. http://www.stopbigmedia.com/chart.php?chart=radio (accessed Oct. 21, 2008).

11. http://www.stopbigmedia.com/chart.php?chart=tv (accessed Oct. 21, 2008).

12. http://www.stopbigmedia.com/chart.php?chart=pub (accessed Oct. 21, 2008).

13. Aphra Kerr, *The Business and Culture of Digital Games: Gamework/Gameplay* (Thousand Oaks, Calif.: Sage, 2006), 55–58.

14. David Goetzl, "Sinclair May Go Private, CEO Says," *MediaDailyNews*, May 8, 2008, http://www.mediapost.com/publications/index.cfm?fuseaction=Articles. showArticle&art_aid=82185 (accessed Feb. 24, 2010).

15. Edward Jay Epstein, *The Big Picture: Money and Power in Hollywood* (New York: Random House, 2005), 117.

16. Ibid., 117.

17. Among industry workers, these costs are often defined as post-production because they take place after shooting, but we are working with a broader definition of production.

18. Joseph Turow, *Media Today* (New York: Routledge, 2008), 400.

19. Edward Jay Epstein, *The Big Picture: Money and Power in Hollywood* (New York: Random House, 2005), 117.

20. Ibid.

21. Diane Garrett, "Red Carpet Becoming More Global," *Variety.com* (April 16, 2007), http://www.variety.com/article/VR1117963193.html?categoryid=13&cs=1 (accessed Dec. 12, 2008).

22. Epstein, *Big Picture,* 118.

23. Information found in Aphra Kerr's *The Business and Culture of Digital Games: Gamework/Gameplay* (Los Angeles: Sage, 2006) was crucial to the development of this section.

24. John Dempsey, "Lifetime Nabs Mother Cable Rights," *Variety.com*, Sept. 23, 2008, http://www.variety.com/article/VR1117992752.html?categoryid=1238&cs=1 (accessed Sept. 28, 2008).

25. John Dempsey, "Twentieth Hits Mother Lode," *Variety.com* (Sept. 14, 2008), http://www.variety.com/article/VR1117992173.html?categoryid=1238&cs=1 (accessed Sept. 16, 2008).

26. Epstein, *Big Picture*, 5, 16.

27. Ibid., 19.

28. Ibid., 355.

29. Angela McRobbie, *British Fashion Design: Rag Trade or Image Industry?* (London: Routledge, 1998), 152.

30. Chris Anderson, *Free: The Future of a Radical Price* (New York: Hyperion, 2009), 57–59.

31. Ibid.

CHAPTER 6

———

Creative Practices and Roles
Involved in Making Media

The early years of the U.S. film industry are often described as the years of the **studio system**. In addition to the tight hold over distribution and exhibition that the studios were forced to relinquish in the late 1940s following the Paramount Decree, a certain arrangement of production also characterized their operations and made filmmaking much more like an assembly-line process than it is today. From the early 1920s through the early 1950s, the studios controlled creative production by keeping all film production personnel—actors, directors, writers, and everyone else—under long-term (typically seven-year) contracts that controlled every aspect of working in film. The studio heads would select what films would be made; assign a producer, director, and actors to make the film; and then reassign them to new projects when that film was completed. Stars could be rented out to other studios, although the studio holding the star's contract would receive the salary difference. The studios even controlled all aspects of publicity and stars' public images.

In this system, the creative workers had very little control of any aspect of their work. They were guaranteed a salary, although Edward Jay Epstein notes that they were paid comparatively little relative to box office revenue at the time.[1] This system allowed the studios to control many of the most substantial production costs.

The contemporary film industry works much differently. A **star system**, in which a few established actors and directors are seen as indispensible to creating a hit movie, has, arguably, replaced the studio system. These individuals are compensated beyond reason, and they wield considerable power in selecting the projects in which to be involved and which are ultimately produced. The breakup of the studio system also expanded the role of the agent in the film industry. Agents are responsible for negotiating deals between studios and "talent," and in many cases, they construct packages of actors, directors, and creative properties (scripts) together in the best interest of the agency.

The transition from the studio to the star system illustrates an immense change in the practice of making movies that required adjustments from the financing of films all the way to what types of films can be and are made in Hollywood. As Epstein notes, "The collapse of the studio system also radically changed the social landscape of the community." The center of wealth shifted from the studio heads to select stars, directors, writers, and musicians. The result, he notes, has been increased studio attention to factors other than pure profit in filmmaking and a desire to produce some works that have high artistic merit or valuable social commentary.

*   *   *

Despite the importance of mandates and operating conditions, these aspects of the media industry alone do not ultimately determine the products that they create. The final layer of the Industrialization of Culture framework involves a wide variety of what we term **practices**. At the level of practices, we begin to attend to particular roles of individual workers in media industries and the day-to-day routines in which they participate. There are far more practices than we can possibly address in just a few chapters, so we group a wide variety of practices into this and the following two chapters. This chapter focuses on some of the practices involved in the actual making of media products. The next chapter addresses the practices required to get the media product to the audience—also known as the processes of distribution and exhibition. The third chapter in this section examines yet other important practices that exist beyond the narrow making and circulating of media production, activities that we term "auxiliary practices" such as audience measurement, advertising, and promotion.

Although much of the book to this point has attended to what might seem massive and unalterable structures of industrial operation, it is important to remember that, in the end, the actual functioning of media industries occurs in day-to-day decisions made by individuals. This final layer of our framework addresses the importance of the people who work in and around the media industries in various roles. Even though one person may seem insignificant when thinking about a vast, multinational media corporation, it is necessary that we also consider these workers as individuals with a certain amount of agency in their decision making that allows them to be meaningful actors in how their companies operate and in the creation of media products.

Joseph Turow delimited many of the activities we discuss as practices as "power roles," and his power-role framework remains a valuable tool for understanding how media systems operate. We intend our Industrialization of Culture framework as an update that streamlines some of the activities he notes, incorporates others, and addresses the different types of **power** that operate in the various levels of industry operation. In this context, power is similar to what we term **agency** in Chapter 1, as in the agency of groups or individuals to shape their environments. In the context of the current chapter, then, power refers to the agency of creative workers to shape media texts.

In this and the next two chapters, we explain many of the practices that are part of the daily operation of media industries. These practices occur because people perform them—people who have their own opinions and perspectives on the world and who make many decisions every day that have meaningful implications for media texts. In the next few pages, we are going to explain some of the many jobs that are crucial to the operation of various media industries, and we will offer some examples of how an individual's decision or perception, what we call her agency, affects media production. Throughout this chapter, it might be helpful for you to "role" play, and once you understand the type of activities that are part of a particular role, imagine the decisions you would make and the consequences they might have.

CREATIVE VISIONS: APPROACHES TO MAKING MEDIA

Nancy is a television writer. Television writing is typically done "by committee," meaning a show's writers brainstorm ideas for episodes together and take turns developing those ideas into scripts. Nancy began her career as a staff writer—a member of the writing team—on a series, supervised by an executive producer, who typically approves the writers' ideas and sometimes does some of the writing as well. After working many years as a staff writer, Nancy became the executive producer of her own show. Nancy created the show—she came up with the idea and pitched it to various networks before finding one that was willing to develop and schedule it.

Nancy is one of those creators whom economist Richard Caves is talking about when he refers to "art for art's sake" as a particular characteristic of the media industries—at least, she is at this point in her career. Nancy has very particular ideas for her show—a specific story she wants to tell that she hopes will make the audience think about the issues she cares about. She has worked in this business long enough to have established herself, and she has saved some money, which leads her to be less concerned with making this show a huge hit and more focused on telling her story precisely the way she wants. Nancy didn't have as much control over what she wrote during the many years she worked as a staff writer. She was often the only woman in the writers' room, so she was given the task of writing the female characters who were the victims in crime stories. She often didn't have the power to determine who was the victim or why, because she was a staff writer on someone else's show. Sometimes she could subtly slip ideas that were important to her into stories—perhaps writing a female character who was more empowered—but the executive producer and the network always vetted her ideas and scripts. Now, as executive producer, she still has to contend with network executives, who may want her to tell a different story than she intends, but she also can argue and negotiate with them. The network executives often suggest changes to Nancy's stories that they think will make the show more successful or expand its audience. Even though Nancy's show is mainly about two women who are in their forties, the network that licenses the show keeps pushing Nancy to include more stories about the teenage daughter of one of the women as a strategy for drawing in more younger viewers.

Nancy has many responsibilities as executive producer. She is mainly concerned with the content of the show, so she spends much of her time talking with the writers and approving their story suggestions or sending them in other directions. She also keeps track of daily production, watching what gets shot every day, and meeting with other creative staff—such as directors and actors—about upcoming scenes. The studio also employs executive producers, who attend more to matters of budget and production logistics to free up Nancy to focus on the creative aspects of the show that interest her. Although these executive producers may not directly influence what stories the show tells, they indirectly influence the creative product through their decisions about how to allocate the budget.

Aaron is also an executive producer. He, too, has worked in the television industry for a long time, but his focus is different than Nancy's. Aaron is more of a businessman. When he has an idea for a show, it is typically because it has a lot of elements that he thinks will make it a successful show. Aaron is less concerned with telling a particular story and more focused on developing shows that will make him a lot of money. Aaron also argues with the network from time to time; unlike Nancy, though, he typically argues with the network in cases in which he feels the network idea is likely to decrease the audience his show could reach. He is less committed to the specific stories his writers tell and doesn't have the same aspirations for his shows to be the kind of stories that stay with people and lead them to think about ideas. Aaron spends less time with his writers than Nancy does, and, as executive producer, he focuses more on budget issues. Aaron also serves as the executive producer of another show, so he spends much of his time attending to issues on that show and working on developing new shows to sell to the networks.

These paragraphs describe two very different approaches to one job in one media industry. Nancy and Aaron may exist on opposite ends of a continuum, as both Nancy's "art for art's sake" approach and Aaron's profit-driven focus are deliberately extreme to illustrate a point. It is likely the case that most creators exist somewhere in between Nancy and Aaron in terms of their desire to communicate particular ideas through media and their awareness of the conventions perceived to lead to profitability. At some point in his career, Aaron, too, may have placed greater emphasis on creating a "great" piece of television, just as Nancy recognized the need to create a track record of commercial success as she started out in her career in order to make having her own show a possibility one day.

The cases of Nancy and Aaron (and every incarnation in between) suggest the wide variation in approaches among what we might describe as the central "creative" personnel of a commercial media product. There is slight variation in the roles of the central creative figure in each media industry, and some industries allow creative tasks to be shared by many different workers. In film, the key creative worker is the director; in the music industry it might be the artist, the producer, or the songwriter. In the magazine industry, a range of editors typically works with a mix of staff and freelance writers to ensure each issue's articles reflect the magazine's overall "voice," although the editor-in-chief ultimately decides what appears in print. We are not suggesting that the only creative role in media industries is that of the creative worker who has final authority. Media productions require an incomprehensibly vast range of creative attention to all sorts of things the audience may not specifically notice but that contribute to the final creative product. Whether they are set designers, those who select costumes, or music mixers, these individuals affect the production of creative products in countless ways. The executive producer, director, or editor-in-chief may have the final say or veto power, but they are typically not responsible for originating the hundreds of ideas and decisions that they accept and that contribute to the substance of the product.

Here we focus on just one creative task—that of creation, an activity that remains relatively common regardless of media. The **creator** is typically the person who holds the guiding creative vision. As you can see in the cases above, that power isn't absolute—creators often negotiate their power with the networks, studios, or editors that enable them to distribute their message—and we'll explore that more in the next section. Creators also cannot divorce their creative tasks from the financial pressures that are part of media production. Creators make myriad negotiations between their visions and the economics of their projects. These concerns might lead an executive like Nancy to revise a script so that a scene takes place on a studio stage, which is far cheaper than shooting on location, and perhaps represents a small negotiation in comparison with entirely eliminating what she feels is an important storyline. Budget and financial concerns also influence how Aaron does his job, although differently. Aaron might not develop a potentially controversial show simply because it is not as likely to succeed or not as likely to sell in international markets.

The different cases of Nancy and Aaron also illustrate the variation in the priorities that might govern someone working in the creative fields and the array of approaches to how creators build and develop creative products. It is frankly difficult to compare Nancy and Aaron, because their approaches to their jobs and what is important to them differ so significantly. A key lesson here is the impossibility of making general statements about how the creative personnel in media industries behave. It is crucial not to assume that all creative workers function the same way and have the same power. Let's say that over his career, Aaron has produced many successful shows that have earned a lot of money for him, the studio, and various networks. This history of success is likely to afford Aaron more control, and a studio or network may be more likely to leave him and his creative teams alone because of that track record, whereas they are more likely to micromanage a newcomer without a proven record. Nancy and Aaron are creative workers who are fairly far up on the food chain. Creative decisions are also available to those with much narrower and circumscribed roles, although they may be much more limited.

INDUSTRY EXECUTIVES: BUSINESS, CREATIVITY, AND INDUSTRY LORE

Unlike in previous eras of cultural production, in which individual creators could develop novels, paintings, or sculptures on their own, the contemporary media industries require many workers doing specialized tasks. Stop and count the number of people included in the credits of a movie sometime or those listed in the masthead of a magazine or the liner notes of a CD. One thing that has always amazed us when we've visited a television production is the number of people it requires—and this is only one stage of the process. In addition to the hundred or so people seen around a set, we also must add many whose names often aren't ever credited, but who still play a crucial role in doing the work required for media creation. We examine many of those roles in the next two chapters, but one broad set of roles fits here in the context of commercial media creation: the role of the industry executive.

"Industry executive" is an imprecise and general term, yet we feel it is meaningful for signaling the many workers who play necessary roles in providing institutional support to creators to enable the development and circulation of media products. Many creators often don't view these workers as enablers at all, and these executives can be viewed as gatekeepers that limit creativity since they also perform tasks such as selecting which projects are developed and making suggestions to the creators about changes to their product. Nevertheless, whether as a help or hindrance, they do play a significant role in shaping media texts.

Some job titles that we'd include in the role of industry executive are "development and programming executives" at television studios, "co-chair and/or CEO" at film studios, and "managing editors" of magazines and newspapers. These roles are primarily "business" roles, meaning that the people working in these positions often have advanced business degrees such as an MBA, but their day-to-day duties involve a fair amount of creative work as well. Unlike the creators we discussed above—who are often driven at least on some level by a particular creative impulse or vision that they seek to communicate—industry executives primarily are charged with maintaining the financial interests of their employer. While many do seek for their projects to tell a good story or intervene in the culture in meaningful ways, industry executives are evaluated on their ability to bring in projects that ultimately yield profits for their studio, label, or publication. The work of the industry executive involves many tricky negotiations because of the peculiarity of media industries and the difficulties of predicting the commercial success of cultural forms that we've already explained.

A key task of industry executives is to interpret audience desires and have their fingers on the pulse of cultural sentiment in such a way as to produce the "right" content at the right time. While this description may be less relevant for executives working in news organizations, who might pay less attention to cultural sentiment than to major political and economic developments, those executives also assign feature articles that are more closely tied to cultural developments and perceived reader interests. Executives have to be immersed in their medium and hyperaware of new trends as soon as they happen while remaining conscious of how established trends may be in danger of passing from fashion. As we'll discuss in the following section, one of the most common strategies for identifying new successes is to reproduce something that was successful in the past—such as using established stars, a known formula, or creating a new version of an existing hit (such as spin-offs in television, sequels in book publishing and film, or different incarnations of a popular magazine brand, such as *Teen Vogue* and *Men's Vogue,* that target varying demographics). The industry executive also must be sensitive to when repetition won't work. Successful creative forms often go through cycles—as in the early 2000s when episodic police procedurals such as the various *CSIs* and *Law & Orders* gathered large audiences. In just a few years though, audiences grew tired of the similarity and predictability, and a successful cycle of shows with more serial storylines and less crime (such as *Desperate Housewives* and *Grey's Anatomy*) grew popular. The film and music industries experience similar cycles in which a new concept (say, gross-out humor movies or boy bands) becomes successful, that concept is replicated many times, and the audience tires and a new trend then replaces the old trend, following the same pattern of replication and burn-out. Industry executives balance their knowledge of the new concepts or acts that come across their desks daily with a sense of what audiences are responding to and awareness of the recent and past history of successes and failures.

One of the earliest sociologists studying media industries, Paul J. Hirsch, notes that one of the key ways industry executives respond to the uncertainties of knowing what is the right project for the time is through deliberate overproduction.[2] Industry executives are responsible for winnowing the thousands of new possible texts they encounter to a handful, knowing full well that maybe only one or two of that handful have a chance to really become a success. Once they've selected the projects to be produced, executives continue to be involved in developing media products—although often one group of industry executives is responsible for the acquisition of ideas, and they then pass the role of development of the projects to another set of executives. Industry executives who work with creators once their projects are under contract balance knowledge of what has worked in the past and what might turn-off segments of the audience or advertisers with the vision the creator puts forth.

A key role of this executive is to offer input, often geared at making the project more commercially successful. For example, creators of television shows typically have to run their ideas by the network's current programming executive before they are developed into a script and again after the episode is shot. The industry executive then gives the creator notes that she may or may not be forced to incorporate. The magazine industry is similar: an editor-in-chief must justify the content of her or his magazine to executives at the publishing company, who may suggest that certain types of content be emphasized or downplayed in order to more effectively appeal to a particular readership. If the executives decide the magazine is not living up to its potential in terms of circulation or advertising revenue, they may even replace the editor-in-chief with someone who will bring a completely different editorial vision to the publication. These examples illustrate the significant creative role available to industry executives.

In addition to those executives overseeing production, other executives, such as those in **standards and practices** departments in the television industry, also evaluate creative products and provide assessments before they are finalized. Standards and practices is the office charged with maintaining network policies about content and making sure that the show being prepared for the network will not result in any kind of legal action—such as for presenting indecent content or defaming an individual or corporation. Standards and practices executives typically rely on a more stringent set of norms than legally is required, and here, too, there is a fair amount of space for the individual executive to interpret standards. For example, the documentary *Anatomy of Homicide*, about the making of an episode of the series *Homicide: Life on the Streets*, depicts a writer's experience negotiating his script with the network's standards executive. The writer explains to the documentary team that he had included more potentially offensive language than he desired because he knew he'd have to take some out. When the standards executive objected to the language, the writer was able to leave in much of what he wanted as long as he took out other words. This process of negotiation illustrates more of the creative work done by industry executives, as it makes clear how standards executives play a role in crafting scripts.

Industry executives don't rely only on their perceptions of likely success and failure; many media industries also employ researchers charged with various methods of audience testing aimed to help executives make informed decisions about audience sentiment. The television and film industries both include pretesting as a standard part of their development practices, which involves showing nearly completed television shows (typically just the first episode, not each one) and films to a test audience. Members of the test audience might have a special remote in hand while watching that they use to constantly adjust a rating of how much they like what they see at that moment, which is tabulated by computer into reports, or they might fill out a survey or participate in a focus group discussion after viewing. In the magazine industry, many editors conduct focus groups to get feedback on a variety of aspects of their publications. For instance, readers in the focus groups might be presented with two different mock covers for the same issue so editors can get a sense of which one may be more successful on the newsstand and why. Editors may also divide focus groups into subscribers versus nonsubscribers to know whether these groups respond differently to particular content or to the magazine's overall voice. There are many reasons why this audience research does not accurately predict the success or failure of a specific media text. For example, familiar stories or character types almost always perform better than unconventional stories in these testing venues, and some of the most successful programs of all times (*All in the Family*, *Seinfeld*) tested terribly. Industry executives consequently don't take these results as definitive, but they add the information to the many other factors they assess.

Just as in the cases of Aaron and Nancy, there are many different versions of industry executives. Some executives are like Jim, who is a real lover of film, grew up watching all the films he could get his hands on, and majored in film in college before attending business school. As a studio executive, he wants his studio to have the reputation for making important and significant films, and he's sympathetic to the creative visions of the creators he manages. He often goes to bat for his filmmakers with the studio heads above him, arguing for increases in budgets or changes in promotional strategy that he believes are necessary for the film to succeed and achieve its potential. At the end of the day, however, Jim's job performance is measured by the economic performance of his division, and sometimes he has to reign in a creator who is going over budget or force a director to edit a film into a more manageable length.

In contrast, there are also executives like Jessica, who never really thought much about films or creative forms, but who was placed in an executive position at a studio after performing well in another division of the studio's conglomerate that was not involved in the media industry. Jessica has a very different approach than Jim. She is very budget oriented. When other executives or creators want to expand the budget on products, she typically wants some sort of proof of how this added investment will make the film more profitable. She is less concerned with making "important" or highly acclaimed films and instead emphasizes commercial hits.

Again, Jim, who might be described as "creative champion," and Jessica, the "bean counter," are extremes and perhaps caricatures of media industry executives. They, however, also again illustrate the variability in the approaches of industry executives and the impossibility of understanding the influence they have on media texts in a singular or consistent way. As with creators, different executives approach their jobs in very different ways, and a single executive may tend to his or her job in different ways at different points in his or her career. This may be related to the need to establish a track record of successes in order to gain more responsibility; the managerial style, system of reward, and general culture of the company in which the executive works; or the degree to which executives (and their families) are dependent on that salary for their livelihood.

Many see the devotion to creating profits at the core of a commercial media industry as a constraint that reduces creativity—and there are many times this is likely the case—but budget limitations can also force solutions and deviations from convention that have creatively productive outcomes. For example, the FX channel's production *The Shield* sought to create a "broadcast-quality" show, but because it aired on a cable channel—with smaller audiences and, therefore, smaller revenue possibilities—it had to find a way to produce the show on a significantly smaller budget. In order to reduce the number of days required to shoot each episode, the production staff experimented with using handheld cameras and natural light that didn't require the extensive set-up time required by traditional cameras and production strategies. The result was a jerky, rough visual style that was uncommon on most television shows but suited to the unconventional storyline of the show, which explored the ethically dubious doings of a police unit that wasn't made up of conventional "good" guys. In this case, the reality of budget limitations forced creative innovation.

Another aspect to consider when assessing the influence of executives on texts is that the path to profits is often unclear, and there is more than one way to increase profitability. An executive like Jessica may consistently try to reduce budget costs, but other executives understand that sometimes going over budget can be the key to both creative excellence and profitability for the studio. What makes being an executive in media industries so challenging is the uncertainty about when returns on those increased expenditures are likely to be realized. Although these kinds of uncertainties exist in all industries, as we've noted in many previous chapters, the unpredictable success of cultural products and their generally high initial costs make them especially risky. Because success is so difficult to predict, it is also the case that there are often a variety of paths that might lead there.

Also, although we might have a romantic notion that a creator with a vision should be left alone and that any suggestion from an industry executive should be seen as inherently likely to compromise that creative vision, leaving creators to their own devices isn't always a good thing. Sometimes, creators and their products benefit from the perspectives and ideas offered by executives. One way that you can judge this tension for yourself is by comparing the version of films released by studios and the "director's cut" typically available as an extra on DVD.

The key ideas to take from this section include the significant creative work performed by those not primarily defined as creative workers in media industries and the many different ways these executives can affect media texts. Executives work within routines, expectations, and environments that allow them agency that is not unfettered—or as we term it, **circumscribed agency**—but which remains meaningful nevertheless. Their actions are structured by parameters such as the need to produce profitable content, but they may perform that task in a variety of ways. Industry executives can be crucial to the success, failure, or the mere existence of various media products. In his book *Desperate Networks*, Bill Carter tells the story of the creation of the reality television series *Survivor*, which ultimately became one of the defining successes of U.S. reality television.[3] The show's creator, Mark Burnett, shopped the series to multiple networks, multiple times, without any executive expressing much interest. Finally, a junior development executive at CBS became intrigued with the series and worked as its champion through the ranks of the CBS development department. The persistence of this one industry executive enabled the existence of this show that became a phenomenal hit, and there are many similar stories across the media industries.

The activities of industry executives are not only curtailed by the profit motive of commercial media, but their activities are also circumscribed by various practices and conventions that are part of how their industry operates. For example, television has long been defined by its schedule, an entirely arbitrary construction that limits the number of shows available, their length, and how many new episodes are created each year. Similarly, films operate with conventions such as the notion of "opening" on Friday nights, featuring "blockbusters" during summer months, and the idea that they should last between ninety and 180 minutes. The music industry long relied on the norm of collecting a group of songs for simultaneous release (the album) that is now being challenged because of the creation of new forms of distribution that make single-song distribution more efficient and more popular among audiences. The point here is that industry executives face a structured range of options and opportunities that have meaningful implications for the nature of the creative products that they are involved in developing.

In addition to working within a system of prescribed norms that limit some of the possibilities for media products, industry executives also work within organizational cultures that reproduce particular ways of thinking about aspects of the creative process and tendencies for success and failure. While "indoctrination" may be too strong a word, there are certain "common sense" ideas and "best practices" that a worker in any industry encounters. We call these beliefs **industry lore**. One example of industry lore that long governed the television industry was the perception that white audiences wouldn't watch a comedy about a middle-class, professional, married, African-American family. Certainly, many creators suggested shows with black casts, and industry executives would say something like, "Oh, you can't do that. It will never succeed, because white people won't watch." Then, eventually, an industry executive decided to take a risk and test the industry lore. In this case, NBC programming executive Brandon Tartikoff challenged it with the production of *The Cosby Show* in the mid-1980s. The show, a conventional family situation comedy about a professional-class, African-American family, went on to spend five years as the most watched television show in the United States.

The record industry of the 1950s provides an example of how prevailing industry lore can shape a variety of industrial structures and practices. At the time, the key to making hit records lay in getting songs played in heavy rotation on popular radio stations, and individual disc jockeys determined the playlist. Industry lore about disc jockeys held that they were highly individualistic, egotistical, and hedonistic. So, record executives turned to independent contractors who plied disc jockeys with money, drugs, and sex, as opposed to trying more conventional methods of industry promotion, such as sales pitches and large conventions.[4] Ultimately, these practices led to the payola scandals of the 1950s that are chronicled more fully in Chapter 7. The question that might naturally arise is, "Were these efforts necessary and successful?" The answer to that is hard to know: most likely, some disc jockeys responded better to the hedonistic approach, while others would have responded better to the more conventional approach, and a large number of them probably would have responded similarly to both approaches. Nevertheless, the point is that industry lore about what disc jockeys were like influenced the amount of money spent on persuading them, the use of outside contractors to approach them, and the particular perks that they were offered.

Or, in the British magazine industry, the failure of several men-targeted publications in the late 1950s through 1960s led to the widespread belief that "men don't buy magazines." Although executives eventually realized they were wrong and began to conceive of men as a desirable audience in the 1980s, that notion limited both the quantity and quality of magazines targeted to men for decades.

As these examples illustrate, industry lore can have significant consequences for enabling certain kinds of text and viewers, while disabling others. Here we see the ideological implications of media industry practices and the real power in the circulation of culture that industry executives can exercise. It is important to note that it wasn't the case that the industry executives sought to ignore African-Americans before this industry lore was proven false—although it is certainly the case that the television industry occasionally faced pressure from activist groups pushing them to add to and diversify their images. While individual executives may have preferred a more democratic approach to reaching audiences, they believed that it was not a good a business strategy and hid behind that justification.

Another thing we can learn is to be suspicious when industry executives claim it would be bad for business" when explaining creative decisions. It may just be the case that no one has challenged the industry lore, as it is often the case that things once thought impossible are now considered good for business. The making of industry lore is a complicated process—and often it may originate from a kernel of truth or something that was true at one point in time. Industry executives are bombarded with often-contradictory information about their products and industry, from detailed statistical focus groups and box offices reports to anecdotes filtered through friends and colleagues. They form perceptions based on this stew of information and often what they know "from their gut." Those with more power pass these perceptions on to those below them and those they mentor, and the industry lore remains in place.

The unpredictability of the media industries ties back in here as well. Often, a product that challenges industry lore may be developed and fail, but it is difficult to know precisely why it failed. It is still the case that many network executives rely on the industry lore that a drama with a predominately nonwhite cast won't succeed (at least by broadcast network standards of success). When shows have challenged this presumption and not succeeded, it has been attributed to the color of the cast, rather than the fact that it might not have been promoted well, might have had a poor place on the schedule, or may not have been a well-produced, -written, or -acted show, regardless of the color of the actors' skin.

TEXTUAL PRACTICES: FORMATS, FORUMLAS, AND ROUTINES

Although it is difficult to separate people performing roles from the practices they attend to in those roles, this final section of this chapter focuses on the routines of media industry workers and the conventions of their industries. Routines transcend individuals, and they are patterns of behavior or established means of completing tasks that are purposively designed to complete the task of creating media texts but also calibrate acceptable limits and meanings regarding how media industries function. The routines also often contain ideas about institutional power, such as how things "are" or "should be" that tie into the discussion of industry lore in the last section. The implications of routines in different industry production processes also relate to the distribution and exhibition process of the particular industries, a topic we explore in the next chapter. Finally, established routines are especially powerful in discouraging innovation and change and tend to lead to supporting "the way we've always done things."

A key practice for managing risk and uncertainty is relying on **formulas** that have proven successful in the past. While we may think of a formula as a precise calculation, such as what you would encounter in a chemistry class, here we use "formula" much more loosely. We consider formulas to include the reliance on known attributes in design and production of a media text. Formulas might include using known stars or creative workers; known products, such as sequels or serials; known formats; and standard features. Before considering these formulas in greater depth, it is crucial to acknowledge that using formulas is often a good business strategy, given that media industries can be characterized by the dictum that "nobody knows." Formulas remain far from foolproof, however. As you'll see, formulas might increase the odds of a media product succeeding—or at least of not failing—but there are also countless cases of media products that rely on formulas failing as well.

Known Talent

One of the most obvious formulas involves the practice of using those who have succeeded in the past or with whom audiences are familiar and regard positively. In many ways, the entire "star system" that characterizes the most successful workers in media industries results from the industry's belief that those who have succeeded in the past are likely to succeed again. With some creative texts, industry workers hope that audiences are so committed to the previous record of an individual that they will purchase, view, read, or listen to a new product simply because that person is involved. Actors identified in Hollywood as members of the "A-list" may not be the most skilled (although in some cases they are), but they earn this distinction because they have established a fan base that consistently turns out for new movies, no matter the subject or reviews. Sometimes the star power of one individual alone can make a movie, although star performer power can be less reliable in other types of media. For example, there have been many cases of A-list stars failing in television series (consider series starring Geena Davis, Jason Alexander, Michael Richards, and Bette Midler). Perhaps this results from the ongoing nature of television series compared with the one-time nature of film viewing; many fans of stars might turn out for the first episode of a star-driven series but choose not to return if the quality is poor. Films don't require repeat engagements. That said, sometimes star actor power isn't enough for films either, and there is a general sense that star power is in decline.

Although star performers quickly come to mind in this formula, all sorts of creatives might be used in this way. We often hear of a new film by Martin Scorsese,

a new novel by Dan Brown, a new series by Steven Bochco, or a new album produced by Timbaland. In the late 1990s, even some magazine editors achieved this
kind of star status, as in Tina Brown's high-profile launch of *Talk* magazine after
her success at the *New Yorker*. Any time you see a media text promoted by emphasizing the individuals involved in its creation, it can be seen as a case of formula
use. Being Steven Bochco or Tina Brown might be crucial to securing the funding
of a studio, network, or investors in order to create a media product, but it isn't a
ticket to success. Most of those who have achieved high-profile successes have also
experienced widely noted failures. A few failures often won't significantly diminish a reputation, however, partly because those who have succeeded in the past are
given so many subsequent opportunities that there are bound to be failures.

Known Products

Another, also very simple, formula relies on known products. In film, we often
see this in the form of sequels. Many noted the summer of 2007 as a particularly
safe film season, as the schedule included *Spiderman 3*, *Pirates of the Caribbean:
At World's End*, and *Shrek the Third*. All three films offered the third installment
of stories about established characters and settings, and, unsurprisingly, all three
films had strong releases. Film sequels are a common and accepted practice that
allows a measure of certainty. Another example of using known products involves
taking a successful media product and reproducing it in another industry—for
example, making the Harry Potter and *Twilight* books into films.

In some ways, what U.S. television viewers accept as a taken-for-granted
norm—that television series return new episodes about established characters and
situations—is also a formula strategy. Many of television's early series were called
"anthology series" and featured an entirely new story each week, much like going
to see a different play. This was especially true in the UK, where the BBC still features a large number of single-episode television plays, many of them penned by
famous writers. The use of serial features—such as the same cast, same setting, and
same story norms—even if the actual story resolves each week, is also an example
of formula use. Television has many other ways of incorporating formulas. The
television spin-off involves taking an established character from one show and
creating a new show around them—as in the famous case of Kelsey Grammer's
Frasier character, who originated on *Cheers* in 1982 and stayed on the air another
nine years after *Cheers*' 1993 conclusion on the eponymously titled *Frasier*. In the
magazine industry, formatting can be seen trying to expand the brand of an existing title, such as *Teen Vogue*.

Another formulaic strategy that became particularly important for the television industry beginning in the late 1990s is the use of **format sales**. Format sales
involve a very particular practice in which the premise, characters, and norms of
a show are sold for production in another country. The most common cases of
format sales involve "reality," or unscripted, programming and game shows. In the
late 1990s, British production company Celador created the show *Who Wants to
Be a Millionaire*, which became a massive hit in Britain. The show soon became

an international sensation, produced at some point in more than 100 countries. Once proven successful in one country, many competitive game and reality shows followed this pattern to various degrees including: *American Idol, Survivor, Big Brother, The Apprentice*, and *The Bachelor* (although countries often change the title of the show). One reason format sales have been so successful is that they allow for the reproduction of the show with local customs, norms, participants, and cultural allusions incorporated in a manner that doesn't happen simply when a show from one country is purchased for re-airing in another country. Most media scholars view this as a better pattern for cultural circulation than the previous norm of simply airing the original (often American) version.[5]

Format sales of reality programming have become so successful that recent years have seen increasing examples of scripted format sales, which are less common because scripted stories are much more expensive to produce and often are perceived as more culturally specific. For example, the series *Coupling, Queer as Folk*, and *The Office* were originally produced in Britain by the BBC, but various U.S. studios purchased the formats and, in the latter two cases, developed the shows beyond the storytelling of their country of origin. Similarly, a UK television production company purchased the format of the series *Law & Order* in order to produce comparable stories with British settings and actors that began airing in 2009, and the U.S. series *Ugly Betty* developed from the format of *Yo soy Betty, la fea*, a phenomenally successful Colombian telenovela. Format sales of scripted shows are not entirely new either: seventies hits *All in the Family* and *Sanford and Son* were based on British formats; the frequency of the occurrence and the level of subsequent success does distinguish present practices from the past, however.

In the magazine industry, U.S. companies such as Time Inc. and Hearst have launched numerous international editions of their magazines. The companies either globally expand through co-venture (in which the publisher maintains a stake in the ownership and helps run the magazine with a local entity) or, when it's more difficult to take advantage of an **economy of scale**, through licensing (in which the publisher simply provides the brand name to a local entity in exchange for a fee and a percentage of the revenue). Dennis Publishing took the latter, more hands-off approach with the men's magazine *Maxim*, which has more than two dozen international editions, although it provided training for the new owners in order to help preserve the quality of the brand. In both approaches, however, decisions must be made about the amounts of local content and U.S. content to include—a balance that often varies by the magazine type. For instance, *National Geographic* generally alters little of its content, as it is already internationally oriented, whereas *Playboy* must carefully fine tune its content to align with local values and norms.[6]

Formats

Another category of formula involves using known **formats**. Do note this is dissimilar from the more specific terminology of *format sales*; rather, using known formats involves reproducing much more general, existing media products. For example, the launch of Oprah's magazine *O* reproduced the well-established women's service magazine format (as well as featuring the star formula); FOX News reproduced the established cable news channel format, but gave it a conservative slant. Format is commonly used in the radio industry to describe the type of music a radio station plays, such as adult-contemporary, Top 40, or country. Identifying the format of a media product is probably the first thing you do to describe what it is, and concepts that seem new often come from combining various existing formats (a cop show that is a musical) or creating a product for a different audience (a fashion magazine, but for men). Formats are a useful strategy because they appeal to the audience's desire for a recognizable product.

Standard Features

A final formula strategy (although there are likely many we haven't specifically noted) can be identified in the **standard features** that develop in media industries. There is nothing that says a feature film must be between 90 and 180 minutes, that television shows are either 30 or 60 minutes (minus time for commercials in many cases), that stories perceived as most important will be on the front of a newspaper, or that pop songs should be three to five minutes long. Similarly, stories do not need to be presented in the conventional three-act narrative structure of television and don't have to end with resolution, but most do. These are examples of the standard features of media texts that have been normalized in U.S. society, and most new media products reproduce these established norms. It is important to reflect on how norms accepted by a culture shape the types of stories told or increase the chances of some being told more often than others.

A case in which standard features were tested occurred in the fall of 2006 when the new "MyTV" network, a loose collection of stations that remained after the dissolution of The WB and UPN networks, offered telenovela style programming during prime time. Rather than the customary offering of one new episode each week, telenovelas offer a new episode of an ongoing story each night—much like the soap operas U.S. viewers are accustomed to during the day. In this case, MyTV used this structure in prime time, asking viewers to tune in Monday through Friday at 8:00 p.m. to follow the story over the course of a few months. This programming structure is quite common throughout Central and South America, but it failed in this case in the United States.

In another case, the ongoing economic crisis in the newspaper industry has prompted papers to deviate from established practices in several ways. Some papers that had long offered daily print editions shifted to publishing a print edition only one or two days per week. Others, such as the Madison, Wisconsin, paper *The Capitol Times*, switched to entirely online formats. Even practices at solvent papers changed. At first, online editions matched what was published and would not be updated until a new print edition was released. As online competition increased, newspapers let go of this mentality and began breaking news online as soon as they were able.

Although relying on formulas offers media industry workers helpful, yet unreliable, tools for dealing with the considerable uncertainty of their industries, formulas have other consequences, as well. Foremost, the reliance on formulas goes a long way toward explaining the significant similarity of media products. Perhaps the biggest criticism by those who argue for structural changes to the way media industries operate is their complaint that commercial media products are "all the same." While we're hesitant to make such sweeping condemnations and wish to acknowledge that even subtle differences can be meaningful, the formulaic conventions of media industries—and our acculturation to these conventions—do make change and difference difficult. Ideas that seem too far "outside of the box," whether because of an unconventional length, an irregular central character, or even just an actor who doesn't match dominant beauty standards (gasp!), simply don't get the funding needed to come into existence.

CONCLUSION

Although we've only been able to scratch the surface of the many ways individuals and organizations, and their conventional practices, contribute to the creation of media products in significant ways, we hope that the cases we have noted illustrate the importance of considering production work at this level. Indeed, there may be hundreds of other cases we could have mentioned: one consequence of allowing for the agency of individuals at this level is that attempting to explain the operation of media industry begins to get very messy. The Industrialization of Culture framework allows for this "mess"—and, as we hope the examples throughout this chapter illustrate, even the workers responsible for day-to-day decisions play an important role in media industry operation.

Acknowledging the meaningful work that occurs at this level makes it nearly impossible to make generalizations about media industry operation. There are two ways of thinking about this: on one hand, if we allow for all of this individual influence, it becomes quite stunning that so much media production ends up being so similar. This similarity indicates how powerful industrial aspects such as routines, industry lore, and norms of practice may well be. On the other hand, though, this type of framework also provides a way to understand those uncommon—but nevertheless important—cases in which these industries produce something that is notably and meaningfully different.

QUESTIONS

1. Imagine you are in a position to make creative decisions on your favorite television show. What specific changes would you make? Would you take the show in a more "art for art's sake" direction or perhaps aim for greater commercial appeal? Why? How might taking such an approach change the nature of the program? What are some of the compromises involved in picking one approach over the other?

2. Formulas may help overcome the risks involved with creating media texts, but they don't guarantee success. Think of an instance in which the use of a formula by a media industry has failed. Why might it have been a failure? Conversely, can you think of a media text that became a hit despite its refusal to utilize any obvious formulas? Was it subsequently imitated, and with what degree of success? Thinking through the numerous ways in which formulas are not fool-proof or necessary should help give you a sense of why media industries are risky businesses.

3. Imagine you are a music-industry executive who must decide which song will be the first single from a CD. To help make up your mind, you hire a team of researchers to provide feedback from potential consumers. What sorts of audience testing will you request, and what information do you think will help you make a final decision? Will you choose the single based strictly on the researchers' report, or will you base your decision on other criteria as well?

FURTHER READING

Many books include assessment of production in the making of cultural goods. Several of these are noted in the further readings for Chapter 1. Some others include: Mark Deuze's *Media Work* (Digital media and society series. Cambridge: Polity, 2007); Sean Nixon's *Advertising Cultures: Gender, Commerce, Creativity* (Thousand Oaks, Calif.: Sage, 2003); Ben Crewe's *Representing Men: Cultural Production and Producers in the Men's Magazine Market* (Oxford: Berg, 2003); Julie D'Acci's *Defining Women: Television and the Case of Cagney and Lacey* (Chapel Hill: University of North Carolina Press, 2004); Serra Tinic's *On Location: Canada's Television Industry in a Global Market* (Toronto: University of Toronto Press, 2005); Laura Grindstaff's *The Money Shot: Trash, Class, and the Making of TV Talk Shows* (Chicago: University of Chicago Press, 2002); and Michael Chanan's *Repeated Takes: A Short History of Recording and Its Effects* (London and New York: Verso, 1995).

NOTES

1. Edward Jay Epstein, *The Big Picture: Money and Power in Hollywood* (New York: Random House, 2006), 8.
2. Paul J. Hirsch, "Processing Fads and Fashions: An Organization-Set Analysis of Cultural Industry Systems," *American Journal of Sociology*, 77, no. 4 (1972), 639–659.
3. Bill Carter, *Desperate Networks* (New York: Doubleday, 2006).
4. Michael Chanan, *Repeated Takes: A Short History of Recording and Its Effects* (London and New York: Verso, 1995), 113.
5. Moran, Albert, *Copycat TV: Globalization, Program Formats, and National Identity* (Luton: University of Luton Press, 1998).
6. "Is Your Brand Well Traveled?" *Folio: the Magazine for Magazine Management*, 33, no. 8 (August 2004), 40–43.

CHAPTER 7

—

Distribution and Exhibition Practices

In early 2004, the music producer and artist Danger Mouse (aka., Brian Joseph Burton) released a collection of songs that came to be known as *The Grey Album*. Mixing lyrics from Jay-Z's *The Black Album* and hundreds of samples from the Beatles 1968 album *The Beatles*, known popularly as *The White Album*, *The Grey Album* was released to a handful of online music stores. Quite rapidly, these files were removed when the EMI Group, which held the copyright to *The White Album*, complained that Danger Mouse had infringed upon its rights. In response, hundreds of Internet websites, organized and encouraged by the activist group Downhill Battle, hosted illegal copies of *The Grey Album* for twenty-four hours, in order to signal their opposition to the corporate interests that dominate the music industry and the ways in which they have responded to sampling as an art form and the Internet as a platform for distribution. More than 100,000 copies of the album were reportedly downloaded during that twenty-four-hour period, now known as "Grey Tuesday" among copyright activists.[1]

The example of Grey Tuesday offers a wide range of lessons for scholars and consumers of popular media. What catches our eye in this story is the way in which new forms of distribution get shaped by existing regulatory and economic conditions, at the same time that they also threaten to alter those very conditions. The new form of distribution is, of course, digital distribution over the Internet, which eliminates the need to ship physical copies of media texts to exhibitors and retailers and also, in theory, eliminates the need for exhibitors and retailers; nowadays, anyone with a broadband Internet connection can download and listen to, read, play, or watch any media text they want, without the inconvenience of having to go to a music store or a movie theater. Additionally, with the necessary technical savvy and enough time, a lot of us can find just about anything we want somewhere online for free.

It's obvious, then, how digital distribution over the Internet threatens to undermine longstanding economic conditions, in which massive corporations with deep pockets cover the costs of production, promotion, and distribution and make their money by controlling the avenues of distribution and exhibition.

Danger Mouse bypassed all of these existing conditions to release an album that became both a popular and a critical success. EMI tried, but largely failed, to stop distribution of *The Grey Album*, demonstrating how existing regulatory conditions also worked against digital Internet distribution but ultimately could not stop it. As one Harvard law professor noted at the time:

> As a matter of pure legal doctrine, the Grey Tuesday protest is breaking the law, end of story. But copyright law was written with a particular form of industry in mind. The flourishing of information technology gives amateurs and home-recording artists powerful tools to build and share...valuable art drawn from pieces of popular cultures. There's no place to plug such an important cultural sea change into the current legal regime.[2]

In other words, the development of Internet distribution requires, in this observer's opinion, changes in the regulatory conditions that govern media copyright.

Although, in this example, changed distribution practices hold the potential to alter long-standing economic and regulatory conditions, most of the time the practices covered in this chapter—namely, distribution and exhibition—have less profound implications. Nevertheless, these processes influence not only the content of the media texts we consume, but also where and when we consume them and thereby the kinds of social purposes that media texts serve.

* * *

DEFINING DISTRIBUTION AND
EXHIBITION PRACTICES

Once a media text gets created, someone needs to distribute, promote, and sell it in order for the text to find an audience and, with any luck, begin to pay back the various stakeholders who invested in its production. We might graphically represent the structure of the distribution and exhibition industries as follows:

Producer   →   **Distributor**   →   **Exhibitor**   →   **Consumer**

Although, we refer to these activities collectively as "Distribution and Exhibition" in the Industrialization of Culture framework, this title can be a little misleading. While some media, particularly film and television, are usually "exhibited" for audiences, others like music, print, and video games are purchased in retail stores. Consequently, it is more accurate to describe these kinds of practices as "retail" rather than exhibition. Nevertheless, we have stuck with the phrase "Distribution and Exhibition" rather than something like "Distribution and Exhibition/Retail" for the sake of simplicity. Throughout this chapter, however, we will pay attention to both similarities and differences among media that are exhibited and those that are retailed. At the outset, we want to emphasize the fact that both exhibitors and retailers respond to a combination of corporate promotions and consumer preferences in deciding what media texts to carry and how to sell them to consumers. They are the primary sites in a commercial media system in which the industry tries to groom the public's tastes and in which the public's tastes influence the industry through consumer purchases and ratings. For both practical and legal reasons, distribution and exhibition are often handled by different companies, and they get treated as distinct sectors of the media industry. In addition, both distribution and exhibition involve a wide range of related activities.

Distributors are basically middlemen; they buy from producers and sell to exhibitors and retailers, and they have little actual contact with consumers. In fact, many casual media consumers have never even heard of some of the largest media distribution companies. For instance, many of us know the television series *Mad Men* (2007–present) and are aware that it is broadcast on the AMC cable network. Few, however, are probably aware of the fact the series is distributed by Lionsgate Television in the United States and abroad. The array of middlemen involved in selling media rights can become dizzying, especially when we begin to talk about worldwide rights that are sold across multiple media platforms. Some producers, for instance, use not only different distributors in different parts of the world, but also a different distributor for television, for Internet, and for DVD rights because these newer distribution outlets change so quickly and earn such small revenues that few distributors have the resources or personnel to keep tabs on all of them.

Distribution includes both the physical (or technological) transfer of a media text to an exhibitor *and* the promotional activities that distributors engage in to convince exhibitors to stock or show specific texts. The way that television programs were distributed in the United States in the 1940s and 1950s offers a good example of the physical transfer of texts. In these early years, independent distributors traveled the country trying to convince each local station to purchase their programming. Stations that agreed would receive their copies of each episode a few days prior to its broadcast date and send it along to another station via mail after the episode aired. These kinds of details may seem far removed from the creation or enjoyment of the texts themselves, but they did have an impact on both: this **"bicycling"** of telefilms effectively isolated the program producers from the preferences of local stations or their viewers, increasing the creator's autonomy but perhaps decreasing the relevance of the programming for the actual viewers.

In many media industries, including music, film, and television, the large corporations that produce media texts also retain their own distribution divisions. These divisions specialize in distributing their parent company's texts, but they also provide upfront funding for other independent producers in return for distribution rights. In other words, these major distributors function at times as banks, lending money in return for a share of the profits. The practice of **deficit financing**, which was discussed in detail in Chapter 5, is an example of this kind of upfront funding, in which major television producers wait until a program enters domestic syndication to make back their investments.

Why do major distributors carry their competitors' products? First, because some of these independent productions can become incredibly popular and lucrative, the major distributors want to get in on a cut of the profits. For their part, independent producers often prefer to work with major distributors because they have the clout to push productions into wide circulation. Michael Moore's documentary, *Capitalism: A Love Story*, for instance, was independently produced but distributed by Paramount Pictures in the UK and France. Second, major distributors use independent productions to round out their **libraries**. Larger libraries generally help increase sales, because they can provide one-stop shopping for buyers. The irreverent Comedy Central sketch comedy *Chappelle's Show*, for example, was a hit among a small, important audience demographic, but was far from a blockbuster television series. Nevertheless, MGM Television picked up the series for worldwide distribution to help fill out its edgy, young male program offerings.

Independent distributors may also sometimes provide upfront funding to producers, but by and large, they approach producers *after* the media text has been created, and try to convince producers to let them distribute the texts. Like their larger counterparts, independent distributors also seek the largest possible libraries, which offer a diverse range of programming from numerous different producers. For example, Rockstar Games, which both produced and distributes (or, in the parlance of the video game industry, "developed" and "publishes") the *Grand Theft Auto* videogame series, also distributes titles for other game developers, perhaps most notably the Bungie game *Halo*, which Rockstar distributed prior to Bungie's acquisition by Microsoft.[3]

Both major and independent distributors often pull out all the stops to convince exhibitors to carry their products, from offering bulk discounts, helping with consumer advertising and promotion, giving free trips and trinkets, and guaranteeing **make-goods** that ensure exhibitors will receive some kind remuneration if texts underperform in sales revenues or audience ratings. Distributor's promotional efforts not only work to convince exhibitors to buy a distributor's products, but also build relationships of trust that help both kinds of companies survive the uncertainties of media markets. Imagine, for instance, that you are a program director for your college radio station, which requires you to decide which songs to play throughout the day. Obviously, you would want a mix of popular contemporary songs, well-loved classics, and probably a good dose of new music. But how do you decide which of the thousands upon thousands of "new" songs to play? Certainly, you could listen to all of the new songs and make your own judgment, and this might be a good method for a nonprofit station. But in a for-profit enterprise, you would want some guarantees that your tastes are not idiosyncratic. One place where program directors seek those guarantees is in trusted distributors and promoters that have good track records when it comes to distributing hit music. That is, over years of grooming their relationships with program directors, music distributors have been able to build trusted relationships that simplify the program director's job and make it seem less uncertain to program new songs with hit potential.

In our framework, program directors would be classified as exhibitors. **Exhibition**, as we suggested at the beginning of the chapter, is not just something that movie theatres do, but refers to a range of activities that work to bring together media texts and their consumers. Organizations that engage in these activities include television channels, online RSS feeds, and even brick-and-mortar music stores. Again, we realize that calling all of these different companies exhibitors may seem awkward. A more accurate, but far less elegant term might be **content aggregators**, which refers to companies that bring together an assortment of media texts for potential customers. All exhibitors do, in fact, aggregate content. However, we have stuck with the term "exhibitor" because it is less jargony than "content aggregator" and because all companies that engage in these activities do deploy some degree of exhibition, whether we mean the actual playing of a film before a theater audience or the display exhibits that surround the newest-release videogames at Best Buy.

One of the most important activities that all of these different kinds of exhibitors engage in is "selection." By definition, exhibitors cannot carry every possible media text, but work to narrow down the consumer's options to a manageable amount of choices. That is, for practical reasons like the size of a store, newsstand, or movie theater, or the limited number of broadcast hours in the day, it is physically impossible—not to mention prohibitively expensive—for most exhibitors to carry every single media text. Of course, on-line retail outlets give us access to a seemingly endless variety of media choices. However, it is instructive to see how these stores also try to guide our selections, in an effort to narrow down our range of choices to a manageable number. Amazon.com, for instance, provides us suggestions about which books to buy when we log on, based on the company's analysis of our previous purchases. Likewise, the display page for each book includes links to other books that have been bought along with the book. These, too, are forms of selection that the exhibitor employs to channel the consumer toward certain products—perhaps because the retailer has a financial stake in these products, or because the retailer seeks to ensure customer satisfaction with the experience. It is important to remember that selection serves two functions: first, it makes the job of selling media more predictable and therefore more profitable; and second, it helps consumers make appropriate choices in an increasingly crowded media marketplace.

Regardless of whether you think that exhibitors' efforts to control our media choices are occasionally appropriate and helpful, it is certainly the case that they employ such efforts. At root, they are a response to the **nobody knows** feature of media commodities that we discussed in Chapter One: if companies cannot predict which media texts will be popular and which will flop, they can at least limit the range of options we have to choose from.

The close business and personal relationships between distributors and exhibitors demonstrate how difficult it is to draw clear lines between these two kinds of industry practices. Instead, this distinction is, in many ways, merely an analytic one that can help us understand the behaviors and consequences of certain kinds of commercial media operation, rather than a classification system with hard and fast boundaries. In addition, for certain media industries, distribution and exhibition practices are minimal and fairly mechanical. This is particularly the case for certain forms of **subscription** media that are shipped directly to consumers, such as newspapers, magazines, and even films via services such as NetFlix. As this last example suggests, the present age of digital Internet distribution has begun to undermine the traditional distribution and exhibition practices in some industries, such as film, as users connect more directly to content producers. In a similar example, the magazine distribution industry, which wholesales to newsstands and retail outlets, has been rocked recently by demands by Wal-Mart to pay for magazines when the consumer purchases them, rather than paying a bulk price upfront to the wholesaler.[4] While this is not an example of Internet distribution, the new Wal-Mart practice nevertheless requires high-speed telecommunications networks like the Internet to link the local checkout counter with computer databases at the warehouse. The relationship between consumers and content providers, it would seem, has changed quite a bit since the days of bicycling telefilms, as has the role of distribution and exhibition practices in bringing texts to audiences.

DISTRIBUTION AND EXHIBITION INDUSTRY ROLES

We can distinguish a variety of different roles that distributors and exhibitors play in the process of bringing finished media texts to consumers. These are listed in Table 7.1. Of course, not all roles appear in all industries; as we suggested above, some of the roles are quite mechanical in certain industries. For instance, in magazine distribution, which is dominated by two national companies, Anderson Merchandisers and Alliance Entertainment, the rights-acquisition role is fairly uncomplicated, because major publishers have only two real choices. By contrast, in international film distribution, the rights-acquisition role with regard to art films is quite complex and highly personalized. Art film distributors spend considerable time and expense cultivating relationships with art film directors, in the hopes that, when they complete a project, they will turn to a trusted colleague to ensure that the film finds appropriate venues abroad.

Sometimes, all of these roles can be found within a single distribution or exhibition company. These are usually the largest companies in a respective industry. The Hollywood **majors**, for instance, tend to both produce and distribute their own television shows and films. Similarly, the major labels in the music

Table 7.1 Distribution and Exhibition Roles

DISTRIBUTION	EXHIBITION
Rights acquisition (from producer)	Rights acquisition (from distributor)
Sales (to exhibitors, redistributors)	Sales/Exhibition/Transmission (to the public)
Promotion (to exhibitors, other distributors, public)	Promotion (to the public)

industry—Universal Music Group, Sony Music Entertainment, Warner Music Group, and EMI—also produce and distribute recorded music. On the other hand, smaller companies tend to divide these roles across several different companies.

The Roles of Distributors

In order to get a clearer picture of how these various distribution and exhibition roles play out and interact with one another in daily practice, it may be helpful to take a couple of concrete examples of real people who work in distribution and exhibition. The first example is someone we'll call Mario, who used to run one of the largest independent television distribution companies in the world, handling worldwide rights to programming produced by other companies, especially well-known, independent producers who had created several popular network series. The company flourished during the days of the **Financial Interest and Syndication Rules**, which prevented the networks from distributing the programming they aired. After the repeal of Fin-Syn in early 1990s, the company foundered, but managed to stay afloat, thanks in no small part to the close relationships that Mario had built with a wide network of television producers. In the late 1990s, the company scored international distribution rights to a popular and critically acclaimed series that had been produced by a Hollywood studio and broadcast on its television network. The studio could have easily sold the program abroad on its own, but chose instead to license the program to Mario.

Why would any producer, especially a major producer with its own worldwide distribution wing, not distribute its own program? The answer is the same for large and small producers: because their efforts are focused on production, they cannot do an adequate job of distribution in a complex, far-flung, and constantly changing environment like international television. Of course, the studio could also have turned to its own international distribution wing, but these executives are focused primarily on high-end programming and large, general entertainment broadcasters, particularly in Europe. The program that Mario handled, by contrast, was not a network blockbuster and appealed mostly to small, startup satellite and cable channels that targeted a particular segment of the viewing audience, rather than the broad audiences that large broadcasters typically seek. As it happened, Mario not only had good relationships with producers that prompted them to turn to him with such programming, he also had good intelligence about potential buyers abroad, as well as good relationships with many of those buyers. In other words, a combination of market conditions, business strategies, and professional relationships worked together to allow Mario to distribute this particular program.

Still, Mario had to work hard to sell the series. He attended several international television trade fairs. He traveled the world making in-office courtesy calls to potential buyers, actively trying to interest them in this and other series. He sent out slick fliers, videotapes with clips from the series, and information about ratings data to dozens of other potential buyers. In other words, Mario took on not only the roles of acquiring and selling rights to this television program, but also the role of promoting it to potential exhibitors.

Three important lessons about the distribution of media texts in general can be drawn from Mario's example. First, the predictability of the distribution market influences how complex the process is in a given industry. When the number and stability of buyers is fairly consistent, distribution is either handled in-house or by established companies that have fairly straightforward relationships with content producers and exhibitors. To take another example from the television industry, the major Hollywood studios and a few large distributors, as well as television stations run by large ownership groups, dominate the domestic American distribution market. These ownership groups include the national networks, CBS, ABC, NBC, and FOX, which focus on stations primarily in the top twenty markets in the country, and independent groups like Sinclair, Nexstar, and Raycom, which own dozens of channels in the top 100 markets in the country. The process of buying and selling rights to television programs in the domestic market, then, consists of fairly straightforward business meetings involving well-known buyers and sellers with few chances for new entrants or surprises. In this way, domestic television distribution is not dissimilar to magazine distribution, while international television syndication is quite a different animal due to quite different market conditions.

A second lesson we can draw from Mario's example is that the more volatile distribution markets are, the more likely it is that distribution will be handled by a complex web of distributors and redistributors. Mario was primarily a distributor, but he did carry a handful of programs the rights to which he purchased from another company and then sold to other distributors. Many other people in international television work primarily as redistributors, picking up rights to programming from another distributor and selling them on to other distributors or broadcasters. This was also the case in the recorded music industry in the early 1960s, before the major record labels developed their own distribution divisions, when local or regional distribution companies would get albums from both major and independent labels and resell them to record stores or other distributors.

Finally, we can see from Mario's example that in volatile and complex rights markets, distributors spend a great deal of time and expense grooming relationships with buyers and other distributors, as well as promoting their companies and their programming to other industry insiders. While most of us are quite aware of how heavily media texts get promoted to the general public, we may be surprised that distributors sometimes have to promote their texts just as intensely to others within the industry.

In predictable distribution markets, the types and range of media texts available to consumers tends to be decided by the companies involved in distribution and exhibition. In other words, the media consumer's choice basically boils down to taking or leaving what established media producers, distributors, and exhibitors offer us. In more volatile markets, by contrast, consumer demand has a far greater role in deciding what media we view, read, listen to, or play, because small, independent distributors and redistributors will find ways to meet unfulfilled demands.

The Roles of Exhibitors

Now, let us turn to an example taken from the day-to-day life of an exhibitor, whom we'll call Larry. Until 2008, Larry owned and operated a newsstand in Pasadena, California, which had been in his family since the 1950s. Centrally located in the old town, his newsstand was a city institution for many years, selling perhaps more magazines and newspapers than any other in the area. Despite the large number of titles and customers at the stand, however, Larry insists that the newsstand was as much a community gathering place as a place of business. Some customers would stop by for hours on weekends to discuss politics and entertainment news. Because of its location in Southern California, not far from the Hollywood foothills, Larry's newsstand featured entertainment industry and gossip magazines more prominently than newsstands in other cities, in the Midwest or East, might have. In addition, the interest in entertainment news provided Larry with corporate clients that bought magazines in bulk to distribute to their employees, as well as conventional foot traffic.

Despite his stand's longstanding success, Larry was forced to close his doors due to two main factors: first, the decline in sales owing to changed city ordinances that prohibited nearby street parking; and second, the fact that his distributor began to favor a nearby newsstand over his. Several other factors helped contribute as well, particularly the bad economy, which depressed overall magazine and newspaper sales; and the explosion of online content, which cut heavily into newsstand sales. Newsstands that continue to operate in Southern California report similar kinds of stresses on their businesses, and one operator even says that she has begun trying to sell titles at car windows when drivers are stuck in nearby traffic.[5]

The fate of Larry's newsstand in Pasadena may seem an isolated case, but it does, in fact, demonstrate the many roles that media exhibitors play. First, Larry must acquire content from newspaper and magazine distributors. When he had trouble fulfilling this role because the distributor began to privilege Larry's competitor, his business foundered. In the print industries, as well as CD, DVD, and videogame markets, exhibitors acquire physical products to sell; movie theaters, television outlets, and radio broadcasters, however, acquire the **rights** to exhibit texts to audiences. Usually, these rights sales specify how long the exhibitor can exhibit the text, or what the **rights period** is, and what media channels (i.e., theater, on-demand, Internet, etc.) the exhibitor can release the text into.

Second, we see how Larry's role as an exhibitor involves more than taking media texts and placing them before an audience; in fact, he actively selected which titles to carry and how to display them, based on his perceptions of his consumer's interests. This practice of anticipating which media texts consumers will want is known as the **surrogate consumer** role, because exhibitors act as our surrogates with distributors, rather than allowing us to make selections based on an objective survey of the distributors' offerings. Put another way, exhibitors *push* certain texts on consumers, rather than letting us *pull* what we want from every available text. In fact, as we will explore in more detail in the following section, exhibitors, distributors, and others all play this surrogate consumer role to some extent. Most of us recognize and accept these surrogates, as long as we believe that they are acting in good faith.

Larry's role as a surrogate consumer was part of his overall effort to promote particular magazines and newspapers to consumers, in particular by selecting which titles to carry and arranging them within his stand. The story of the newsstand employee who tried to sell to drivers stuck in traffic is also a part of this effort at promotion, and it demonstrates too how all promotion involves selection: after all, she can carry only a tiny fraction of all the titles the newsstand sells. All of these efforts at selection are attempts to shape consumer demand as much as they are reflections of that demand.

Together, the roles that distributors and exhibitors play in bringing completed media texts to consumers demonstrate a high degree of selection and shaping of consumer demand. As with much we've discussed throughout this book, these practices reflect the efforts to decrease the high risks inherent in the media industries, particularly the nobody-knows principle. That is, if media companies cannot predict the popularity of their products, they can at least try to limit access and shape demand.

DISTRIBUTION AND EXHIBITION PRACTICES

In their various roles, distributors and exhibitors engage in a wide range of practices designed to shape both media content and consumer behavior in order to maximize profits and minimize loss. We identified some of these above, such as using promotional techniques to influence which media texts we consume; in this section we detail the range of these practices more fully.

Distribution and exhibition are risky undertakings, and they can be richly rewarded. In the television programming industry, for instance, the distributor typically takes about 25 percent of the profits "off the top," which means that they get a percentage of **gross sales**, or total sales revenues before overhead and other costs of production are subtracted out. In the late 1980s and early 1990s, *The Cosby Show*, for example, earned more than $4 billion in domestic syndication markets, which probably netted its distributor, Viacom, roughly $1 billion. At the same time, distributors have to make substantial investments in media products (sunk costs) before they know how popular those products are going to be in order to secure distribution rights from the producer. For exhibitors, making the wrong acquisitions choices can advantage competitors, and also mean that valuable space in the retail outlet, the theater, or the program schedule might be taken up by unpopular media texts, drawing attention and space away from potentially more popular ones. The commercial organizations that handle the distribution and exhibition of media products have developed several business strategies to try to deal with these financial risks and rewards.

One strategy that both distributors and exhibitors engage in is akin to the **intentional overproduction** that characterizes the media production business.

We might call this strategy **overstocking**. As we have already noted, one of the ways that commercial media organizations deal with high production costs and uncertain sales is through creating a large number of products, with the understanding that only a handful will become successful. At the national television networks, for instance, out of every 300 ideas for new series, only about 2 or 3 percent will be made into full **pilot episodes**, and of these pilots, only about one-quarter or one-third will be made into full series. Thus, the network develops numerous more projects than it needs or could use in the hopes of finding just a few that seem likely to succeed.

Distributors help guarantee overproduction because they subsidize production and pay producers for rights to much more product than they can ever hope to sell. They overstock media products for the same reasons that producers overproduce: in the absence of reliable predictors of what might appeal to exhibitors and consumers, distributors carry as wide a range as possible in order to increase the possibility that some of their properties will hit big. In addition, having a large number of titles helps increase the overall value of a distributor's library, as we explained above. Distributors combine the practice of overstocking with **differential promotion** of the material they acquire. Differential promotion refers to the fact that distributors tend to shower praise, attention, and money on only a small fraction of the products they acquire, specifically, those songs, artists, films, and television series that they believe have the greatest potential to become hits. These products benefit from large promotional budgets and strong-arm promotional efforts designed to cajole exhibitors, retailers, and even critics to give those products privileged treatment. By contrast, distributors largely abandon texts that they see as potentially unsuccessful, releasing them to the public with little fanfare or promotional support. The seventh installment of the crude but popular *American Pie* movie series, *American Pie: Book of Love* (2009), for example, bypassed theaters and pay-per-view television channels and was released directly to DVD because its distributor, Universal Pictures, thought it unlikely to attract many viewers in other outlets. Differential promotion is one of the most obvious ways in which distribution works to determine what media content is popular in the United States and abroad: by making a big noise over one media product, a distributor can help create positive "buzz" about it, at the same time, the clamor can drown out excitement over unendorsed products.

Exhibitors, too, engage in differential promotion, except that their lopsided promotional efforts focus primarily on consumers, rather than other commercial enterprises. This differential promotion includes advertising certain texts more prominently in other local media outlets; differential pricing, coupons, and rebates, such as the common practice of charging more for 3D movies than for 2D; and the exhibitor's placement of different texts, whether we mean placement in stores and newsstand or placement on a television schedule or in certain types of theaters. In fact, a main aim of a distributor's promotions is not simply to get exhibitors to carry its products, but to get exhibitors to feature them prominently as well. Some distributors even offer ready-made consumer promotions for the texts they sell, such as recording plugs for a buyer's radio station made by well-known musicians.

All of these efforts to promote media products to one another and consumers can lead to a good deal of money, favors, and even graft within the distribution and exhibition industries. The federal government has even shown occasional interest in the methods that distributors employ to get exhibitors to treat their texts favorably. In one of the most notorious examples, known popularly as **payola** scams, music distributors in the 1950s and 1960s gave cash, drugs, and prostitutes to popular DJs in order to get them to play their songs and rave about them on air. More recently, in 2007, four of the largest radio broadcasting companies—Clear Channel Communications Inc., CBS Radio, Entercom Communications Corp., and Citadel Broadcasting Corp—were fined $12.5 million by the FCC for accepting money and gifts in exchange for promoting songs distributed by several major and independent record labels.[6]

Windowing: A Special Case of Media Distribution

One of the most unique aspects of media commodities and the industries that support them is the practice of **windowing**, which refers to releasing new products on a staggered schedule, differentiated by medium or territory. For instance, non-blockbuster films are sometimes released through **platform** windows, in which theaters in large cities receive copies to screen before theaters in smaller towns, which may or may not receive prints, depending on how well the film does in larger communities. In the music industry, individual cuts are often released to stores and radio stations before an entire album is. While windowing is not common in the gaming industry, because of the reliance on retailers rather than distributors, some video games do have staggered release dates in different parts of the world. *Guitar Hero 5*, for instance, released on September 1, 2009, in the United States, but not in Australia until two weeks later.

Windowing serves two basic economic functions: first, it is an effort to build excitement, word of mouth, or "buzz" about new media products in order to drive people to consume them. When it comes to platforming movies, for instance, one of the purposes is to build up positive press coverage of a film in larger cities that might bring in audiences around the country. Platforming also reduces the risk in cases where texts fail to perform. For example, if a film does not open strongly on early screens, then its distribution may be limited or it may be removed from theatrical release and sent directly to home video. Second, windowing ensures that distributors can squeeze the maximum amount of profit possible out of media products. The major determinant of when to release a text in a particular window is the price that the consumer will pay. For instance, movies start out at theaters, where each audience member pays in excess of $10 per person. Next, they will show up on pay-per-view, where groups of audience members can watch the movies, probably for less than $10. Similarly, the movie may move to a second-run theater, where tickets cost much less than $10. Finally, a very popular movie at the end of its distribution windows may show up on a local television station on a Sunday afternoon, scheduled against an NFL game; the audience pays nothing to watch it, and the local television station has probably paid very little to air it.

We can distinguish between **upstream windows**, or distribution channels that occur earlier in time, and **downstream windows**, or those that occur later. Table 7.2 gives a list of the typical order of distribution windows for a typical blockbuster film, where the upstream windows are at the top of the table, and downstream windows are at the bottom.

A broad variety of factors influence decisions about how exactly to order distribution windows and when to release a text into a downstream window. Increasingly, windowing is a complex practice that is tailored to each individual text. The most important factors that influence the order and timing of windowing are: 1) per capita revenues in each window, 2) differences in potential audience size in each window, 3) the degree to which audiences will consume the programming in downstream (later) windows, 4) the loss of interest among viewers following a product's initial release, and 5) how vulnerable the distribution channel is to illegal copying or piracy.[7] In addition, for many media products with large promotional budgets, such as blockbuster films, distributors want to take advantage of the buzz and increased audience awareness that advertising creates before it fades by moving through later windows more quickly.

Windowing always involves a trade-off between holding a text in upstream windows, where it generates higher per capita revenues, and releasing it into a downstream window, where the audience is quite likely to be larger. Distributors want, for example, to wait until every person who is willing to pay $10 to watch a movie in the theaters has gone to see a film before releasing it to pay-per view, where an entire family can watch it for $8. If a distributor releases into the downstream window too quickly, consumers who might have paid full price may wait and pay the lower price. Wait too long, however, and consumers who might have paid the lower price in the downstream window may have lost interest and moved on. This is what we meant when we said that windowing is an effort to wring maximum profits out of media content: it is a very careful calculation to try to get us to spend the maximum amount of money we are willing to spend by giving us multiple times to spend that money, in decreasing quantities. Outside of the film and television industries, windowing is a less common practice, because fewer venues for accessing other forms of media content exist. Online newspapers and

Table 7.2 Typical Windowing Order for Blockbuster Movies

First-run Theaters
DVD and Internet
Video on Demand and Pay-Per-View
Subscription Cable (HBO, Showtime)
Second-Run Theaters
National Television Network
Local Television Stations and Ad-Supported Cable Networks

magazines, however, have taken to posting portions of new stories online before their print release in an effort to drive print sales, a strategy that is somewhat reminiscent of windowing. Also, the book publishing industry has long released paperback books after hardcover versions, although this practice, like windowing in film and television, is shifting toward more and more simultaneous releases across windows.

For some kinds of media content, the channel of distribution matters little to audiences and end users. It generally doesn't matter, for instance, whether we receive a new hit song via CD, an online store, or a peer-to-peer sharing network, or whether we watch a recent film at home on HBO, pay-per-view, or DVD. For other kinds of media, however, the channel of distribution matters very much. Take action and fantasy films: you've probably heard friends insist on watching certain kinds of spectacular films in the theater, in order to fully experience all the graphics and special effects. Perhaps you, yourself, are one of these people who likes to watch spectacular films in the theater, whereas you don't much care whether you watch, say, a romantic comedy at home. Such distinctions in viewer behavior go to our third point above—that the organization and duration of windows depends on how likely viewers are to consume programming in a downstream window. Note, however, that these norms can change. For example, depending on one's setup, it's possible today to almost recreate the theater experience at home with BluRay DVDs and HDTVs, increasing the number of people willing to consume spectacular films in a downstream window and, likely, shortening the theatrical window for such films. To put this in the language of the Industrialization of Culture framework, here we see how changing technological structures alter distribution and exhibition practices.

The fourth point above—that windows are determined by the degree to which the channel of distribution is vulnerable to piracy—is perhaps most obvious in the trepidation with which music, film, and television distributors approached digital Internet distribution for a number of years. Due to the ease and high quality of digital reproductions (see Chapter 10 for clarification), digital release windows are extremely vulnerable to piracy, or illegal copying and distribution. Because windowing basically builds walls between different types of distribution platforms and audiences, platforms like the Internet that tear down those walls are particularly troubling. Different industries have taken different approaches to the dangers that Internet distribution poses to conventional windows: the music industry, for instance, has gone after websites and individuals who share files illegally with multimillion-dollar lawsuits, while the movie industry preferred to hold back completely on digital distribution until technologies developed that protect copyrights, even on digital copies, with a variety of mechanisms.

Some in the industry question whether digitization and Internet distribution have forever undermined the idea of windowing, and they foresee windowing slowly eroding as a business strategy. Increasingly, movies are being released to DVD and on-demand channels on the same day, and there is speculation about the possibility of pre-releasing certain films to on-demand channels *before* their theatrical releases, charging consumers perhaps $100 or $150 for the privilege of being the first to see, for instance, the final installment of the *Harry Potter* movie series. In fact, some powerful people in the media industries, such as Steve Jobs, the founder of Apple, argue in favor of such developments. The industry term for this unbundling of media texts from their traditional distribution platforms is known as **disaggregation**. In a disaggregated media environment, consumers would be able to access any media text through any device or distribution channel they wanted, essentially eliminating windowing. Powerful media corporations fear disaggregation, however, because control over which distribution platforms carry which texts at which times is central to their current business models. These corporations are fighting to maintain the practice of windowing, and they have had some success, encouraging technological advancements that make digital copies more secure, developing their own distribution sites where protected content is available, and trying to devise business models whereby people will pay for downloaded content. It remains to be seen, however, whether the days of the release window are numbered.

Distributing News

Until now, we have focused on distributing and exhibiting entertainment media, to the near complete exclusion of news media. This is because the very nature of news, which quickly gets obsolete, makes it difficult to distribute in ways that most entertainment media get distributed. Think, for example, of the programs that clutter your home DVR: chances are that, even if you are a heavy news consumer, you don't keep recordings of news programs much more than a day or two, while you may keep entertainment programs for days or weeks on end before you watch them. Because no one is really interested in yesterday's news, news content tends not to have the kind of long distribution tail that much other media does.

Still, like all media content, news must be distributed before it can reach the reader, viewer, or listener. Harkening back to the days when the telegraph was the main technological device for delivering the news, these distribution organizations are popularly known as **wire services**. Wire services operate as both cooperatives and for-profit organizations, and some, such as China's Xinhua News Agency, are government funded. Cooperative news wires collect and share stories among member news organizations, while for-profit services charge media outlets such as Internet websites and newspapers, television, and radio channels, for news stories. Among the best-known cooperatives are the U.S.-based Associated Press (AP) and the Paris-based Agence France-Presse (AFP). Under these cooperative arrangements, contributing members, such as newspapers, make their stories available for other newspapers around the country and around the world while also using stories from other contributing members in their own newspapers. Currently, these cooperatives also employ their own staffs of reporters and sell their members' stories to news outlets that do not contribute; in other words, most cooperative newswire services today combine both cooperative and commercial practices.

Online news sites have been a boon to the newswire services because most of them rely on syndicators to supply all or most of their content. Similarly, RSS feeds and other such direct-to-user types of news distribution primarily draw on content from newswire services. Thus, while the Internet has facilitated the explosion of websites through which users can access news content, it has not diversified the news content to the same degree, because it continues to rely on syndication models that have informed both newspaper and television news practices for decades. Of course, blogs and other kinds of amateur reporting have also taken off in the era of the Internet; perhaps most famously, when CBS's *60 Minutes* ran a story about then-President George W. Bush's alleged efforts to escape military service in the 1970s, bloggers within hours were able to call into question the legitimacy of several evidentiary memos. The vast majority of the hard news that we access online continues to come from traditional newswire sources, however.

The use of newswires has been relatively uncontroversial, but along with increased concentration of ownership in the newspaper industry, some observers have begun to question the impact of newswires on diversity of news content. That is, due to competition from a variety of other news sources, but particularly Internet websites, advertising dollars have begun to migrate away from newspapers, and many papers have hit rocky financial times. Eliminating small newspapers, consolidating ownership, and relying less on paid reporters and more on newswire subscriptions for stories have all proved to be cost-effective ways of dealing with the contemporary environment. As fewer and fewer people own newspapers across the country, however, and as those newspapers carry increasingly similar content, people who believe in the importance of diverse news content for the proper functioning of democracy begin to worry.

THE CULTURAL IMPACT OF DISTRIBUTION AND EXHIBITION

All of the activities we've been describing in this chapter address how we as consumers experience media texts, as well as the content of the texts themselves. In this way, distribution and exhibition profoundly shape the social significance and uses of media texts.

Most obviously, distribution and exhibition practices are attempts to influence consumer behavior in ways that increase profits for distributors. One of the most successful examples of these attempts is the way in which exhibition strategies among television broadcasters, specifically the construction of the program schedule, encourages viewers to watch particular programs and channels that they otherwise might not watch. Among insiders, these strategies are known as **lead-in** and **carryover effects**, both of which operate by using particularly popular programs to try to increase viewership of surrounding programs. For instance, when *Friends* was one of the biggest hits ever for NBC, the network typically launched new series immediately following it, betting that viewers would stay tuned after *Friends* ended and give the new series a shot. This is an example of a carryover effect. Likewise, programmers have noticed that viewers will often tune in to programs *prior to* especially popular programs—at least, they tune in to the last few minutes of the prior program. This is known as a lead-in effect.

In fact, television programmers have been perhaps the most creative and effective of all media industry professionals when it comes to using exhibition as a way to control audiences and, thereby, reduce economic risks. For years, for instance, television networks in the United States scheduled their commercial breaks in tandem with one another in an effort to prevent us from changing channels when a commercial came on. After all, why change the channel when you know that you're just going to encounter another commercial? When some cable channels, such as TBS, started challenging the broadcast networks, part of their strategy was to stagger commercial breaks so that viewers would, in fact, be tempted to change to TBS when a break started. More recently, television networks of all types have adopted a variety of strategies to try to keep viewers from changing channels when programs end, including running program credits on a split screen during a final scene or promotion for an upcoming series, as well as eliminating breaks between series and simply transitioning from one series to the next with a brief fade-to-black.

As mentioned, the practices of television programmers are just a highly evolved example of the ways in which all exhibition and retail media outlets try to influence social behavior. Theater owners decide which movies to screen, and how many screens to devote to each movie, thus influencing not only how popular movies are, but also whether or not we have a chance to see them. Music and game retailers, likewise, make decisions about what to shelve, which promotional displays to erect, and where to place items and promotions within the store. Conglomerated magazine companies use direct mail to promote to their subscribers other, similar titles. All of these practices have been shown to influence purchasing decisions.

We have already discussed the ways in which distribution influences our media consumption throughout much of this chapter, particularly through windowing and promotions that encourage us to maximize spending in order to gain privileged access to media content. In addition, distribution affects the very texts themselves, through both windowing and cross-platform branding. Because of the importance of downstream distribution windows for increasing profits, producers working in upstream windows need to take into consideration the textual and industrial practices in downstream windows while in production. For instance, in the 1960s, music album producers and artists limited songs to fewer than three minutes in length, because that was the maximum length that most radio stations would play. When television became a major revenue stream for movie distributors, directors were forced to move characters closer to one another in two-shots, because television had a boxier screen: without such a change, one of the two characters in a two-shot would have been cut off the TV screen! More recently, when premium cable outlets such as HBO and Showtime began producing their own television series, which they subsequently began selling into basic-cable syndication, producers had to carefully shoot scenes with profanity, graphic violence, and sexually explicit imagery, so that these could be easily edited out for syndication without affecting the overall clarity of an episode's storyline. This practice of anticipating the aesthetic demands of downstream windows during production is part of a larger process of **remediation**, which we discuss in greater detail in Chapter 3 and below.

Cross-platform branding is another distribution strategy that influences the content of media texts. Rather than simply accounting for downstream windows, in cross-platform branding, producers carefully build the look and feel of different types of media into a text from the beginning. In these instances, the process of remediation is more pervasively apparent than it is in conventional windowing arrangements. For instance, the children's television series *Dora, the Explorer* looks and sounds like a conventional videogame, because online and computer games are a central component of the overall branding and promotional strategies of the series' distributor, Paramount. Similarly, since mobile telephone ringtones have become a multibillion-dollar business, musicians around the world have begun to write music and tune their instruments in ways designed specifically for the main ringtone markets in East Asia, Europe, and North America.[8]

Much as the other conditions and practices explored throughout this book, distribution and exhibition influence certain elements of media texts under certain conditions; they do not determine everything about the media we enjoy. Nevertheless, as the examples in this section demonstrate, distribution and exhibition do have direct and identifiable effects on media content.

CONCLUSION

As the vital link between producers and consumers of media, distribution and exhibition are important and powerful practices, but ones that most of us have never really considered in much depth. Far from being mechanical or simplistic processes, distribution and exhibition typically involve a good deal of business acumen and creativity to successfully manage. Whether at the local theater, at home watching TV, at the Best Buy browsing computer games, or on iTunes buying music, both the media content we encounter and our watching/listening choices have been shaped by media distributors and exhibitors. While these cultural gatekeepers are not all-powerful masterminds manipulating culture and society, neither are the processes of production and consumption wholly absent of their influence.

Clearly, distribution and exhibition practices show us that the commercial media industries do not merely give the public the media content we want. Rather, to varying degrees, these practices influence where and when we consume media texts, how much we pay for them, and what kinds of texts we get to choose from in the first place. In other words, distribution and exhibition groom our tastes and shape the programming we enjoy.

The important social question that distribution and exhibition practices raise is the degree to which the media we consume and our own personal tastes are shaped by large media companies to fatten their bottom lines. In general, we see a trend *away* from straightforward efforts to control our behaviors due to changes in technological conditions of distribution, which have turned distribution and exhibition into practices centered more around the pull of consumer desires than the push of corporate control. Today, the emphasis of the commercial media industries centers more on surveilling, aggregating, and predicting our media preferences than on limiting our choices, as was once the case. Indeed, as we explore in the next chapter, the number and variety of auxiliary industries involved in various forms of consumer and audience research have mushroomed since the introduction of digital distribution technologies.

QUESTIONS

1. You are a distributor responsible for selling the television series *How I Met Your Mother*. Gross profits for selling the series in one-year amounts to $200 million, of which $100 million is **net** profits, or the amount of profit left after deducting production, distribution, and promotional costs. Assuming you have a conventional contract with the producer, what are your company's total distribution profits? (Answer: $50 million).

2. Imagine you have created a new media product and plan to release it on a staggered schedule taking into account the four factors that influence windowing. How would you window it, by medium and territory, to best maximize the audience demand and size? What upstream and downstream windows exist for this type of product? Depending on the particular product you have created, is windowing a useful practice? Why, or why not?

3. Consider the work of countless surrogate consumers who "guide" you through your media choices. In what ways are they helping you make selections? In what ways are they limiting what you can consume? How has digital distribution changed the influence of surrogate consumers?

4. Think about the implications of a disaggregated media environment. Which traditional distribution platform would you most like to see unbundled and why? What might be the economic consequences of the disaggregation for that particular industry and for consumers? It may be helpful to think about the unbundling that has already occurred through online stores such as iTunes and Amazon.com, which allow people to buy songs a la carte instead of demanding that they purchase an entire CD. How has this changed the way you buy music and what have been the consequences for the music industry?

FURTHER READING

Other than research on movie theaters, the study of media distribution and exhibition is less well-developed than the other conditions and practices we explore in this volume. On film exhibition, see Epstein's *The Big Picture,* and Barbara Wilinsky's *Sure Seaters: The Emergence of Art House Cinema* (Commerce and mass culture series, Minneapolis: University of Minnesota Press, 2001). Also, Ina Rae Hark's edited anthology *Exhibition, The Film Reader* (In focus, Routledge film readers. London: Routledge, 2002) offers a good collection on the scholarship in film studies on exhibition.

General overviews of distribution and exhibition in the commercial media industries can be found in Paul J. Hirsch's "Processing Fads and Fashions: An Organization-Set Analysis of Cultural Industry Systems," *American Journal of Sociology*, 77, no. 4 (1972), 639–659, and Joseph Turow's *Media Systems in Society: Understanding Industries, Strategies, and Power* (Longman, 1997).

Timothy Havens' *Global Television Marketplace* (London: BFI Press, 2006); Toby Miller et al.'s, *Global Hollywood 2* (London: BFI Publishing, 2005); and Paul Torre's "Block Booking Migrates to Television: The Rise and Fall of the International Output Deal," *Television and New Media*, 10, no. 6 (2009): 501–520, all address aspects of the international distribution and exhibition of American films and television.

NOTES

1. Matthew Rimmer, *Digital Copyright and the Consumer Revolution: Hands Off My Ipod* (Northampton, Mass.: Edward Elgar Publishing, 2007), 130.
2. Bill Werde,, "Defiant Downloads Rise From Underground," *New York Times*, Feb. 25, 2004, http://www.nytimes.com/2004/02/25/arts/music/25REMI.html?pagewanted=1 (accessed Feb. 24, 2010).
3. Business Wire, "Take-Two Interactive Software's Rockstar Games Announces Oni for the Playstation 2," March 16, 2000, http://www.factiva.com (accessed Feb. 3, 2010).
4. Ed Christman, "Magazine Distributors Clash With Publishers," *Billboard* (Feb. 5, 2009), http://www.billboard.biz/bbbiz/content_display/industry/e3id425eb6001d58ee75185dcf0bcceee17 (accessed Jan. 26, 2010).
5. Sharon Knolle, "Death of L.A. Newsstands," *L.A. Weekly* (May 27, 2009), http://www.laweekly.com/2009-05-28/news/death-of-l-a-newsstands (accessed Feb. 2, 2010).
6. John Dunbar, "FCC Unveils Settlement with Radio Firms," *USA Today* (April 13, 2007), http://www.usatoday.com/money/economy/2007-04-13-2144814802_x.htm (accessed Feb. 3, 2010).
7. Adapted from Bruce M. Owen and Steven S. Wildman, *Video Economics* (Cambridge, Mass.: Harvard University Press, 1992).
8. Sumanth Gopinath, "Ringtones, or the Auditory Logic of Globalization," *First Monday* 10, 12 (2005), http://firstmonday.org/htbin/cgiwrap/bin/ojs/index.php/fm/article/view/1295/1215 (accessed Sep. 1, 2010).

CHAPTER 8

—

Auxiliary Practices

Arguably, some of the most important media workers don't play a direct role in the creation or circulation of media. Yet the work of these individuals can make or break a media company, or at least the careers of many working in them. Their phone numbers are on the speed dials of all of the most powerful media executives, yet most media consumers never know their names or even the names of their companies. These companies provide the shared currency upon which media industries operate—they declare winners and losers, all without occupying a personal stake. They are audience measurement companies.

Have we oversold the case? Doubtful. In his 2005 *New York Times Magazine* article profiling the new technologies and procedures being developed to measure radio and television audiences, Jon Gertner wrote:

> Change the way you count, for instance, and you can change where the advertising dollars go, which in turn determines what shows are made and what shows then are renewed. Change the way you count, and potentially you change the comparative value of entire genres (news versus sports, dramas versus comedies) as well as entire demographic segments (young versus old, men versus women, Hispanic versus black). Change the way you count, and you might revalue the worth of sitcom stars, news anchors and—when a single ratings point can mean millions of dollars—the revenue of local affiliates and networks alike. Counting differently can even alter the economics of entire industries, should advertisers (thanks to the P.P.M. [Personal People Meter]) discover that radio or the Web is a better way to get people to know their brand or buy their products or even vote for their political candidates. Change the way you measure America's culture consumption, in other words, and you change America's culture business. And maybe even the culture itself.[1]

The importance of impartial data about media use isn't particular to the broadcasting industry—other media industries have their own companies or arrangements upon which they collectively agree to believe. Given that nearly every media industry spends at least some of its time chasing a **constructed audience**, those who report the behavior of the **real audience** earn particular importance in media industry operation.

* * *

We use this chapter to include a sampling of the other important, even essential practices for the operation of media industries that are not directly involved in the making or circulating of media texts. We use the term **auxiliary practices** to categorize those involved in these practices. Auxiliary—meaning, "to give support" or "secondary"—captures the nature of a wide range of additional media industry roles and practices. Indeed, it is impossible to include them all, as each media industry has a distinct range of particular practices in addition to a core set held in common across industries. We focus on four auxiliary practices that are central to the operations of the media industries: audience ratings, worker representation, promotions and marketing, and translation and localization. We develop each example with enough depth so as to make clear their activities and significance. Highlighting some of these auxiliary practices might also inspire some new ideas about career paths for those interested in doing work that relates to media industries but is less centrally involved in actual media creation.

AUDIENCE MEASUREMENT: THE CURRENCY OF ADVERTISING-BASED MEDIA

Building on our opening case, let's further consider the task, roles, and importance of audience measurement companies. Nearly every media industry has some sort of audience- or consumer-measurement entity, although what gets measured, why, and how does vary. You may be most familiar with the television audience measurement company Nielsen Media Research, as the name "Nielsen" has slipped into the popular awareness more than those of most measurement companies. Perhaps you were once a member of a "Nielsen family," those selected to be part of the nationwide sample of viewers from which the viewing of all audiences is extrapolated. One of the biggest surprises to our students is, often, the size of the Nielsen sample. Until fairly recently, Nielsen used a national sample of 1,200 households to base viewing figures for a nation of nearly 100 million people. The expanding number of channel offerings and viewer adoption of technologies such as VCRs, DVRs, and video on-demand have made measuring television viewing more complicated. Nielsen consequently has had to develop new panels to measure different aspects of television use and has expanded its nationwide sample to 5,000. While we do appreciate the wonder of properly deployed statistical measurement techniques, it remains somewhat questionable whether even this enlarged sample can accurately report the viewing of audiences around the nation.

Nielsen now uses a number of mostly technology-based methods for counting viewers; in some cases, however, Nielsen still uses some pretty low-tech methods. The beginning of audience measurement, which dates to radio in the pre-television age, was little more than announcers imploring listeners to send in a postcard with their names and maybe some limited information about themselves. A next stage involved telephone polling, in which audience measurement services would call a sample of homes and inquire about what they were watching or listening to at that moment, or perhaps the night before. Companies including Nielsen also made use of **diaries**—small notebooks that would be sent to a sample of viewers who were then asked to fill them in by writing down everything they watched over a two-week period and then to return them by mail.

A substantial advance began in the late 1950s and has arguably just recently become fully functional. In 1959, Nielsen began implementing a device called an "Instantaneous **Audimeter**," a mechanical device that recorded what channel the television set was tuned to on a minute-by-minute basis. At first, viewers had to send these meters back, and their tabulations would be figured with some delay, but by 1971, Nielsen introduced its "Storage Instantaneous Audimeter," which could be connected to the set and would relay tuning information nightly to a data-processing center over a telephone line. The next big development arrived in 1987, when Nielsen introduced the **People Meter**, a technology that expanded the ability of audimeters by adding a mechanism to report who was in the viewing audience. While audimeters only reported what channel the set was tuned to, the People Meter added another crucial layer of information by requiring viewers to indicate who in the family was viewing with the click of a remote. The most recent development in this history began in the early 2000s as Nielsen began introducing Local People Meters in the largest cities in the country in order to provide over-night data about local television stations.

We develop these paragraphs on Nielsen's evolving methods with such depth because how audiences are measured is crucial to understanding the meaning of the data that get produced. For example, until the Local People Meter, Nielsen continued to rely heavily on diaries in order to assess the viewing of local markets and used diaries with audimeters in order to have some information about who was watching. Consider how frustrating it might be for a network programmer or advertiser to know only how many homes watched, but not who within those homes viewed? Or consider your own likelihood of filling out a diary. Would you do so diligently? Would you lie? Certainly, those who rely on audience data have no illusion that there isn't a fair amount of inaccuracy in measurement methods that rely on the viewers themselves. What they don't have, however, is any systematic way to account for these inaccuracies.

In the radio industry, Arbitron is the primary measurement company, though at one time Nielsen and Arbitron competed in both television and radio measurement. None of the technologies that make television measurement more accurate exist for radio, so radio is still measured predominately based on a sample of listeners selected by Arbitron, who are asked to complete a week-long diary of their radio listening. Arbitron (initially in partnership with Nielsen) has been working on a technological advance called the Personal People Meter or PPM. This device is worn like a beeper by people in the sample and can record information about any radio or television signal that the person comes in contact with through inaudible codes embedded in the broadcast. Arbitron plans to replace its diary system with PPMs in the top fifty radio markets by the end of 2010.

The challenges of audience measurement—and the information that is particularly desirable—change some as we move into those industries Miege identifies as following a "publishing" model, which sell a measurable physical good such as a CD, magazine, or movie ticket (see Chapter 5 for clarification of industries that follow the publishing model). Yet key differences exist among these kinds of industries as well, particularly whether the media product is supported either entirely or partially through advertising, because audience size and composition are crucial factors in determining the cost of advertising. In the magazine industry, magazine companies pay organizations such as the Audit Bureau of Circulation (ABC) and Business Publications Audit of Circulation (BPA) to regularly inspect their shipments and certify that the number of issues a company claims to circulate is indeed true. As in the case of television, however, magazine advertisers are not only interested in how many people subscribe, but also want to know something about those subscribers. Sometimes magazine companies compile this information themselves, but more often, they contract such reader surveys to a media research firm.

The recording industry uses a couple of services in order to keep track of the performance of its industry. Since 1991, Nielsen's SoundScan system has automatically recorded music sales at participating retail outlets in order to compile a weekly list of top sellers. (Incidentally, SoundScan is not the data used by the Recording Industry Association of America in its certification system. So, for instance, if you hear that the RIAA has declared a CD "platinum," the certification doesn't indicate that one million copies have actually been sold but rather that one million copies have been shipped to retailers.) The industry seeks information about frequency of radio play as an indicator of popularity, and contracts with various firms that monitor radio stations electronically in order to develop a count of the most played songs. Similarly, the film industry collects its basic performance data from box office reports that come out at the end of each weekend, but they also employ audience measurement services from companies such as the National Research Group, which survey audience awareness of and interest in upcoming films.

An important difference between the cases of the recording and film industries' use of audience research and those of radio and television is that the data from Nielsen and Arbitron become particularly important because those audience figures determine the price of advertising. In the case of the recording and film industries, data about audience behavior are used primarily for the information of the industry about the performance of their acts and to develop release and marketing strategies, because these industries derive most of their revenues from consumer purchases rather than from advertiser sponsorship.

While different sectors of the media industries engage in varying degrees of audience research after a media text is released, all of them conduct research prior to and during the development of products. This type of research falls under the general category of **market research**, which includes a wider range of practices as well. Nielsen and Arbitron are big players in this type of market research, although countless other firms also subcontract for them and conduct original market research for various clients. All of these researchers take media products at various stages of completion and elicit responses from members of targeted demographic groups, in an effort to integrate audience preferences more fully into the final product, thereby increasing sales. As you might imagine, the creative people in the industry are often wary of these efforts to influence their creative expression. Undoubtedly, this type of market research is one of the clearest examples of how commercial interests can alter a society's cultural life.

Market research firms typically handle an array of clients, including advertisers and manufacturers, as well as media companies. Using surveys, focus groups, and specialized techniques designed for specific products, market research firms specialize in gathering the responses of a small group of research subjects, who represent the intended demographic for the client, and using those responses to test the popularity of the products and make adjustments before they go into production. For products with an ongoing life cycle, such as television series and magazines, follow-up market research is often done as well. For films and recorded music, however, once a movie or album is released, follow-up research with the intent of changing the product is impossible.

Market research makes much more widespread use of focus groups and other non-quantitative forms of audience analysis than does post-release audience and performance research, because there is time for the qualitative impressions of potential audiences to feed back into the production process. In recent years, Las Vegas has become a hotbed of market research, especially for the media industries: because of the popularity of Las Vegas as a travel destination for people from all walks of life, the city gives ready and quick access to just about any demographic group. Market research for media products includes having audiences watch or listen to a brief media clip and fill out a survey; watching a television show or film in a special theater that allows you to give feedback on how much you like or dislike the program in real time; tracking subject's eye movements as they watch a commercial; and discussing textual elements such as characters, plots, singers, and genres in small focus groups. In addition, market researchers often use cable television, the U.S. mail, and the Internet to deliver movies and television shows to potential consumers and test their responses.

We know very little about how market research activities feed back into the production, selection, promotion, and performance of media texts. Todd Gitlin in 1983 reported that, when it comes to decisions about whether to green-light particular television series, market research was mainly used to verify executives' gut feelings; if a show that they liked performed poorly in testing, however, they rarely cancelled the project.[2] While anecdotal evidence suggests that, nowadays, market research has more influence in decision making than it did twenty-five or thirty years ago, we are not aware of any recent research that examines this question in depth. However, one thing is certain: the technological changes of the past two decades, combined with growing pressure to shave costs and squeeze profits in the media industries, have led to a marked increase in the volume of market research conducted before the release of media products. Undoubtedly, this explosion of information has had an impact on the business of media and the texts that the media industries produce.

AGENTS, LAWYERS, UNIONS AND OTHER REPRESENTATION

Like workers in many industries, media industry workers often rely on some sort of official representation of their collective and individual interests. By "representation," we mean a variety of unions, guilds, agents, business managers, and lawyers whose primary task involves facilitating the ability of media industry workers to ply their trades. In the cases of unions and guilds, large organizations represent the collective interests of many workers, while agents and lawyers typically negotiate individual contracts and working conditions of clients on a case-by-case basis.

To work in almost any aspect of production in film or television requires membership in a union or guild (even if you also employ an agent). In general, guilds represent the so-called **above-the-line** workers, who tend to be the most prominent creative workers involved with a project, such as a film director or television star. These guilds include the Screen Actors Guild, Writers Guild of America, and Producers Guild of America. Meanwhile, **below-the-line** workers, or those who are more involved with the technical aspects of media production, typically belong to various unions such as the Communication Workers of America or International Alliance of Theatrical Stage Employees and Moving Picture Machine Operators.[3] In both cases, however, the function of the union or guild is the same. These collective bargaining organizations establish a baseline of compensation and benefits for workers—what is often known as **scale**—as well as basic working conditions (such as the maximum number of hours per day and the number of hours between "days," which is important because of the long and irregular hours required by production).

Additionally, many of those who create media goods—talent, writers, and producers—also employ agents. Agents function as intermediaries between the worker and the media organization, and are responsible for negotiating individual terms of employment. Agents keep track of projects moving through the "pipeline" and try to "attach" their clients to projects that are good for the overall career trajectory of their client. Agents have steadily become increasingly central to the development process as large talent agencies have developed a veritable "stable" of clients including actors, writers, directors, and producers, and have also taken to purchasing rights to various creative projects (scripts for movies or television shows). The agency then puts together a package deal that might include the creative property, the director, and most of the major acting roles, and then tries to sell the whole package to a production studio. Inevitably one aspect of the package will be particularly attractive, which allows the agency to leverage work for additional clients (and earn an even higher fee).

In addition to employing agents to manage careers, working in the upper-echelons of the media industries also requires the services of lawyers and law firms and various personal business and promotion staff. The particular nature of media goods as intellectual and creative products often requires specialized legal services for drafting contracts and reserving rights. In fact, an entire legal specialty known as entertainment law or media law has developed within the legal profession to address the needs of media workers. Meanwhile, media organizations such as studios, labels, and networks also maintain legal staffs to handle their side of contract arrangements in-house, as well as a range of intellectual property and workplace-related matters.

FINDING AUDIENCES: THE WORK OF PROMOTERS, MARKETERS, AND CRITICS

An old riddle that asks, "If a tree falls in the forest, and there is no one around to hear it, does it still make a sound?" has a relevant application to the work of media industries. This version might go something like, "If a media company pours millions of dollars into a project, and no one sees/hears/reads it, does it matter that it was made?" Although creating media projects is often a multi-year and multi-million-dollar enterprise, just making the product does little to guarantee that the final product finds an audience. In order to make sure media workers do not toil in vain, media industries employ a wide range of publicity and marketing specialists to make sure that audiences find their products. Additionally, they try to co-opt the work of others they cannot directly employ—such as critics—to further the spread the (hopefully good) word about their products.

Public Relations and Marketing

Employing public relations and marketing professionals is a common practice in all industries, not just media industries. We include public relations and marketing as auxiliary practices of the media industries not to suggest these activities are unique to these industries, but to highlight the importance of these activities to the success of media industries' goods.

Public relations and marketing share a good deal in common: both industries exist primarily to communicate certain messages about a client in order to achieve a particular end. In general, the key difference is that the work of public relations professionals typically does not call attention to itself as a sponsored message nor does it call attention to the sponsor. Media companies may employ public relations firms to sway public or political opinion on important issues. For example, the Recording Industry Association of America (RIAA) employed more than a dozen public relations firms to help lobby Congress for stricter piracy provisions throughout the 2000s and to help try to change public opinion about illegally downloading music.

Marketing, on the other hand, typically involves much more direct promotion of particular films, television shows, albums, and other texts produced by the media industries. Media industries' marketing efforts are so vast that they do some of the marketing work in-house through the marketing staff of the studio, label, or publisher. Rather than as auxiliary practices, we would categorize this marketing activity as part of the distribution and exhibition practices explored in the previous chapter. Such in-house work typically includes devising the basic marketing plan for a new release and arranging to have advertising purchased. Typically, the marketing effort also includes all sorts of promotions such as live appearances by stars or performers, premieres, and other events. This more specific event planning and star handling work might be contracted out to marketing firms that specialize in more particular types of promotional activities. It is this out-of-house marketing work that we categorize as an auxiliary practice.

There are truly countless activities that are part of promoting a new media good. The recording industry long employed firms with expertise in securing radio airplay for new singles; the film industry often subcontracts the work of developing film trailers; both the television networks and production studios increasingly employ legions of workers who help develop online promotional content that helps enrich the viewer's possible experience with a show. One thing all these examples have in common—whether technically public relations or marketing, and whether done inside or outside the media conglomerate—is that in all cases, these promotional efforts are paid for as part of the creation of the good, and the costs can quickly become a substantial portion of the budget. Edward Jay Epstein explains that one of the reasons why marketing of media texts is so difficult—and therefore why such vast sums go into this activity—is because, unlike an industry like the packaged goods industry, media goods need to succeed immediately.[4] A film that doesn't open strongly will quickly find its remaining promotion budget slashed and be pulled from distribution on a wide range of screens. Increasingly in the music industry, a major label will not even release a CD until one of the songs on it becomes a hit, resulting in many albums that are delayed, reworked, or permanently shelved when their first and second singles do not chart well or fail to garner significant airplay. Likewise, a new television show that doesn't connect with a sizable audience in its first few weeks on the air may quickly be cancelled or shuffled off to another timeslot, making it even more difficult for audiences to find. Various entities in media industries may engage in **intentional overproducion** in hopes of finding a hit, but, as we discussed in the previous chapter, not all media products are promoted equally.

Critics

The role of critics is quite different from PR and marketing workers in key ways, although we can also understand them as playing a role in creating media audiences. Critics typically write about a certain media industry, and they often review its products for a general audience of readers. It is important to understand that critics are not employed by the media industries they write about, yet a positive review or a feature story about some aspect of a media text can nevertheless provide quite valuable publicity. Critics' relationships to media industries are complicated by the fact that they often work *in* media industries, but typically for newspaper or magazine publications separate from the media they "cover"—most often television, film, or music. In theory then, these critics are independent of the media industry and free to register both positive and negative assessments of the products they review. At the same time, however, because of increasing **conglomeration** in the media industries, it is possible that critics may work for the same conglomerate that ultimately owns the rights to the text the critic is reviewing.

Media industries most certainly do try to co-opt critics to do their publicity work for them with varying degrees of explicitness. Music-label publicists have been known to try and exert influence by treating critics to lavish dinners, providing them with VIP concert packages, and inviting them to press-only events where new and established talents perform. Other publicists do not grant interviews with A-list artists unless the critics have been supportive of the artist in the past or unless, for instance, the article will appear on the front page of a newspaper or the cover of a magazine. One of the most egregious abuses can be found in the phenomenon of the film-industry junket. In advance of the opening of a big film, a studio will invite a hundred or so critics and journalists to an all-expense-paid event that offers them the opportunity to hear creative workers and the stars talk about the film. In these junket settings, the journalists often are explicitly told what they can and cannot ask questions about and those who violate the decorum of the celebratory environment the studios try to maintain can find themselves uninvited from future events. As a result, these events tend to produce results similar to the promotional work the media industries directly pay for—and indeed, these junkets are no small expense.

As a point of contrast, a group of television critics has been successful in maintaining a more rigorously journalistic environment for its direct interactions with the networks as a result of forming a collective organization. The Television Critics Association (TCA) holds two annual press tours in which critics who write for papers and magazines from around the country converge on Los Angeles for ten days to three weeks, during which different networks present panels promoting current and new series and also present their executives for questioning. Rather than the networks (or studios in the case of film), the TCA vets the list of attendees, which ensures that no critic is "uninvited" as punishment for rigorous journalism, such as asking tough questions or writing negative reviews. The critics also travel at their own expense, somewhat reducing the degree to which they can be perceived as beholden to the networks.

Arguably, in the current era of great plentitude of media texts, critics' value to media industries comes as much from their ability to draw the attention of audiences as does their assessment. In fact, when interviewing a group of television critics about how they approach their work, one of your authors repeatedly encountered critics who noted that, rather than writing a negative review of a show, they simply write nothing at all because there are too many good or interesting works to write about.

LOST IN TRANSLATION: ADAPTING
MEDIA PRODUCTS ABROAD

The final set of ancillary industries may be rather unknown to most of you, unless you have spent some time abroad watching TV, or are one of those rare American moviegoers who are willing to watch foreign films. These are the translation or language transfer industries that make it possible to watch films and television and read magazines from other language cultures. Of course, not all of the media industries we cover in this book utilize translation services: the radio and recorded music industry, for example, typically does not translate songs and videos, although there have been numerous examples of songs being translated and remade in foreign lands, both by local musicians and the original artists. However, given the uncommonness of this practice, the kinds of organizational structures and patterns of practice that we generally associate with the phrase "industry" have not developed. Instead, popular music translation tends to be done on an ad hoc, case-by-case basis. Further, it is increasingly the case that artists will not simply translate their songs into other languages but will also, often with co-writers, create entirely new material in other languages.

The television, film, and advertising industries, by contrast, have a long history of being translated into many different languages, along with well-developed industry structures and main players in most countries. At first glance, the process of dubbing or subtitling may seem simple and mechanical—and, indeed, the common way of referring to these processes within the American television industries as "language transfer" encourages such a mechanical view of the process. As anyone who has ever tried to translate a poem or a piece of short fiction can tell you, however, translation is as much an art as a skill. In fact, subtitling and dubbing have a significant impact on the success or failure of imported media culture.

As with almost everything we've studied thus far in the commercial media industries, the degree of attention and care that dubbing and subtitling get depends on how important the commercial success of the particular program is for the company that pays for dubbing. According to one often-told anecdote, during the 1980s, Pepsi began marketing its soda drinks in China, but the market was not yet a large consumer of Pepsi, and so it made little sense to spend heavily on developing new marketing campaigns or even translating the American campaign. Consequently, the company translated its slogan "Come Alive With the Pepsi Generation" as "Pepsi Brings Your Ancestors Back From the Grave."[5] How this alleged mis-translation may have affected sales is uncertain, but, hopefully, the case clearly demonstrates the importance of good translation.

Beginning in the 1990s, as cable television was introduced across Latin America and U.S. cable channels began expanding into the region, good translations became more and more important, as well as more costly, for the distributors. Rather than handle translations in-house and in the exporting country, major television distributors began to outsource those activities to local firms that employed people with a better grasp of the local language, as well as better writing skills.

Unlike in our conventional view of outsourcing, however, it actually proved more expensive for distributors to ship these jobs abroad. One prominent, early example of this process was the dubbing of the animated series *Duckman* (1994–1997), an irreverent and profane cartoon that was the precursor to *Beavis and Butthead* and *South Park* and was also one of the first hits on the Cartoon Network. Turner Broadcasting, the owner and distributor of *Duckman* and Cartoon Network, had recently launched a channel in Mexico and was trying to build that channel's reputation around the series. So, Turner hired a local firm that subsequently brought in a group of writers and comics, not only to translate the words of the script, but also to rewrite the script for local references, tastes, and senses of humor. The subsequent popularity of the series in Mexico led other distributors quickly to follow suit.

As we saw in Chapter 7, and will return to on a global scale in Chapter 11, the trade in media products takes place between two distinct entities—distributors, or sellers, and exhibitors, or buyers. Even when these two entities are owned by the same conglomerate, as was the case with *Duckman* in Mexico, the seller and the buyer must still agree on who will pay for the dubbing. This is no small issue, either, as top-of-the-line dubbing can cost as much as one-third of a distributors' profits. Typically, in larger language communities in which distributors expect lucrative sales, the distributors will cover most or all of dubbing costs. This is because distributors expect to sell into multiple markets that speak the same language, and also to sell the dubbed version to several buyers in each market. In smaller linguistic markets, especially those countries that do not pay high license fees for media imports, the buyers will shoulder a larger burden of translation costs. Today, most Spanish-language translation for U.S. product is translated by firms in Miami, which not only can draw on actors with native ability in a range of Latin American dialects, but which also tend to be able to keep a pulse on both U.S. and Latin American cultural and linguistic trends.

Translation costs also differ within countries and firms, depending on the type and quality of the translation. Subtitling is generally quite a bit cheaper and quicker than dubbing, because it does not require a studio to hire multiple voice actors and because it's technologically simpler. Dubbing, meanwhile, not only tends to be more carefully translated, but also requires multiple actors to come into the studio to voice different characters. Often, at least in European countries, prominent local theater and film actors take on dubbing projects during the off-season. This not only adds to the expense of dubbing, but also leads to the common practice of certain dubbing actors being associated with certain Hollywood stars—although the demands of the industry are altering this practice. For instance, a well-known local actor would voice Clint Eastwood in all imported Clint Eastwood films; if that actor happened to be unavailable, the process would have to wait until he had time.

In most markets nowadays, new Hollywood films tend to be subtitled in the theaters, because the timing of release **windows** among distributors does not leave enough time for translation studios to dub them. This tends to be the case even in countries in which audiences prefer dubbing to subtitling due to conventional, historical practice. That is, particularly in Europe, different nationalities and language cultures tend to have a preference for *either* subtitling *or* dubbing; this preference developed over the twentieth century, and depended upon a variety of cultural factors. In Denmark, for instance, dubbing is generally viewed as something done for children's programming; adults, most Danes feel, can read subtitles. By contrast, in Hungary, whose language is radically different than English and other Germanic languages, both adults and children tend to prefer dubbing. These cultural differences in translation preferences, however, are being erased by the needs of the Hollywood studios to have precise control over blockbuster release dates.

In television, historical preferences for dubbing or subtitling still tend to prevail, because release dates are not as carefully timed as they are for theatrical releases. In dubbing countries, a range of qualities and prices tend to be available, including subtitling, "cable-quality," "broadcast-quality," and "theatrical-quality." The quality of the dubbing is determined by expectations of how popular the import will be among viewers. Unsurprisingly, these expectations are often self-fulfilling: the more one spends on dubbing, the better the quality, and the more likely audiences will watch.

The translation industries are currently undergoing significant change, in part due to the increasing coordination of release windows for both television and film, but also due to technological changes. One of the biggest problems with dubbing has always been the mismatch between image and soundtrack, something which has led to endless mockery of Chinese "Kung Fu" movies among American audiences. Digitization, however, promises to reduce, even eliminate, this dissonance, because it can allow for the subtle manipulation of both audio and video tracks to match one another's timing more precisely. In addition, high-end dubbers often try hard to write translated scripts in a way that reduces the difference in lip and mouth movements between the original and the translated languages. Together, these innovations seek to reduce—perhaps, one day, even eliminate—the traces of translation that today are so obvious in dubbed media texts.

Finally, we want to say a word about magazines, many of which also have multiple language editions and rely on translation industries. Although, in order to remain competitive in the local market, most localized versions of global magazines tend to include primarily locally sourced articles, they also fill out their pages with articles translated from other versions of the magazine, particularly the English-language, U.S. versions. Much like their counterparts in the television and film industries, these magazines, too, primarily rely on auxiliary firms to provide those translations.

The practices of the media translation industry demonstrate some of the difficulties that media texts face when trying to cross cultural and linguistic boundaries. Translation is part of the larger practice of media **localization**, which we discuss in Chapter 11 as a prevalent industry practice in an increasingly global media environment.

CONCLUSION

Auxiliary media industries develop because it makes more sense, from both an economic and an organizational perspective, to move those processes away from the central production, distribution, and exhibition entities. In theory, the core media industries could perform all of the auxiliary functions described here. For practical reasons, however, some things, like television ratings, would lose much of their legitimacy if done in-house, because advertisers would always suspect that the broadcasters padded their numbers. Organizationally, then, it makes sense to export these processes to outside firms in order to maintain the appearance of independence.

In addition to independence, a couple of other concerns work in favor of letting auxiliary industries develop. One is cost: why, for instance, take on the extra costs of dubbing or marketing when those costs can be off-loaded to a third party? Another reason has to do with the limitations of organizations when it comes to innovation. Successful commercial organizations put a good deal of thought and effort into innovating their core product line—in our cases, the media texts themselves. Any attempt to work in multiple product areas risks losing one's edge in core products, at the same time that an organization is unlikely to be able to keep up with innovations in its peripheral product lines when it faces competition from others.

At the same time, while both economic and organizational logics favor the outsourcing of certain processes, outsourcing also leads to decreased control. In addition, lack of control also leads to greater complexities and costs in what might have been fairly straightforward, in-house processes. For most organizations operating in the commercial media industries, then, the question becomes what aspects of their operations to keep in-house, and which to leave to auxiliary organizations. Different companies in different locations and time periods come to different decisions about these issues. For instance, Disney tends to outsource its dubbing in major markets, but demands the right to select who will voice its characters in every language, because it wants to retain brand consistency of characters across national and linguistic boundaries. This, in turn, stems from the enormous merchandising revenues the company earns from its most popular characters. In addition to these considerations, changes in the economic, technological, or regulatory conditions of the media industries often work to create or eliminate the practice of off-loading particular operations to firms in auxiliary industries.

The practices carried out by the auxiliary media industries are not specifically represented in the Industrialization of Culture framework. Instead, they are included with production and distribution/exhibition under the general category of practices. It is important to realize that, however, just as the media industries have specific mandates and operating conditions that influence their day-to-day practices, so do the auxiliary industries, and operating conditions of the auxiliary industries may differ markedly from those of the media industries. It is at the level of practices that these auxiliary industries intersect with the media industries most frequently, which is why we have focused in this chapter primarily on how non-core industry practices affect the business practices of the media industries.

QUESTIONS

1. Pick an industry and list other auxiliary roles. Reflect on how these roles can affect the nature of the products of that industry. Also, think about why those roles are performed by auxiliary companies—what might motivate the media industry to take on that role itself or to keep it external?
2. Consider the importance of the real audience in the Industrialization of Culture framework. How might knowledge of who actually consumes a media text (instead of who is imagined to consume it) change the way that creative workers conceive of and create the text? How could that knowledge be used differently by those involved in an industry identified by Miege as "publishing" versus "written press" or "flow"? How might knowledge of a media text's real audience change the way people in distribution and exhibition do their jobs? How might marketing be approached differently?
3. Think about the similarities and differences among the roles of critics, public relations representatives, and marketers. Do you see them as essentially serving the same purpose? Do you think one may be more influential in terms of how financially successful a media text is? What about in terms of how creatively successful a media text turned out to be? Which seems most important to potential consumers and which seems most important to the industry—why?
4. How does the work of critics differ from public relations and marketing professionals?

FURTHER READING

A more detailed exploration of audience measurement can be found in Hugh Malcolm Beville's *Audience Ratings: Radio, Television, Cable*, rev. student ed. (Hillsdale, N.J.: Lawrence Erlbaum Associates, 1988); Philip M. Napoli's *Audience Economics: Media Institutions and the Audience Marketplace* (New York: Columbia University Press, 2003); and James G. Webster's *Ratings Analysis: The Theory and Practice of Audience Research*, 3rd ed. (Mahwah, N.J.: Lawrence Erlbaum and Associates, 2005). Surprisingly little has been written on the role of agents and other forms of representation in the media industries. Tom Kemper's *Hidden Talent: The Emergence of Hollywood Agents* (Berkeley: University of California Press, 2009) offers a valuable historical view.

For more on the role of television critics, see Amanda D. Lotz's "On 'Television Criticism': The Pursuit of the Critical Examination of a Popular Art," *Popular Communication: International Journal of Media and Culture*, 6.1 (2008), 20–36; and "Seventeen Days In July at Hollywood and Highland: Examining the Television Critics Association Tour," *Journal of Popular Film and Television*, 33.1 (2005): 22–28; for work on film critics and junkets see Sharon Waxman's "Fade to

Black," *American Journalism Review* (June 1997,), 32–37 and "Spoon-fed News," *American Journalism Review* (October 1998,), 36–39.

For more on dubbing and translation, see Caroline-Isabelle Caron's "Translating Trek: Rewriting and American Icon in a Francophone Context," *The Journal of American Culture*, 26, no. 3 (2003): 329–355; Chiara Ferrari's "Dubbing *The Simpsons*: Or How Groundskeeper Willie Lost His Kilt in Sardinia," *Journal of Film and Video*, 61, no. 2, (Summer 2009); and Markus Nornes's *Cinema Babel: Translating Global Cinema* (Minneapolis: University of Minnesota Press, 2007).

NOTES

1. Jon Gertner, "Our Ratings, Ourselves," *The New York Times Magazine*, April 10, 2005.
2. Todd Gitlin, *Inside Prime Time* (New York: Pantheon Books, 1983).
3. The distinction between above-the-line and below-the-line workers dates back to the early days of film financing, when budget sheets had an actual line drawn between costs associated with creative work, which had to be paid before production, and those associated with technical skills, which were incurred during or after production.
4. Edward Jay Epstein, *The Big Picture: Money and Power in Hollywood* (New York: Random Ouse, 2006).
5. David A. Ricks, *Blunders in International Business* (Cambridge, Mass.: Blackwell, 1993), 83–84, 159.

CHAPTER 9

—

The Growth of the Symbolic Economy

U ntil now, our book has focused mostly on processes and practices that are directly centered on the media industries, especially those that are internal to the industries themselves. In this final section, which encompasses this and the following two chapters, we look at three forces of change that originate outside the media industries, but are reshaping those industries in profound ways. Each of these forces—the growth of the symbolic economy (this chapter); the shift to digital forms of communication (Chapter 10); and the globalization of the economy (Chapter 11)—originates outside the media industries and portends much broader historical changes, of which changes in the media industries are but one small part. In many cases, these three forces interact, making it difficult to explain changes as "just" because of any one of them; rather, changes occur because of a combination of globalization, digitization, and the development of the symbolic economy. These "forces of change" are transforming the very societies in which we live and—not surprisingly—the media industries that are a part of those societies as well. They are taking place at every level of the Industrialization of Culture framework, from the way that governments imagine industry mandates to the way that media professionals perform their day-to-day work. In addition, these changes alter the power relationships between organizations, governments, workers, and audiences. While we do not offer a painstaking analysis of all of the changes that each of these forces is causing at every level of the framework, we do explain some of the most prominent changes that are taking place at each level.

We also want to say at the outset that we try very hard not to engage in idle speculation about what the media industries will look like in the future. We avoid this as much as possible because we are well aware of how badly almost every scholarly speculation about the future goes wrong. This seems to be particularly true of speculation about media technologies—probably because most people overestimate how "new" new technologies really are at the same time that they tend to underestimate how transformative the truly new elements of new technologies can be. The journalism historian David Nord tells a cautionary tale in this regard about the editor of the *New York Herald*, Frederic Hudson, who in 1873 predicted that:

> ...the next stage of journalism would be the truly national newspaper, a newspaper laid on breakfast tables everywhere in the land, every morning, simultaneously. And what technological marvel would make possible such a national newspaper? Pneumatic tubes, Hudson prophesied. Enormous compressed-air "dispatch lines" would run from New York to San Francisco and to points north and south, blasting bundles of the *Herald* across the continent as fast as the sun could sweep across the sky. This, then, was Hudson's future: *USA Today* delivered by tube.[1]

So, one reason that we want to restrain our predictions about what the media industries will look like in the future is that we don't want to look silly to our grandchildren. More practically, we realize that the future of the media industries will be shaped by the people who work in and consume media—by people like you and us—and how we act and react in light of the major changes that are sweeping society. So, what we want to offer here is not a set of predictions, but an analysis of how these forces have already begun to change the nature of the media industries, their relationship to society and culture, the role that they play in our everyday lives, and the contents of their products.

*   *   *

Phil is an animation editor for William's Street production house in Atlanta, a major supplier of programming for the Cartoon Network's Adult Swim adult animation block. His job involves taking storyboards, voice tracks, and images and creating a rough cut of an entire episode of a series, which then gets finalized by an outside company. Most of his work involves computers: he receives voice and image files electronically, edits them together on his Macintosh computer, and sometimes even submits his final edits electronically.

Although he has worked in his current position for several years and considers himself well compensated, Phil also faces long stretches of time when he goes without work and without pay. He loves the laid-back atmosphere of his workplace, the flexible hours, and seeing his name in lights—or, more accurately, dots—on the television screen. He also, however, endures occasional long nights and early mornings during "crunch time," an arrangement that becomes more and more difficult to accommodate as he has gotten married and started a family.

While Phil works squarely within what we have defined as a media industry—specifically, the cable television industry—he is also undoubtedly a computer software expert, not all that different from someone who specializes in database management or statistical analysis software. Furthermore, his working conditions—casual work environment, flexible hours, high pay with unpredictable periods of unemployment, and long hours during crunch time—are remarkably similar to conditions in both the gaming and software development industries. Increasingly, the lines between media work and information work is blurring, in part due to technological **convergence**, and in part due to corporate **conglomeration**.

People disagree on what we should call this new economic engine that runs on the production, collection, processing, analysis, and presentation of information and entertainment and the hybrid jobs that they produce. Some prefer the term "knowledge economy." Others call it the "creative industries," Still others use the terms "information economy" or "cultural economy." In our view, all of these terms favor either the information *or* the creative side of this major economic shift. Which is why we have chosen the term **symbolic economy** to refer to the explosion of jobs and industries that involve some form of symbolic manipulation as their central tasks, whether those symbols are audiovisual stories, music, numbers, or consumer research data.

The phrase "symbolic economy" is purposely ambiguous. In general, it refers to those kinds of commodities that primarily serve communicative, informational, or entertainment-related functions, such as the media industries, the fashion industry, and the telecommunications and computer industries. We discuss the definition and possible objections to this classification in more detail later in this chapter. The symbolic economy is the outgrowth of a much broader shift in economic conditions over the past several decades, which has seen the decline in mass production and distribution and a growth in more flexible forms of production and distribution, known as **post-Fordism**. Again, we will clarify what exactly this term means in a minute. But, in order to help you navigate this chapter, we want to introduce both of these terms—the symbolic economy and post-Fordism—and their general characteristics as soon as possible. In what follows, we will first explain the general changes to the economy known as post-Fordism and how they have affected the media industries, then we turn our attention to examining how these new economic conditions helped pushed a range of industries, including the media industries, toward center of twenty-first century economic life.

Industry and government experts agree that the jobs of yesterday based on the manufacturing of physical goods are gone forever. While in 1950 nearly one-quarter of all workers in the United States were employed in factory work, operating machinery, or day labor, that percentage had dropped to less than 15 percent by the year 2000. By contrast, the number of jobs in information-technology is forecast to grow by nearly 25 percent by 2016. While many of these jobs are in industries such as software engineering or communications network management, increasingly, they also require expertise in computerized presentation software and audio and video editing to make presentations to clients, managers, and stakeholders. To put this another way, while media production students used to pursue jobs mainly in broadcasting or in-house corporate videos, today, companies of all descriptions want people with these skills. At the same time, of course, competition among job seekers is getting more intense. This simultaneous growth in both the availability of media industry jobs and competition for those jobs means that media workers today have greater flexibility when it comes to where and when they work, but they also must make greater sacrifices in terms of unpaid overtime and they lack the job security of their predecessors. This chapter aims to explain how and why these changes in media work have taken place, as well as to explore how the rise of the symbolic economy has altered other conditions and practices of the media industries.

HISTORICAL CHANGES IN CULTURAL PRODUCTION

As we have already noted throughout this book, the media industries today tend to be for-profit endeavors. Adjectives like "for-profit" or "commercial" or "capitalist," however, often seem to mask as much as they reveal about the nature of these institutions, their working conditions, and the kinds of texts they produce. The cultural scholar Raymond Williams, in fact, has identified three distinct periods in cultural production: the patronage era, the market professional era, and the complex professional era.[2] The specific names of these different eras, however, is probably less important than the recognition that 1) cultural production always needs to be funded in some way, and the funding mechanism will influence the texts that get produced; and 2) funding mechanisms take on the dominant economic forms of their time, and they tend to change over time.

The **patronage era** of cultural production was the dominant way of funding creative works from the Middle Ages through the nineteenth century. Patrons commissioned artists, musicians, playwrights, and so forth to create cultural texts for their particular needs. Patronage grew out of an agricultural and artisanal economic system common during the era, in which landed aristocrats heavily taxed economic activity that took place within their domains. These were generally the only members of society who had the disposable income necessary to pay for cultural goods, and they offered the only markets for cultural workers.

The **market-professional era** began in the nineteenth century as trade and industry became increasingly important dimensions of the overall economy, and as a new class of businesspeople began to gain power and disposable income in Western societies. As part of their efforts to establish their legitimacy, these nouveau riche businesspeople often became collectors of art and culture. During this time, individual artists and producers began to be able to sell their wares on newly developing cultural markets. This development required creative workers of the time to serve as both businesspeople and creators, selling and promoting their work to potential clients, and giving them greater control over their creations than they had generally enjoyed in the patronage era.

In the **complex professional era**, which began in earnest in the 1950s, creative workers began to become salaried employees of organizations devoted to creating culture, rather than independent or contracted workers. As these organizations have become larger, more diversified, and more global since the 1950s, their impact on working conditions and media texts has likewise become more and more complex. This is particularly evident if we consider how cultural texts have changed through time. In the patronage era, the kind of culture that got produced was closer to what we today would call creative art, or forms of cultural expression that require a single artist. In the market professional era, creative art produced by a single artist remained the dominant form of cultural production, although some division of duties begins to occur as trade professionals—someone like a gallery owner—emerged to display and sell artistic wares. The media of the complex professional era—the newspapers, magazines, films, music, and television we've mainly discussed throughout the book—require vast staffs to create and distribute. This labor is not interchangeable, but is based in distinct skill sets. Thus, media creation requires an expert in camera work who knows nothing of sound scoring or editing, etc.

So the organization of the media industries in any era grows out of the dominant economic forms of the time, which should lead us to ask whether the dominant forms of economic activity have changed at all since Williams initially came up with this typology in the late 1970s. This is a question that media industry scholar David Hesmondhalgh takes up and answers in the affirmative, and we, too, believe that significant macro-economic changes have taken place in the past three decades that have had a serious impact on the media industries, the texts they produce, and the roles they play in society.[3] This change has many features and has been given many names, including post-Fordism, the Long Downturn, and Economies of Signs and Space.[4] First, we will summarize these changes briefly, and then we will discuss in detail how they have altered media industry mandates, regulatory and economic conditions, and creative and distribution practices.

Williams identifies the 1950s as the time in which the complex professional era of cultural production began to take off, because it was during this period that the world economy began steadily growing after World War II. The period from the 1950s through the 1960s was a time of predictable and consistent economic growth, particularly in the United States, which led to reliable interest rates, inflation rates, wages, and more. This was a period of mass production, mass distribution, and mass consumption, and the media, particularly television, played a central role in holding this system together with the glue of mass advertising, which helped create consumer demands for the products of mass production around the country and around the world. Large corporations of this era invested massive amounts of capital upfront and waited months, even years, before they recouped those investments.

The automobile industry is perhaps the quintessential example of how American industry, including the media industries, worked at this time. Automobile manufacturing was a highly centralized activity, with workers living in close proximity to massive factories where almost every car in the nation was made, after which the cars were shipped around the country to retail outlets. Standardization was a given, and consumers in every part of the country faced basically the same choices when purchasing a car. Manufacturers, meanwhile, had to make large investments in research and design, factories, materials, wages, transportation, and advertising before their new models ever turned a single penny of profit. Finally, and perhaps most important, manufacturers generally produced high-ticket items that were designed to last for many years; at the time, durable goods like cars were the main economic engines of the American economy.

Because of Henry Ford's pioneering role in organizing this type of automobile mass production, industries or economies that emphasize centralization, standardization, long-term profit horizons, and durable goods are sometimes referred to as **Fordist**. During this period in history, Fordist principles were the main ones by which most industries operated, including most of the media industries. Television and film production were centralized in Hollywood and funded mainly through large, up-front capital investments, not unlike automobile manufacturing. Texts tended to be standardized and aimed at common cultural tastes and sensibilities. This was the era of mass entertainment, when "everyone" in the country flocked to the same movies or switched on the same programs, leaving the impression that the nation as a whole possessed similar tastes, experiences, and aspirations, even if this impression was predicated on the exclusion of most women and citizens of color.

The record industry, too, was organized along Fordist principles at the time, although a number of independent labels and publishers thrived, as well, and often introduced the most innovative musical acts and movements, including Motown, R&B, and rock. Still, most popular musical recordings were financed with long-term profit windows in mind, and they were nationally distributed by the major record labels. The major labels employed a large number of musicians in their studio bands and also contracted with popular musical acts, who were limited to recording only with that label. Vinyl albums and later electromagnetic tapes were pressed in large factories and distributed nationwide to retail outlets. Again, much of the cultural output of the Fordist music industry reflected the preferences of a general, national listening audience, rather than the cultural tastes of subgroups. In addition, the magazine and radio industries, which were clearly Fordist in their organization in the early decades of the twentieth century, had already begun to adopt post-Fordist principles by mid-century, due in large part to competition from television. That is, in response to television's power as the new mass medium of its day, the magazine and radio industries began targeting small demographics and shifted their focus from a general readership or listener to formats built around particular interests, such as classical music or fashion. Foreshadowing more recent events across the media industries, some of the most successful magazine formats began to focus on subjects that have persistent, cyclical turnover, such as fashion, gossip, or the entertainment industry.[5]

The newspaper industry was perhaps the only media industry not organized along Fordist lines in the postwar period, due largely to the particularly local emphasis of this medium. Certainly, some of the largest national newspapers, such as the *New York Times,* published a good deal of general-interest national news and centralized both news gathering and newspaper publishing activities in particular locations, not unlike the automobile industry. Even these newspapers, however, contained a large amount of local news, and they published different editions in different parts of the country by mid-century. Most newspapers around the country have been predominantly local enterprises, reporting on local stories and featuring local advertising. In this sense, newspapers as an industry have not generally gone through a comparable transition to post-Fordism, although they have certainly faced substantial challenges and changes, especially with the introduction of digitization, which we explore in Chapter 10.

DEFINING THE POST-FORDIST ERA

Beginning in the mid-1970s, the stability of the postwar economy began to erode. The immediate precipitating event was the 1973 oil crisis, during which oil-producing countries in the Middle East refused to sell oil to the United States because of its support of Israeli military forces in the Yom Kippur War. This seemingly isolated event caused oil and gas price in the United States to spike, forcing an already weak American economy into a deep recession. What came to be known as "stagflation"—stagnant economic growth combined with currency inflation—caused interest rates to more than double by 1974. While interest rates had generally hovered between 4.5 and 5.0 percent throughout the 1950s and 1960s, rates near or above 10 percent became commonplace after the oil embargo.

These high interest rates slowly worked to undermine Fordist principles of industry organization and contributed to the rise of industries involved in symbolic production. High interest rates made it much more difficult and risky to pour massive amounts of money into product development and production and then wait months and years before seeing a return on those investments. At least as important as high interest rates is their unpredictability, which makes profits similarly unpredictable. In the last few years, as interest rates have dropped to near zero, they have nevertheless remained rather erratic, keeping firms skittish about borrowing too much money for too long a period. As is often the case with major economic changes, it took years for changes in the way that firms operate to percolate through the system as a whole and develop a new standard for how money is made. Nearly forty years later, however, many of the changes that began in 1973 have taken root and become commonplace. These changes are often loosely referred to as "post-Fordism."

Post-Fordism is characterized by a complex web of centralizing and decentralizing tendencies, which differ among forms of goods and industry types. Most industries have decentralized production and now produce goods closer to where they will be retailed, cutting down on transportation costs and decreasing the lag time between production costs and sales revenues. The American automobile industry, for example, now has manufacturing plants around the country. These plants specialize in producing cars that get sold in the immediate vicinity (although not exclusively so). This arrangement has the added benefit that each plant can produce only as many cars—and the kinds of cars—that are needed in that specific region. In this way, decentralization of manufacturing helps eliminate waste and overproduction. Observers have taken to calling this process **mass customization**, which focuses on producing commodities that are more tailored to local market conditions than their mass-production predecessors. Mass customization calls attention to the fact that these commodities are still produced in factories for large numbers of people, not crafted for individual consumers, but that they are more tailored to buyer preferences than mass-produced goods. Post-Fordism couples mass customization with **just-in-time production**, or the effort to produce goods as close as possible in time to the moment they are purchased. This effort cuts down on the lag time between payment of production costs and revenues from sales, which is an arrangement well suited to an era of unpredictable interest rates.

Post-Fordism in the media industries similarly takes the shape of mass customization and just-in-time production. Beginning in the magazine industry and slowly spreading across almost all media, mass customization begins with the identification of **niche** audiences and the design of texts specifically targeted at those niches. As mentioned, the magazine industry is perhaps the most evolved when it comes to creating niche media. If we look, for instance, at magazines targeted at pregnant women—already a pretty well-define niche audience—we find *Fit Pregnancy* for women interested in maternity fashion and staying in shape during pregnancy; *Pregnancy* magazine, aimed primarily at first-time mothers; *Pregnancy and Newborn*, aimed at both pregnant women and new mothers; and *American Baby* for new and expectant mothers primarily in the 18- to 34-year-old demographic. And this is only a partial list.

Just-in-time production in the media industries primarily takes the form of collapsing **distribution windows** so that consumers can access the newest films, television programs, and games through a range of different **platforms** at the same—or nearly the same—time. The recent acquisition of NBC Universal by Comcast creates the opportunity for the newly formed conglomerate to release blockbuster movies in the theaters, on pay-per-view cable, and online at the same time, a move that some observers see as the very near future of the media industries. In fact, many of these changes in release windows have already taken place, as we saw in Chapter 7. They permit distributors and producers to recoup their production investments as quickly as possible, rather than waiting for profits to trickle in over months and years as each new window opens.

We can see how both niche media and collapsing release windows take advantage of changes in the technological conditions that the media industries face, in particular digitization and the increased channel capacity it makes possible. Digitization allows distributors to deliver any media content via any distribution technology at the same time that it compresses the information that travels through those distribution channels. Together, these conditions have led to an explosion of new distribution channels for media texts, including satellite, cable, and Internet, which are used to deliver television, movies, games, magazines, newspapers, music, and more. With more and more channels for receiving media and more and more flexibility in how we receive them, niche audiences become easier to identify and target. We explore digitization in more detail in Chapter 10. At the moment, we simply want to note how changed technological conditions make niche media possible. In addition, we want to point out that these technological conditions did not simply change on their own; instead, they were part of a sustained effort by large corporations, including the heavy hitters in the media and telecommunications industries, who were seeking to adjust to the new opportunities and perils of a changed economic environment.

The Growth of the Symbolic Economy during Post-Fordism

What we have called the symbolic economy—that is, industries involved primarily in the production and reproduction of symbolic, rather than material, commodities—is particularly well suited to the demands of post-Fordist economic arrangements. Symbolic commodities tend to have more rapid turnover times than industrial commodities, especially the durable goods that served as the base of the Fordist industrial economy.

Now, you might rightly object that these industries actually *do* produce material goods: the fashion industry, for instance, produces clothing, a material good that has long been an important part of the world's economies. Likewise, the computer industry produces a good deal of hardware that is at least as important for computing as is the more symbolic commodity, software. On the other hand, you might also object—rightly, again—that even durable goods have symbolic elements to them. In the 1950s, for instance, refrigerators and dishwashers weren't simply home appliances, but also symbols of a family's upward mobility. The automobile also, the epitome of Fordism, possesses a good deal of symbolic power, suggesting everything from the male virility of a sports coupe to the family values of a minivan to the environmental consciousness of a hybrid.

Despite these very reasonable objections, however, we continue to believe that distinguishing something we are calling the "symbolic economy" from earlier kinds of industrial economies, and arguing for the former's growing importance in the world's economic activities, makes sense. While fashion certainly has utilitarian functions and dishwashers have symbolic significance, the relative balance of utilitarian and symbolic elements is quite different: that is, we would argue that fashion is *mainly* symbolic, with some utilitarian elements, while dishwashers are mainly utilitarian, with some symbolic elements. The focus of economic activity in the United States and other post-industrial countries has shifted in the past forty years from mostly utilitarian to mostly symbolic commodities.

The symbolic economy includes industries as diverse as fashion, software engineering, heritage, and, of course, the media industries. In all of these cases, the commodities being bought and sold are not so much tangible goods as cultural and communicative ones. These cultural and communicative goods tend to have much shorter shelf lives than tangible goods, even though they also continue to earn revenues for years after their initial release. Fashion changes biannually; new television series and new episodes appear in fall and in late winter; new movies are released throughout the year, but tend to congregate around particular events, such as summer and the end of the year; new computer games get released in advance of the holiday shopping season. In the case of all of the media industries we study in this book, the texts that they produce must consistently be replaced by new texts much more frequently than new refrigerators or cars need to be replenished. In this way, these industries consistently—and with some predictability—get new infusions of consumer cash several times per year. With durable goods, by contrast, only a small percentage of consumers would purchase new items in a single year. For this reason, the media industries, and the symbolic economy in general, lend themselves well to the pressures for frequent turnover and short-term profits that characterize the post-Fordist era.

Media and communications industries also permit surveillance and commercial targeting of consumer niches, which serve the just-in-time production schedules of consumer goods more generally, again making them central to contemporary economic activity. That is, as profit margins have gotten slimmer, producers of all kinds of goods focus more intensely on that portion of the public that consumes the majority of their products, as opposed to the more scatter-shot approach to advertising and corporate communication that reigned until the 1980s. New media outlets offer companies numerous options for communicating with specific consumer segments, while permitting them to collect and analyze vast amounts of data about those consumers. Wal-Mart, for instance, reportedly has a data warehouse with more than one-half a petabyte—or more than 500 terabytes—of information, although only an undisclosed percentage of that figure consists of consumer records. While Wal-Mart does not release information about the contents of its data warehouse, it is widely assumed that every credit card purchase ever made in its stores is cross-referenced by name, and individual buying patterns are mined for what they reveal about our purchasing habits, the kinds of coupons we respond to, and so forth. Online, the amount of information that is available about us increases exponentially, due to the digital footprints we leave everywhere we go. In fact, the vast amount of data that corporations collect about us in order to understand, shape, and exploit our purchasing habits led to the development of **data mining** in the 1990s, a term that captures well industry-wide perceptions about how valuable information about consumers' habits has become for today's businesses. The development of practices such as data mining are relevant to media industries because they make the old advertising practices of paying a lot to reach a lot of people (many of whom have no interest or need for the product) less valuable, replacing them with much more targeted approaches that advantage those advertising opportunities that are more "addressable," which many of the traditional media industries are not.

The symbolic economy therefore refers to *both* the tendency for industries that produce culture to move to the center of economic activity, *and* for consumer goods industries to rely on telecommunications and computer industries to segment and track the general public. These efforts also lead to the creation of advertising and media designed for specific consumer niches in order to position products properly for those consumers.

The shift from mass media to niche media and the growth in the amount and flexibility of distribution channels have ushered in a new set of economic conditions, regulatory conditions, and production practices. Let's break down each of these changes one by one so that you can see them play out on the different levels of the Industrialization of Culture framework.

POST-FORDISM AND CHANGES IN ECONOMIC CONDITIONS

Increasing **conglomeration** and **consolidation of ownership**, along with changing relationships among large and small media organizations has been the hallmark of the post-Fordist era. Conglomeration of different types of media industries under a single corporate umbrella allows firms to focus less on limiting distribution and more on owning **copyright**. In previous decades, companies dealt with the high risks of media production by controlling how many media texts competed with one another at any given time. To some extent, companies continue to pursue this strategy today. For instance, the major Hollywood studios release a limited number of blockbuster movies each year and try to stagger those releases to some degree so that competition is comparatively low. This strategy of creating **artificial scarcity** of media texts helps guarantee that even relatively unpopular texts will garner at least some revenue, because people have so few options to choose from. By contrast, the focus on owning copyright and diversifying into a wide range of media industries allows contemporary conglomerates to worry less about controlling the amount of media available, and concentrate instead on scanning the entire media landscape for popular texts or trends. Once those texts or trends get identified, the multimedia conglomerate can leverage those stories, characters, musicians, or genres across multiple media outlets. The 2009 blockbuster *Avatar*, for instance, which tells an adventurous tale of fighting to protect the environment in a futuristic world, led to the release of a video game of the same title a month after the movie's debut. This ability to profit from the same idea across several media outlets is the basis of contemporary efforts to reduce the economic risks of media production.

During the Fordist era, companies primarily operated in a single media industry with little or no cross-over with other industry sectors. So, NBC was a television company, *The Chicago Tribune* a newspaper company, and Disney a movie company. Today, by contrast, each of these companies is part of a conglomerate that also has holdings in several other media industries. Disney, for instance, owns numerous movie studios, a broadcast television network, cable networks, theme parks, magazines, and newspapers. In addition to conglomeration, the largest players in each industry have tended to consolidate their positions as they have gobbled up competitors into conglomerates and entered into a range of cooperative projects with their competitors. We will have time to discuss the social implications of these developments more fully at the end of this chapter, and we already covered some of these debates in Chapter 5. Here, we want to emphasize how these changes have arisen from the business challenges and opportunities of the present era.

Going back to Chapter 1, remember that uncertainty is one of the main characteristics of media industries, and that firms deal with uncertainty in a number of ways. During Fordism, controlling the audience's access to media texts by controlling distribution helped limit competition and made profits more predictable. Network television is the quintessential example here. Until the 1980s, in most parts of the country, viewers had access to only three national networks, through their local affiliates. During prime-time hours, viewers had a choice of three programs to watch, nearly guaranteeing that even unpopular programming would attract tens of millions of viewers. This arrangement made it possible to keep advertising rates relatively high and ensured that the networks more or less recouped the **license fees** they paid to producers. Other media industries operated by similar principles. Hollywood controlled which films got access to movie theaters initially by owning the theaters, then, after 1948, by managing an elaborate, nationwide distribution network that could deliver films in consistent numbers, of consistent quality, at reasonable prices. These arrangements led to an **oligopolistic** industry structure in most media industries, as powerful players limited distribution in order to combat uncertainty.[6]

In today's media environment, firms tend to focus less on controlling distribution and more on owning copyright and managing successful media **brands**. Brands, in this instance, refer to particular characters, story worlds, or recognizable elements of texts that can be exploited across multiple media, sometimes referred to as **transmedia** storytelling. The first prominent example of this recent corporate strategy dates to 1989, when Time, Inc. and Warner, Inc. merged and developed the Batman character as a new, cross-platform brand that could serve multiple departments of the new conglomerate. Batman appeared as a newly revived comic book character in the conglomerate's DC Comics company, as a movie soundtrack featuring Prince that was owned by Warner Music, and as a blockbuster movie produced and distributed by Warner Bros., as well as a range of Batman-related merchandise that the conglomerate licensed to others to develop and sell.[7]

Conglomerates, then, are designed to take advantage of potentially popular texts that appear in any one medium by leveraging them through all other media in which the conglomerate operates. Today, those media often include games, movies, television, and, sometimes, print. Each of these outlets also serves as a possible promotion for other outlets, each of which engages the audience and earns revenues but that also drives audiences to different media outlets, where they will spend even more money. These, in theory at least, are the **synergies** that conglomerates enjoy in the post-Fordist era.

The example of the Batman movie series and its related media texts and merchandise demonstrates the synergies that large media conglomerates dream about and occasionally enjoy. Our telling of the story may leave the impression, however, that these kinds of synergies are always carefully engineered, top-down projects that manipulate unwitting audiences with texts that serve corporate, rather than public, desires. While many people do believe this version of how contemporary media industries operate—and even though this does sometimes occur—more frequently, the process of developing synergistic texts is far more haphazard. Most conglomerates still retain fairly loose control over textual development at their various subsidiaries, but once one of their creations "hit," they leverage the various characters, storylines, and so forth throughout their various media holdings. This is why owning copyright is such an important aspect of post-Fordist media operation. It allows the development of transmedia worlds—seen more recently in the *Harry Potter* and *Twilight* franchises—for eager fans to engage with many contexts of storytelling.

In addition to conglomeration and consolidation of ownership in the media industries, post-Fordism has also led to the seemingly contradictory growth in smaller, independent media companies. Generally, these smaller companies enjoy a good deal of independence, but they also operate in the riskier parts of the business, especially developing texts for new or niche media. As soon as these companies become successful, they frequently become the object of conglomerate take over. The social networking site MySpace, for instance, was purchased in 2005 by the News Corporation conglomerate at a time when it was the most popular social networking site on the Internet. Today, of course, in a demonstration of the truism that conglomerates can't simply force their will on the public, the popularity of MySpace has been eclipsed by that of Facebook, which continues (at this point) to be an independent company.

So the structure of the media industries during post-Fordism can be summed up as follows: a small number of global, multimedia conglomerates control the most lucrative segments of each of the industries, with a large number of smaller, independent companies operating at the margins of each industry. Don't, however, let the word "smaller" fool you. One of these independent companies, the game publisher Electronic Arts, earned more than $4 billion in 2008.[8] Others, however, are indeed small operations that employ only a handful of people. Both conglomerates and independent organizations have symbiotic relationships with one another. Not only do independents take on riskier endeavors and tend to get bought out once they turn profitable, they also will license particularly lucrative properties to and from conglomerates to distribute and cross-develop into other media texts.

The *Harry Potter* series is an interesting case study of textual synergy in a conglomerated media world. The book series was originally published by Bloomsbury in the UK and was licensed to Scholastic Publishing for printing in the United States. Both Scholastic and Bloomsbury are among the largest publishing houses in their respective nations, but both remain independent companies. After the first book, *Harry Potter and the Philosopher's Stone*, became a popular book in the UK and the United States, Warner Bros. optioned the movie rights to the series, as well as rights to the movie soundtrack, which it has published under its Warner Music label. Warner Bros. also holds worldwide rights to distribute the movies to television, film, and home video outlets. Meanwhile, Electronic Arts purchased rights to develop Harry Potter computer games, and the toy manufacturer Hasbro bought rights to create merchandise, including rights for candy, trading cards, role-playing games, and electronics. While Warner Bros. is the only company in this list that is a member of a global media conglomerate, the others are still large companies that stand atop an oligopolistic industry. The Harry Potter brand and its related media texts, however, are broad and complex enough to involve a number of much smaller, upstart companies as well. For instance, although Entertainment Arts published the first *Harry Potter and the Philosopher's Stone* computer game, it was developed by a group of much smaller companies, including one company founded by a British high school student in 1982, Argonaut Games.

POST-FORDISM AND CHANGES IN REGULATORY CONDITIONS

The shift from isolated media industries dominated by an oligopoly of firms to the integrated media conglomerates we know today could not have taken place in the United States without changes in the regulatory conditions that govern the broadcasting, telecommunications, and newspaper industries. Generally, these industries had been separately regulated prior to 1996, and competition among firms in different industries was forbidden. Telephone companies, for instance, could not own cable companies, and the same company could not own both a broadcaster and a newspaper in the same market. These regulations grew out of efforts to ensure competition and diversity of viewpoints in the media. Regulators worried, for instance, that a single entity owning both a newspaper and a broadcast station in the same city could control the public's access to important, unbiased news in a way that might damage democracy, as you might recall from the discussion of localism as a regulatory goal from Chapter 4.

The Telecommunications Act of 1996 removed many of the barriers to competition and cross-ownership among media and telecommunications companies operating in different industries, at the same time that it removed **ownership caps** on the number of television or radio broadcasting stations that one entity could own. Since 1996, a number of other cross-media ownership regulations have fallen as well. Today, as many of you probably know, telephone and cable companies can operate in each other's markets, with cable companies offering phone service over cable and telephone companies offering television packages over the phone lines. These changes required altering not only federal, but also state and local, regulations, which often had further jurisdiction over cable television. The **duopoly rules**, which prevented a single organization from owning more than one broadcasting station in a single market, and the TV-radio cross-ownership regulations, which prevented a company from owning both television and radio stations, were repealed in 1999. And, the **Newspaper-Broadcast Ownership Rule** was relaxed in 2007 to permit a company to own newspapers, television stations, and radio stations in the same market under certain conditions.

Each of these changes has been hotly debated, and a coalition of **media activist groups** has successfully challenged some of these decisions, some of which we covered in Chapter 4. For our present purposes, however, it is important to keep in mind two major facts: first, that the changes that have taken place in the economic conditions of the media industries could not have occurred without changes in the regulatory conditions; and second, that changes in the regulatory conditions were only possible because of larger changes in the economy and politics of the nation, specifically the economic difficulties since the 1973 oil embargo and the shift to the right in American politics in the 1970s and 1980s following the Vietnam era.

PRODUCTION AND DISTRIBUTION PRACTICES IN THE POST-FORDIST ERA

The shift from mass to niche marketing and from mass production to just-in-time mass customization has led to the development of niche media, or texts designed specifically with one segment of the audience in mind. Again, it is important to keep in mind that, although this trend existed in media industries prior to the 1980s, particularly in the radio and magazine industries, it did not become dominant across all of the media industries until much more recently, aided very much by the new economics of digital distribution. These niche media often take advantage of newly developed digital distribution methods and industry organizations, particularly globalization, to reach audiences and rework the kinds of texts that the media industries produce and the ways that they finance those texts. Thus, it is clear that all of the forces of change we address in this last section interact in their consequences upon the media industries.

As we explore in the next chapter, Joseph Turow distinguishes between what he calls **society-making media**, which are designed for all members of society, and **segment-making media**, which target only a small segment of society. The former, which were most common during the Fordist era, are characterized by their broad appeal and their inoffensiveness to most of the public. On the other hand, these kinds of texts have been critiqued as not terribly captivating or interesting. Niche media, by contrast, aim to be highly appealing to members of the target group, but of little interest and even offensive to people beyond that audience segment. Early gangsta rap music offers a good example. Coming into prominence in the late 1980s with such artists as NWA and Ice T, as well as Dr. Dre's label, Death Row Records, the sexual, violent, and (to some) offensive lyrics of gangsta rap drew immediate criticism from parental watchdog groups which in turn, not surprisingly, increased the popularity of the genre with certain teenage fans. Though an underground musical movement with deep roots in African-American urban life at the time, gangsta rap became popular with teenage and young adult listeners around the country and, eventually, across the globe. The major record labels were heavily involved in grooming and popularizing the genre, including Warner Music, which carried one of the pioneers of the genre, Ice T, and acquired Death Row Records in the mid-1990s.[9]

Part of the reason that niche media like gangsta rap have become prevalent is that they can deliver **pure demographics** to media outlets and advertisers. "Pure demographics" refers to segments of the audience that are relatively absent of members of other demographic groups. This purity is important because it helps corporations build consistent brand identities. Imagine, for instance, how suburban teenagers might have reacted to gangsta rap if their grandparents, too, had been fans. Media texts and genres that can establish clear taste boundaries among demographic groups are said to have **edge**. Not all media industries seek edgy media texts under all conditions, however. Instead, media corporations, particularly the major ones, carry a combination of both edgy and broad-appeal programming, or they own media outlets that reach a variety of narrowly defined groups. At the same time that Warner Bros. music was busy popularizing gangsta rap, for instance, its television production wing was producing such general-appeal programming as *The Fresh Prince of Bel-Air*. Or, think of the range of cable channels owned by Viacom: Nickelodeon, MTV, Spike, and TVLand. Each channel targets a very particular, yet different, segment of the audience. The dual strategy of focusing on both society- and segment-making media is an example of how media conglomerates continue to hold on to the programming and distribution practices of the past in an effort to minimize the financial risks of new economic and technological conditions. It also demonstrates how, despite much of their rhetoric, most large media organizations are not leaders of new media trends, but followers.

As we have already mentioned, the trend toward niche media is largely a product of changes in the advertising industry, the needs of business in the new economic order, and new technological conditions that made new distribution and exhibition practices profitable. In particular, new forms of distribution and exhibition/retail have led to an abundance of media texts that once were much scarcer. Magazines stands, for instance, have become crowded with titles that, as we've mentioned, are often remarkably similar to one another. Researchers have found that most magazine-stand customers glance at a cover for about ten seconds, during which time the cover must signal who its primary audience is, distinguish itself from its nearby competition, and convince the buyer to purchase it. As the costs of magazine publishing and distribution have declined, the number and variety of titles has exploded, increasing the number of competitors and requiring magazine publishers to seek smaller and smaller niches. One publisher in the 1990s, for instance, explored whether women golfers constituted a distinct and large enough demographic to warrant a magazine of their own.[10] Other media industries have seen similar explosions in distribution and exhibition channels that have led to increased competition for the audience's attention. Edgy texts that deliver pure demographics are the industry's response to this new competitive landscape.

THE SOCIAL AND CULTURAL CONSEQUENCE
OF THE SYMBOLIC ECONOMY AND POST-FORDISM

Most observers of the media industries agree that the demands of post-Fordism and the new opportunities of the symbolic economy are reshaping the media industries' conditions and practices. Debate exists, however, over the social and cultural consequences of these changes. At one extreme, critics see a collapse of social cohesion and an erosion of creative expression; at another extreme, proponents see increasingly tailored media texts and growing flexibility and independence of media workers. As in most of these debates, we advocate a position between these two extremes. We would characterize the present moment as one in which, on balance, media workers probably have less creative control than before, while audiences have better access to more relevant media texts at the same time that their experiences, tastes, and behaviors are increasingly monitored, repackaged, and sold back to them.

One of the main debates about the media industries today has to do with social cohesion: is the trend toward differentiation of segments and media experiences undermining our shared sense of national community? And if so, do these developments weaken our nation and our democracy? Critics tend to blame all sorts of social ills—from voter apathy to poverty, racism, and even depression—on the decline of social bonds that has been facilitated by the disappearance of society-making media. In this formulation, the media industries are often cast as both a symptom and a cause of social decay. Ken Auletta, one of the best known journalists who studies the media industries, for example, argues that, despite their limitations, the national television networks, prior to the introduction of cable, offered a common set of cultural experiences that most Americans shared.[11] Some go as far as to claim that the new media environment will one day result in each of us reading our individualized version of the daily newspaper, or the *Daily Me*.[12] Michael Curtin, by contrast, insists that such shared cultural experiences were never more than a myth—that millions of Americans, including women, gays and lesbians, and African Americans, felt quite excluded from the television fantasies of yesteryear.[13] In his view, the present media landscape is merely more aware of and responsive to the divisions that have always marked American society.

While Curtin's critique is surely accurate, it is also the case that today's media audiences coalesce around a wide range of geographic designations, including the local, the regional, the national, and the transnational in ways that were impossible four decades ago, except perhaps in the magazine and radio industries. In this way, the kinds of social groupings that the media encourage extend beyond the national, to include racial, economic, political, gendered, and sexual groups, to name but a few. These new kinds of grouping can be seen as socially positive, because they can permit us to imagine and explore the links we may have to people in remote parts of the world in much more complex ways than was once possible. However, some profitable media niches are regressive, even offensive, such as white supremacist forms of black metal music, which celebrate white racial purity and Nazism.

WORKING IN THE SYMBOLIC ECONOMY

The new economy has not only altered the media texts we receive as audiences, but also the work environment of people employed in the media industries. Unionization and permanent work have decreased and **casual work** has grown as companies have tried to cut costs by hiring independent workers on a project-by-project basis. As we clarify in more detail in Chapter 11, global **outsourcing** of media jobs, made possible by the globalization of media conglomerates and the spread of high-speed telecommunications networks to many parts of the earth, has been a major driver of the changing work conditions in American media industries.

These changes have led to more **flexibility**, creative control, and higher pay for some creative workers, while others have experienced significant job insecurity and lack of creative decision-making power. Flexibility is one of those buzz words in the media industries, and business more generally, that is used to mean a lot of different things. We've used it to describe the structure of the media industries today, as well as the way we access media. Here, we refer to flexibility in employment practices, which may *sound* good at first, but has ambiguous consequences. Flexibility refers to the use of casual, contract labor, rather than full-time, unionized employees. For some workers, this can mean that they have more control over what they do and when they do it; for others, it means that unscrupulous employers can more easily exploit them. Specifically, **above-the-line** workers have enjoyed the benefits of flexibility, especially well-known actors, directors, musicians, producers, and other high-end workers, who used to be tied to long term contracts with major labels, studios, networks, and so forth. For **below-the-line workers**, these changes have meant long periods of unemployment or underemployment, such as Phil experiences as an editor at Williams Street. Workers such as Phil may earn competitive salaries when they are working; but others have seen a decline in their real wages since the days of unionization ended.[14] Still, new talent continues to stream in to media industry jobs every day. Media industries prefer casual employment (as opposed to contract workers on salary) because it allows them to directly link costs with textual production. Often, casual workers do not receive the same benefits as contract workers, such as health insurance, retirement contributions, or wages for sick and vacation time.

Many media and media-related jobs today have a good deal of appeal, as well as their share of drudgery. From computer software development to gaming to animation, many companies offer flexible work hours, good pay, and a relaxed work atmosphere, sometimes featuring workout facilities and other desirable perks. In return, however, the fun atmosphere of work requires employees to work **crunch time**, a period of intense work that lasts sometimes more than two weeks and longer, during which time people work as much as eighteen hours a day and some even sleep at work. Crunch time is necessary in some instances because inexperienced companies underestimate how long certain production-related tasks might take. On the other hand, Nick Dyer-Witheford and Greig de Peuter find evidence that even experienced companies make routine use of crunch time merely as a way to lower costs, because their workers are paid on salary, not hourly wages.[15] Crunch time occurs in all of these industries and makes it difficult for employees to have a life outside work, particularly as they grow older, get married, and start families. For these reasons, employees in these kinds of industries tend to be overwhelmingly young and male.

In news media, by contrast, the changes of post-Fordism have led to similar kinds of casual work as well as the tendency to rely on single reporters to write, shoot, and edit their own stories. Because of the ubiquity of computers and computer skills, as well as the shift to digital media production, one or two reporters can now, reasonably, complete work that used to rely on a camera crew, a writer, and a reporter, as well as an editing and post-production crew. Of course, the quality of the reporting under these conditions is a legitimate concern, as are the jobs of people who work behind the scenes and below the line in television news.

Again, as with everything else in this chapter, we are dealing with industries in transition, and some aspects of work in some media industries have changed very little, while other kinds of jobs are gone or irrevocably changed. We have no crystal ball with which to look into the future of media industry work. If current trends continue, however, we should see increasing outsourcing, growing casualization, increasing wage disparities between above-the-line and below-the-line workers, and the continuation of crunch time and periods of unemployment in most industries, as freelance workers finish one project and seek out the next or permanent employees are briefly laid off between projects.

CONCLUSION

Large-scale changes in the way that the economy operates have profound consequences everywhere, including the media industries. While today's media environment is characterized by tailored media products, global multimedia conglomerates, deregulation, flexible work arrangements, casualization of the labor force, and increased consumer surveillance, these changes are extensions of earlier historical processes rather than a radical break with the past. Moreover, these changes are fundamentally tied to economic change, not to technological changes such as the growth of Internet access and digitization, though these changes certainly helped facilitate the economic changes we are witnessing.

Often, for those of us who have seen our media options expand and who now enjoy greater control over where and when we consume media, it is sometimes hard to see the potential downsides to the current media environment. Unlike a democratic media system, however, which would expand everyone's access and choices, a commercial media system still values the most lucrative audiences over others, particularly young, well-off consumers with large disposable incomes. Moreover, the price of increased media choice is decreased privacy. Perhaps the most troubling aspect of this decreased privacy is that few of us are aware of just how much information we give away and how much companies today know about us. Conveniences like a home DVR or digital cable box can also record and store information about which shows we record; which we watch; which ads we skip and which we watch; when we fast-forward, rewind, and pause; and much, much more. We, in fact, give media service providers permission to collect this information when we order the service and sign their privacy policies.

The remainder of the forces of change that we explore in this section—digitization and globalization—are both related to these large-scale economic changes. Post-Fordism is arguably the most advanced of these forces of change, meaning post-Fordist economic operations have been most thoroughly integrated into the conventional operation of the media industries. Thus, in many cases it is difficult to determine discrete adjustments of digitization and globalization, as each often incorporates aspects of the post-Fordist practices emerging over the last three decades.

QUESTIONS

1. Consider a media text that you consume often. In what ways does it reflect—through its content, production, and so forth—the adoption of post-Fordist principles? Can you explain why it is the product of an industry in the symbolic economy?
2. Why couldn't the changes that have taken place in the economic conditions of the media industries during post-Fordism have occurred without changes in the regulatory conditions?
3. Think about a media text that you believe would be characterized as niche. Why do you believe it is niche instead of broad-appeal? How does it create edge? What pure demographics do you think it delivers to media outlets and advertisers? Conversely, think of a broad-appeal text and explain why it does not have edge and what sort of demographics it delivers.
4. We described debates about the cultural and social consequences of the symbolic economy and post-Fordism. Do you believe the consequence is that the trend toward differentiation of segments and media experiences undermines our shared sense of national community? And if so, is that necessarily a bad thing? In what ways might the consequences be culturally and socially positive? Similarly, given our discussion about crunch time, flexibility, outsourcing, and so forth, do you feel the consequences on work life and opportunities is positive or negative?

FURTHER READINGS

For general overviews on post-Fordism, the symbolic economy, and the media industries, see David Harvey's *The Condition of Postmodernity: An Enquiry into the Origins of Cultural Change* (Oxford: Blackwell, 1989); Sharon Zukin's *The Cultures of Cities* (Cambridge, Mass.: Blackwell, 1995); and Michael Curtin, "On Edge:

Culture Industries in the Neo-Network Era," in *Making and Selling Culture*, ed. Richard Ohmann (Hanover, N.H.: Wesleyan University Press, 1996), 181–202.

For discussion of post-Fordism in particular media industries, see in *film*: S. Christopherson and M. Storper's "The City as Studio; The World as Back Lot: The Impact of Vertical Disintegration on the Location of the Motion Picture Industry," *Society and Space*, 4 (1986), 305–320; and Asu Aksoy and Kevin Robins' "Hollywood for the 21st Century: Global Competition for Critical Mass in Image Markets," *Cambridge Journal of Economics*, 16 (1992), 1–22; and, in *music*: David Hesmondhalgh's "Flexibility, Post-Fordism, and the Music Industry," *Media, Culture & Society*, 18 (1996), 469–488.

NOTES

1. David Paul Nord, "The Ironies of Communication Technology: Why Predictions of the Future Often Go Wrong," *Cresset*, 49 (March 1986), 9–20, 9.
2. We rely here on David Hesmondhalgh's (2001) revision of William's original terminology, which replaced what Williams called the "corporate professional" era with the phrase "complex professional." This revised terminology is an effort to de-emphasize the importance of the modern corporation in the era, and to play up the importance of the complexity of organization life in the present era, which was Williams' main concern. David Hesmondhalgh, *The Cultural Industries* (London: Sage, 2002).
3. Hesmondhalgh, *The Cultural Industries*, 2002.
4. David Harvey uses the phrase "post-Fordism" in *The Condition of Postmodernity: An Enquiry into the Origins of Cultural Change* (Cambridge and Oxford: Blackwell, 1989); David Hesmondhalgh uses the phrase "The Long Downturn" in *The Cultural Industries* (London: Sage, 2002); and Scott Lash and John Urry use the phrase "Economies of Signs and Space" in *Economies of Signs and Space*. (London: Sage, 1996.)
5. David Hesmondhalgh, "Flexibility, Post-Fordism, and the Music Industry," *Media, Culture & Society*, 18 (1996), 469–488.
6. Michael Curtin, "On Edge: Culture Industries in the Neo-Network Era," in *Making and Selling Culture*, ed. Richard Ohmann (Hanover, N.H.: Wesleyan University Press, 1996), 181–202.
7. Eileen Meehan, "Holy Commodity Fetish, Batman! The Political Economy of the Commercial Intertext," *The Many Lives of the Bat-Man*, ed. Roberta E. Pearson and William Uricchio (New York: BFI-Routledge, 1991), 47–55.
8. Electronic Arts Inc., United States Securities & Exchange Commission 10-K filing, March 31, 2009, EDGAR Online (accessed Sep. 17, 2010).
9. Curtin, "On Edge", 181–202.
10. Ibid.
11. Ken Auletta, *Three Blind Mice: How the TV Networks Lost Their Way* (New York: Random House, 1991).

12. Fred Hapgood, "The Media Lab at 10," *Wired*, 3, no. 11 (Nov. 1995), http://www.wired.com/wired/archive/3.11/media.html (accessed Sep. 1, 2010).

13. See note 9 above.

14. Gillian Ursell, "Working in the Media," in *Media Production*, ed. David Hesmondhalgh (Berkshire, England, and New York: Open University Press, 2006).

15. Nick Dyer-Witheford and Greig de Peuter, "'EA Spouse' and the Crisis of Video Game Labour: Enjoyment, Exclusion, Exploitation, Exodus," *Canadian Journal of Communication*, 31(2006), 599–617.

CHAPTER 10

—

Digitization

The modern recording industry can trace its origins to the late 1890s. In their desire for musical entertainment at home, people purchased wind-up music boxes and player pianos before the advent of the record player and its growing accessibility at the end of the nineteenth century. Over the last century, many fundamental aspects of the recording industry have remained the same, although the delivery technology by which favorite songs and artists reached eager listeners evolved from records, to tapes, and finally to compact discs. The most recent evolution of that history—the availability of digital music files—has introduced far greater consequences to the operation of the recording industry.

Although compact discs are also a digital format, this delivery technology largely continued the norms of industry operation because they still required the transfer of music to a physical form that record labels manufactured and then distributed to stores around the world. The digital music file, and its online retailers such as iTunes, substantially disrupted these norms of distribution in the recording industry. Economic models had to be reassessed as substantial manufacturing, distribution, and shelving costs were eliminated as listeners embraced the ability to purchase individual tracks instead of complete "albums," which had dominated music distribution in previous delivery technologies. Divorcing the sale of recorded music from a physical form (a technological condition) also made it much more difficult for the recording industry to manage its circulation, and the relatively small size of audio files made illegal sharing over the Internet rampant (a regulatory condition with economic consequences). The sale of physical forms of music still remains substantial. In 2009, the Recording Industry Association of America (RIAA) reported that digital downloading accounted for 41 percent of total music shipments (obviously, this does not factor in illegal downloading).[1] The quick increase in this means of distribution has made the industry well aware that a new era of operation is upon it.

* * *

A development that may be the single most revolutionary event in the operations of all media industries has occurred in your lifetime. By the time you were old enough to use media on your own, this revolution had already swept in, so it is likely that you don't even recall what it was like to use media before this monumental shift. Perhaps older siblings or your parents have told you tales of the challenging nature of the "bad old" days of media use before modern conveniences and capabilities. We are speaking, of course, of the wide-ranging consequences wrought upon media industries by **digitization.**

In terms of the "forces of change" discussed in this section, digitization is not as far along as the transition to a symbolic economy that we explored in the last chapter. Nevertheless, it is most certainly here, and we've already noted many examples of the changes it is bringing to media industry operations throughout the book. While all media industries have experienced some adjustments in their established operations, few have figured out what the new norms of their industries will be. A wide variety of experiments can be found across media industries as they struggle to innovate and respond to the new ways audiences—enabled by this massive change in technological conditions—seek to access and engage their products. It is likely that all of the disruption to established media operations by digitization have not even been realized, as the capacity of digital networks continue to expand.

UNDERSTANDING THE DIFFERENCE
OF DIGITAL MEDIA

But what is digitization? Or more precisely, what distinguishes digital media—since chances increasingly are good that you aren't really sure why anyone would make the distinction of saying a "digital" camera instead of just calling it a camera, since digital versions of cameras and other technologies have rapidly become the norm? Digitization refers to a technical process or a technical specification describing the way media are recorded and/or transmitted; digital media are those media that translate the content of media—be it images or sound—into digital code, a language of ones and zeroes. This digital language has many advantages, particularly that it uses space efficiently, maintains quality, and operates as a common language that allows different types of machines to speak to one another. It is difficult to overstate the ways in which digitization is changing media, as it has (and continues to have) enormous consequences to the degree that it has created new media industries and irreversibly altered the operations of "old" media.

Although this elaboration may be decreasingly relevant, allow us to say a few words about analog media in order to make the distinction of digital clearer. Media using an **analog** method of recording store signals in a manner that represents the message using an "analog," or direct facsimile, of the original. To explain the concept, Dominick, Sherman, and Messere, encourage us to: "Think of the grooves in a phonographic record. As the needle travels through the grooves, it vibrates in a pattern similar to the vibrations made by the guitar string or vocal cords it represents."[2] In the case of analog tape media, this "analogy" of the original is created through a process of magnetizing the tape in patterns that represent the audio or visual signal. Film works because chemical changes in photographic film are altered by light exposure so that a representation of the image in front of the camera appears on the film. In all of these cases, receiving the message on the media form—whether tape or film—required a machine that could decode the analog language, such as a record needle, the heads of a tape player that read the magnetic coatings, or the chemical developing process for producing a film negative.

There are strengths and weaknesses to both analog and digital recording. In terms of media industry operation, analog had considerable limitations. For one, analog recording requires transfer to a physical medium (such as a tape, film, or paper). Because they are tied to a physical form, analog media take up considerable space, which requires more storage resources for producers and limits users by decreasing portability. Early videotape, for instance, required nearly twenty miles of tape to record a single hour of programming and required large vaults for storing originals. Or, remember how little music you could conveniently carry with you when you had to carry CDs (although already a digital improvement over tapes) compared with the volume of music you carry in a digital player. From an industrial perspective, this is an attribute that adds expense to production, because it necessitates the creation of this physical medium (which has some per unit cost) and adds costs associated with transporting it to consumers and shelving it in a retail location.

Degradation of quality is another limitation of analog media—although this is significant in different ways to media users than media industries. A common practice among media studies teachers in the analog era was to share videotapes, as it was easy to make a copy of another's tapes to gain access to recordings not available for commercial purchase. The quality of the recording, however, was always notably decreased from the original, which prevented this from being particularly useful in comparison with the pristine quality of digital copies that lose nothing in their transfer. This limitation of analog media was actually quite valuable to media industries, as it decreased the attractiveness of making, illegally selling, or otherwise circulating copies.

For those of us who knew the analog age, though, probably the main advantage of digital media that we appreciate each and every day is the interconnection among our technologies enabled by digital recording. As we noted, digital code operates as a common language across many machines that could not speak to each other in the analog age. The common digital language allows digital television recorders, computers, and audio recording devices to all speak to each other, while digital media also enable the distribution of information over the Internet, allowing for quick and "perfect" transmission of a media product without physical transportation.

Convergence is often the word used to describe the new connections among media enabled by digitization, first in terms of technical language, but increasingly in terms of media products and the media industries themselves. Convergence can refer to many different aspects of media industries, and it is a term used with varying specificity. Sometimes, convergence refers to the coming together of cultural or technological forms, such as the convergence of television and the Internet evident in online streaming and distribution. Sometimes, convergence is used in place of conglomeration to reference the coming together of once discrete media industries or corporations. And, sometimes, convergence indicates the merging of communication systems—as in the instance of cable providers offering Internet and phone services. Media scholar Henry Jenkins, a leading thinker in this area, deliberately reminds us that convergence is more than a technological process. He argues that convergence also "represents a cultural shift as consumers are encouraged to seek out new information and make connections among dispersed media content."[3] This insight is important for media industries because it suggests that particular strategies—such as those that enable personalized experiences with media—have increased value in the age of digital media.

Another important insight from Jenkins is of the difference between **delivery technologies** such as tapes, CDs, or MP3 files that facilitate the distribution of media content, and *media* such as recorded sound, printed words, or visual images. By making a distinction between delivery technologies and media, Jenkins gives us language that helps us avoid **technological determinism** and stops us from dwelling on silly assertions—such as the notion that introduction of new media will "kill off" existing media. As we've seen countless times now, radio did not kill the newspaper, television did not kill radio or cinema, and so on. Rather, in each case—and as we see now—new delivery technologies can make existing delivery technologies obsolete or require reconfiguration, but the media themselves persist.

The existing media industries often must make substantial adjustments in their norms and operations to respond to new delivery systems—as was the case for radio after the introduction of television. As more and more homes purchased televisions, established radio shows transferred to the new medium (as radio was much like television today, distributed over a national network with an evening schedule of comedies and dramas). Certainly, few who had the choice to listen to *and* watch their favorite stories would want to settle for radio alone. Subsequently, the network era of radio ended, as the networking of content dissolved and was replaced by an emphasis on locally operated stations featuring music or talk. The radio industry rebuilt itself on attributes that distinguish it from television, particularly that people can listen while doing something else (with emphasis on creating portable radios and introducing it to cars) and as a more locally specific form. Half a decade after its predicted death, radio lives on.

You can likely think of countless examples of the convenience that sharing a common digital language provides. One that springs quickly to mind for us is the realization that it would have been much more tedious if we had been writing this book together a mere fifteen years ago. In a digital age, we can quickly trade drafts back and forth over the Internet—editing and reviewing each other's work effectively in real time. In the era before digital distribution channels (we'll at least assume the existence of computers; even we can't imagine having to retype everything on a typewriter), one of us would have to finish a draft, print it out, and mail it to the other. Digitization produces consequences for many aspects of media industry operation, but its enhancement of the ability to separate a media product from its physical form and transport it to any wired location in the world in seconds (building on the revolution of telegraphy, telephony, and broadcasting before it) may be the most substantial that we've realized to this point.

Given the big role digitization likely plays in your own life, imagine what it has done to the media industries. This chapter explores both the ways digitization has changed media industries that had established norms of operation as analog media as well as the broad range of "new" media industries that have developed as a result of the opportunities digitization allows. We certainly can't address all of the effects, nor have all the consequences of digitization emerged. As is the case with the topics covered in other chapters in this section, digital recording and transmission is a central cause of adjustment and developing change for media industries.

The implications of digitization are also much greater than those evident here. We particularly focus our discussion upon the consequences of digitization for the operation of media industries, but it also adjusts commercial practices in many industries and even the operation of governments. We approach this chapter more from the perspective of media industries than the standpoint of the individual user/consumer, although we do address the experiences of users in the final pages of the chapter. Digital media may seem common and conventional to you today, but in truth, the so-called "new media" industries enabled by their creation are still relatively emergent and have not yet established the conventions of operation that allow us to develop sophisticated and coherent understandings of their behaviors in the same way that the longer duration of other media industries allows. It is also the case that norms continue to evolve very quickly in the new media industries, which makes it inevitable that some of what we address will be outdated before this book even is printed. This chapter consequently pays considerable attention to how digitization challenges norms of operation established for the analog era and is a bit more tentative in some of its assertions and claims in discussing new media than it is when explaining the operation of media industries that have refined their norms over decades. One of our goals in creating the Industrialization of Culture framework is that it serves as a relevant tool in just these instances, as a way to guide you through the salient aspects of the operation of emergent industries, or to help you understand the differences in a single industry before and after the introduction of digital technologies.

The remainder of the chapter attempts to cover the breadth of digital change by subdividing into areas of production, distribution, and consumer use. Although this provides a convenient way of introducing some order to a vast topic, we must be clear that the significant consequences of digitization result because of the intertwined nature of these areas. In other words, the shifts in production introduced by digitization are sizable alone, but in combination with digital distribution, these effects increase exponentially.

DIGITIZATION AND SHIFTS IN PRODUCTION

The transition from analog recording and distribution of media to digital techniques has had considerable consequences for the production norms of media industries. Many of these changes have been gradual and been experienced by various industries on different timelines. It is difficult to address all of the potential adjustments wrought by digitization on any single industry—let alone all of them—as in many cases, digital technologies have substantially reconfigured even the most mundane and particular of operations, such as revolutionizing special effects work in video media or radically changing the workforce needed to publish a newspaper. Instead we focus more on broad practices that are likely relevant to many media industries.

Some consistency in consequences can be seen if we organize media industries in terms of whether they are primarily print, audio, or video media, because the associated technological differences and requirements of these media provide various lessons and indicate different levels of integration of digital development. For example, the technological tools required by print are minimal compared with video, and the size of the digital file means that print has had easy digital distribution for some time, while this is a fairly new development for video (with audio falling somewhere in between in both necessary technology and file size). Consequently, at the moment we write, newspapers and magazines are facing different trials than music and video industries and are at a different stage in working through new capabilities and challenges. Similarly, the struggles the recording industry experienced with file sharing and adjusted distribution models during the early 2000s were not a concern for video-based media until later that decade, but now the film and television industries face these challenges as well. It is difficult to know at this still early moment in the digital revolution whether all media will follow a similar path or if there will be significant long-term difference in the adjustments wrought by digitization for these media.

Print

It is a combination of production and distribution adjustments that have particularly affected print industries. For many consumers, the nature of their use of print media has changed because digital technologies enable instantaneous update and delivery of content, although online access to print media does not neatly replace use of the original print source. Consider the situation of most local papers. In terms of pre-Internet competition with other media, one of the biggest limitations was the paper's tendency to get "scooped," since it could only deliver information once a day, while radio and television could offer live news or newscasts updated at intervals throughout the day. An Internet version of that paper allows it to break stories and share information throughout the day.

A key challenge print media have faced in adapting to new digital capabilities has been figuring out the relationship between their online and print content and what economic strategy to use during a period with considerable uncertainty. Many of us expect to pay for our print versions of print media, including the newspapers that arrive at our door in the morning or the magazines we receive in the mail or purchase at kiosks. As the Internet has enabled print media to have online versions, however, many of us expect to click on links or search and read stories for no cost at all. Although the online version does not have the expense of the paper and physical distribution of the print version, there are still costs involved in its creation. Many print media titles have struggled to develop a profitable Internet strategy as it has grown increasingly necessary to make content available in this form, yet advertisers have not moved into the online space with fees adequate to support new costs or fully compensate for the decreasing readership of the physical form. In the previous moments of transition, established media have been able to use existing media to help fund the nascent form during broad-scale adoption. For example, CBS was able to fund its early years in television from the ongoing revenues of its still successful radio network. The extent to which the emergence of digital technologies would disrupt existing economic models and business practices caught the print and music industries before they had established viable alternatives. The television and film industries have had more time to develop strategies and to learn from other industries' mistakes, but it remains to be seen if they will do so.

The competitive arena of print media is also changing because of competition from "print" media that don't have a physical version—and it remains difficult to evaluate the impact of these new journalistic outlets. On one hand, some note that "amateur" news and commentary outlets may now compete with "traditional" media, but that online media still only reach a subset of the population. A chart in Chris Anderson's book *The Long Tail*, shown in Figure 10.1, shows blogs, including Boing Boing and Engadget, were more popular (based on incoming links from other sites) than many established media sites, including PBS and CBS News, although the established media brands of the *New York Times*, CNN, and *Washington Post* still dominated.[4]

Yet, in some cases, web-based journalistic outlets and blogs are breaking news or drawing more readers than the online version of long established print media. It is important to realize that the number of readers isn't the only relevant way of measuring how blogs and other variations of new journalism produce important consequences for the media industries. We now witness constant examples of news being broken on sometimes-obscure amateur media; the news is then picked up and covered extensively by traditional media; for example, when you see CNN noting that "The Drudge Report (or even just "Online sources") reports...", as happened repeatedly during the 2008 presidential race. Such developments indicate the importance of considering the many ways the easy production of "print" media in the digital era can affect media industry operation.

While some observers are optimistic about the possibility for a greater diversity of voices in journalism in an era when "anyone can be a publisher," we need more time to assess what really is happening as a result. The truth is that very few of these new publishers break through to a large readership, and it is also worth exploring how expanded popularity of an amateur media outlet requires it to evolve and whether it takes on characteristics of "traditional" media in that process. In other words, as amateur productions increase in scale to the point

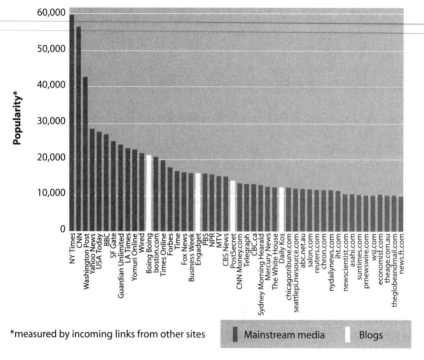

*measured by incoming links from other sites

Mainstream media   **Blogs**

Figure 10.1 Mainstream media and blogs compete for attention online.

that they become more than vanity projects, it is important to assess whether they maintain industrial aspects that differentiate them from conventional media industries. For example, when the news and commentary blog the *Huffington Post* launched in May 2005, it was largely run out of the home of its founder, Arianna Huffington, (granted, it was a mansion) and its operations likely differed considerably from established media entities. A little over a year after its launch, it had secured $5 million in venture funding to expand its staff, and it raised $15 million by November 2008 as it moved into local news and investigative journalism, seeking to be the "Internet newspaper."[5] Such funding and success, though, may have also led it to operate more like the traditional media industries it once contrasted.

Audio

Digitization has had significant implications for the recording industry—as a result of changes in both production and distribution. Joseph Turow explains that considerable fragmentation in production has occurred, partly because digital technologies have made professional digital recording technology more accessible.[6] He notes that studio rates—the cost for time in the recording studio—which typically ran as much as $50,000 for an album, have been cut in half in recent years because of the greater competition spurred by affordable, professional-quality equipment.[7] Some emerging artists can even create decent-quality recordings in basement studios for much less.

These decreases in the costs of professional or near-professional recordings have significant implications for aiding those who are trying to break into the recording industry. Paired with the possibilities that the digital distribution of music enables, entirely new routes into the recording industry are being created, even if at this point, those routes still seems to lead to the established recording studios for many artists who ultimately achieve "success." The availability of decent, affordable digital audio production technologies (paired with do-it-yourself distribution such as MySpace) has revolutionized the common methods for finding new artists. In the last few years, it has become increasingly common for record label executives to find new artists by trolling MySpace and the artists' websites to hear samples of their work (as opposed to searching out new acts in bars, coffeehouses, and small venues). Many artists (such as Ingrid Michaelson, Lily Allen, the Arctic Monkeys) have broken onto the national scene after signing with labels that found them online, although stories about artists breaking into the top of the charts off of MySpace (without a label) seem largely mythic at this point.

Video

Think about the visual difference in the films and television shows that dominate industry production now in comparison with those of the 1980s and before. Digital technologies account for many of the differences—particularly the wide range of what were once most certainly considered "special effects" that are now increasingly commonplace. The development of high-quality digital recording technologies that could be merged with digital editing effectively created entirely new universes for visual storytelling, all with much better quality and at a fraction of the cost of older effects efforts. Or, consider the refinement in videogame images. The latest versions of games are stunningly realistic and appear far removed from predecessors such as Pong or Pac-Man, as evident in Figure 10.2. Digital technologies shape advances in gaming production as well.

In fact, television scholar John Caldwell argues that the development of various digital technologies as well as a changing competitive environment (or economic conditions in our terms) were responsible for fundamental shifts in the aesthetics of television.[8] He coined the term "televisuality" to describe the new attention to aesthetic style that became increasingly de rigueur for television shows beginning in the 1980s. Much of this style—everything from the sophisticated graphics and crawls that now commonly fill our screens to television shows that approximate the production values of studio films—owes its existence to a digital technology. More recent television storytelling has expanded these early moves of the 1980s. Shows such as *Heroes*, *Lost*, and many others rely heavily on worlds created on computers instead of in front of the camera.

This is most certainly true in film as well. Consider that the film *Lord of the Rings* (2001) used computer animation for more than 1,000 separate shots, a total of 70 percent of the film.[9] Such films combine "digital compositing," which blends computer generation with live actors using "motion capture" technology to create complicated visual imagery (also used in television and video games). This shift

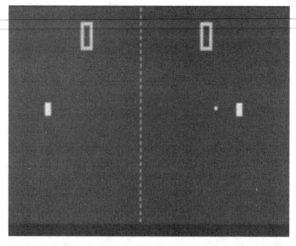

Figure 10.2 Refinement of digital imagery in video games. An image from Pong versus 2010's Red Dead Redemption.

has had significant implications for the type of labor involved in filmmaking and the budgets of contemporary films. For example, George Lucas' original 1977 *Star Wars* lists 143 graphic technicians in the credits while his 2003 *Attack of the Clones* prequel required 572.[10]

As in the cases of both digital print and audio technologies, new capabilities have reached the amateur video producer that allow for the creation of what was near-professional grade video just a few years ago at affordable costs. Digital video shooting and editing is increasingly a basic form of expression familiar to many of our students, and it is hard to believe that little over a decade ago, college editing classes involved the cutting and splicing of tape. Basic computer software packages routinely include applications that allow casual users to create audio/visual products that rival those of professionals in a previous era. As we note above, the production of professional video has also changed as result of these technologies (which does enable the perpetuation of this gap), but it is a significant development that video production tools are now accessible to a greater variety of creators.

The wider availability of audiovisual production tools has helped fuel global outsourcing, a development that we look at more closely in the next chapter.

Outsourcing, in turns, alters both the production practices and economic conditions of the industry. A case in point is contemporary animation. Animation is a time-consuming and labor-intensive process that requires the creation of thousands of images, backgrounds, and objects. Consequently, a good deal of this heavy lifting is subcontracted to foreign countries where workers earn significantly less than in the United States, particularly India. Outsourcing is made possible by two recent developments: first, the spread of cheap computers and computer storage, which makes it feasible for companies in the countries to create the massive digital audiovisual files that animation requires; and second, the development of high-speed digital networks, which allow those large files to be transferred back and forth between the originating and outsourcing nations. These developments allow the production houses to retain close supervision of the production process, including making decisions and corrections along the way, even while the physical production occurs thousands of miles away.[11]

Because of developments like the global outsourcing of animation, we are perhaps more skeptical than those who forecast an amateur revolution and overthrow of traditional media industries as a result of access to production tools. Still, it is important to acknowledge the growing coexistence of amateur and professional media content and the significant role digital production and distribution capabilities have had in enabling these developments. While amateur production may not overthrow the established media industries, it does provide new routes into industry work that may begin to change the make-up of the industry. At the least, the work of amateurs may challenge industry workers to imagine their work in new ways.

DIGITIZATION AND SHIFTS IN DISTRIBUTION

As we saw in Chapter 7, distribution encompasses the activities and processes involved in transporting the completed media product from its site of production to the audiences who seek to consume it. In the case of many media industries, this traditionally involved transferring—often to paper, vinyl, tape, or disk—the contents of the media product, and then physically transporting it to a store. Once at the store the product would sit on a shelf until someone came to purchase it. Digital technologies introduce many tools for eliminating various inefficiencies in this process.

Digital technologies eliminate the need to transfer the product into a physical form as well as the need for a "bricks and mortar" store for displaying and transacting sales. Much of the waste of the analog era developed from the uncertainty surrounding the likely success of a product relative to the efficiency of creating many physical copies at a single moment in time. For example, a record label or book publisher would want to "run" a number of copies all at once without knowing what sales might be like. Often, they guessed wrong (remember the problem of "nobody knows" explained in Chapter 1) and were left with thousands of copies. In another case, consider the film industry's need to make thousands of copies of a film for it to open in theaters nationwide on the same day—a strategy used to maximize its promotional strategy. In 2003, the average cost of making prints for a studio film was $4.2 million.[12]

Digital technologies introduce two solutions for this: 1) they eliminate the need for physical copies, and 2) they enable the efficient production of limited, small runs of products. The music industry provides the best illustration of the first solution. Digital technologies have enabled those who so desire to have music collections without any physical copy. Listeners can create vast libraries of music simply through downloading music from online retailers. This is similarly the case of formerly "print" industries such as magazines and newspapers. Now readers can call up stories of interest and read them in their entirety without printing a single piece of paper.

In some cases—music, magazines, and newspapers—media consumers have willingly forgone the physical version of media products in exchange for the convenience and quick and ready access provided digitally. In some cases, users have not had a choice, as in the many newspapers that have shifted to online-only versions in recent years in response to the failing economics of their previous business models in the era of digital media. Other industries have not yet seen that willingness to trade delivery technologies—for one, the book industry (although perhaps that too is about to change with the introduction of more friendly technology). Digital media, however, also provide media industries with strategies that aid the distribution of physical media as well; both the music and book industries have particularly benefited from the second solution noted above. Because of the convenient storage of digital information and the purity of new copies, these industries can now "print" to order.

It is hard to say which is the more significant change: the elimination of the creation of physical media products, or the adjustments in these industries that result from not needing a physical place to exhibit and sell them. Chris Anderson, the *Wired* magazine editor who proposed the term **"long tail"** to describe the shift in distribution practices related to online media, has done most of the thinking on this second aspect.[13] The long tail describes the slope to the curve of graphing **Pareto's principle**—also known as the "80/20 rule," which shows that in most industries, 80 percent of the profits are made from 20 percent of the products. (See Figure 10.3.) In the case of media industries, this illustrates the value media industries can find outside of the blockbuster hits that have dominated industry operation in other eras. The peak of the slope illustrates the very few products purchased by vast mass audiences. At the other end of the slope is the long tail, or the many products that are purchased only by a few. Although few purchase any one of these products, the many titles/albums/etc. purchased by a few add up.

Anderson argues that digital distribution—and the savings that come from not having to maintain brick-and-mortar stores, having efficient ways to search for products, and, in some cases, not having to manufacture physical copies of products—significantly shift economic strategies of media industries away from blockbusters and toward niche products. (See Figure 10.4.) Anderson draws on

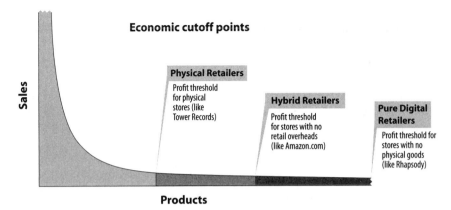

Figure 10.3 Slope of available goods from different types of media retailers (from *The Long Tail*).

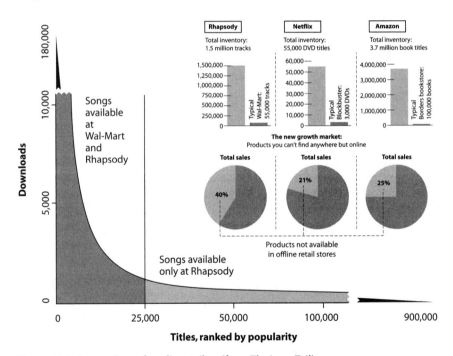

Figure 10.4 Comparison of media retailers (from *The Long Tail*).

various data that suggest that the **Fordist** tendency toward mass culture, which we addressed in the previous chapter, resulted from the inefficiencies of delivering niche products that digital distribution enables. Amazon.com's automated book suggestions and the music available at iTunes are good counter examples of more efficient, **post-Fordist** distribution practices (although Anderson relies on the online music distributor Rhapsody in his illustration).

Anderson's theory of the long tail for media industry products continues to be tested as new media industries mature and old media adjust their practices. In many cases, it remains too early to commit concrete new practices to print, as it is still unclear how these industries will continue to evolve. Anderson recently augmented his argument about digital distribution by posing a new economic model—that of giving away content for free—as the future of media industries—as mentioned in the conclusion of Chapter 5.[14] He imagines how many of the direct pay media industries might reconstruct their economic practices to be more profitable by giving away content or enabling certain services while deriving greater economic value from others; for example, it might be more profitable for theaters to eliminate the cost of admission to films and make money from concessions (although the theater owners already rely on this to a considerable degree), or for pop stars to give away their music (as they do in China) and profit instead from public appearance fees or advertisements. At the core of his argument is the assertion that "information wants to be free." Anderson's solution, then, is to give it away in cases where there is no marginal cost (cost for the creation of another unit)—as is the case when products are distributed digitally—but to charge for physical copies in the cases users want them, or by converting users from a basic free version to a premium paid version. In this strategy, users can do certain things for free, but to engage with the full array of capabilities, need to pay a fee—typically a subscription.[15] For example, the professional networking website LinkedIn (sort of a Facebook for executives) is free if you just want to post your profile, but requires a monthly fee in order to access information such as who clicks on your profile. Others using such "freemium" pricing tiers include Flickr, Skype, and Pandora. For Anderson, then, digitization reduces the marginal cost of media distribution to such a degree that offering "free" content might become a viable economic strategy.

This leads to one of the key challenges that media industries face as a result of digital distribution—namely, **piracy** or other means of circumventing the established economic model by illegally sharing or circulating media in violation of **copyright**. Again, those core attributes of the products that media industries create—such as their "public" nature and the way that one person's "use" does not "use up" the product—lead this to be particularly challenging. All of the advantages of digital distribution in terms of convenience for users have amplified the problems associated with maintaining copyright and legal circulation of these products.

The established media industries in many cases seek to maintain the same terms of payment and use that supported them in the analog era. While generally willing to create routes of digital distribution for paying customers, they are eager to make sure that allowing such distribution does not enable illegal sharing. The basic properties of digitization make this difficult. As you'll recall, the quality of the product is much more easily maintained with digital copying, and many of these products can be efficiently shared over the Internet in a matter of seconds—a phenomenon widely observed in the early days of online music downloading. In an analog era, the quality of the product degraded in the copy and required a physical form for sharing.

Understanding the dilemmas of digital distribution is complicated, as the issue involves a nexus of economic and regulatory conditions, the debate is multi-sided, and a lot of uncertainty exists regarding the consequences of both new and old ways of operating. In one corner are many of the old media industries (particularly the recording industry) that have detailed economic models and practices built on pre-digital distribution norms. These industries would happily expand their profitability by adding revenue from digital distribution, as long as they can replace each dollar they lose from the sale of physical products in the digital market. In another corner, you have new media-industry entrepreneurs who seek to use tools of digital production and distribution to remake these industries by taking advantage of new technological possibilities and eliminating inefficiencies built up in the old media. The consumer of media products is in yet another corner. Some want cheaper media products, while others are willing to pay, but want greater accessibility, convenience, or ease of use. Finally (although there are likely others yet), we have a disjuncture between "industry" (entities such as studios, record labels, and networks) and "artists or creators," as one of the consequences of digitization is an increased ability to make and distribute texts without industry middlemen. Some creators want a greater share of the profits that are currently taken by the industry, while others seek an environment of greater creative freedom.

The properties of digital media—such as the elimination of a physical product—require new economic and regulatory conditions, and in many cases, these new conditions have not yet taken shape. A key question remains whether digitization affects media industries in a manner different from other industries because of the particular properties of the products produced, and if so, exactly how. Many other industries could not get by without a physical version of the product they exchange, so it is reasonable to understand these developments as fairly specific to media industries.

DIGITIZATION AND CHANGES IN USE

If we consider the consequences of digitization from the perspective of established media industries, we see how challenging these developments have been, and continue to be. The spread of digitization happened despite the efforts by established media industries to maintain traditional practices and behaviors. In this case, new capabilities were largely introduced by the computing and consumer electronics industries that had less of a stake in preserving the ways of the past. The revolution we're observing couldn't have been imposed by these industries alone, however. The adoption of the new technologies by users—and their continued desire for greater convenience, choice, and control in media use—also played an important role. Any effort to imagine how the media industries of the future will operate must consider the capabilities audiences most desire and how the economics of the industries will then change if those capabilities are made possible.

We turn then, in these last pages of the chapter, to some of the ways in which users of media products experience digitization, the outcomes that it has upon our daily engagement with media, and the social and cultural consequences of media that take advantage of the opportunities digitization allows. As this section indicates, the road of new media is already littered with companies that had great ideas, but failed to connect with the desires of media users—or failed to connect at the right time. Although the Industrialization of Culture framework does not particularly highlight the role of media users or consumers in any particular level, we have tried to acknowledge the influence that they nevertheless provide. To some degree, the emerging patterns of use, behavior, and media engagement that audiences support provide key conditions for assessing the consequences that digitization has forced upon old media and which new media entities are surviving and thriving as a result. Digital technologies also provide valuable mechanisms through which the media industries can connect with audiences and obtain greater and more immediate feedback about their products. So, even though we've tried to focus our attention throughout this chapter on the consequences of digitization for media industries, it is fair to say that shifts in media use by consumers are playing a key role in adjustments of industry operation, as well.

Digitization allows many changes in the use of media products. As we already noted, the affordability and quality of digital technologies better enables those who traditionally only consumed media products to produce and circulate them as well—even if not on the scale of the conventional media industries. Although digitization arguably produces many other consequences, perhaps its greatest outcomes can be loosely categorized into the areas of expanded choice of media, the fragmentation of audience as a result (which also occurs as a result of post-Fordist economic practices), and increased convenience in accessing media. Emerging shifts in digital media may provide one of the best illustrations of the many, multidirectional influences that shape the creation of media products. The technological capabilities provided by digital media make some things possible, but users take up these abilities based more on their needs and desires than on what particular corporate interests might have desired from an economic perspective or than what was permissible via established regulatory structures. The very different nature of media industries today and the products increasingly available cannot be traced through simple, causal developments, but can only be explained as the result of a confluence of shifts in technology, economic models, regulatory mechanisms, and consumer activity.

Choice

A consequence of digital recording, production, and distribution in the media industries has been an exponential increase in choice among available media products. Consider the music industry. Once bound to the choices available in brick-and-mortar distributors, listeners have ready access to many more recordings far down the long tail with great ease. On the production side, the affordability of "garage band" recording software enables amateurs to record their music and easily make it accessible (although this doesn't guarantee that anyone actually listens to it).

Or, consider the expansion in choice that digital technologies have enabled in cable television. The possible compression of television signals through digital transmission has allowed cable service providers to offer many more channels than analog transmission allowed, as well as services such as on-demand content. The expanded choice in cable (a newer part of an old medium) has led to changes in broadcasting, as well. Broadcasters have adjusted their content and pushed boundaries in form, style, and attitude in response to being forced to compete with cable and its specificity in targeting tastes.

Although still largely economically unsustainable, digital distribution has offered print readers far greater choices and access to articles in more discrete forms. As people interested in all things television, we now enjoy the opportunity to read the columns of critics who write for papers around the country. We also have a much easier time finding articles of interest as a result of digital digests that link to a wide range of "print" sources. While this has been a boon to our ability to find more interesting pieces of criticism, the limitations of the current economic model mean that the papers whose columnists we read earn only a few cents of advertising—and at this point, this revenue is often not enough to compensate for the number of readers cancelling subscriptions and the associated decreasing advertising revenue. Even the most established media continue to experiment with economic models for accessing content. *The New York Times* recently announced that it will start charging "frequent users" of their site to access stories and columns starting in 2011; if you look at too many articles in one month, you'll have to pay to look at additional ones.[16] Such efforts respond to the need of media industries to earn enough to pay their staffs; many journalists have found themselves laid off in newsroom cuts or at papers that have shut down operations entirely in recent years. Thus, the choice enabled by digital distribution must be traced throughout the industrial framework to appreciate the extent of consequences.

Fragmentation

A key consequence of the greater range of media content in the digital era is the **fragmentation** of media use. In thinking about media and culture at a very broad level, the most unprecedented aspect of the change in media use today results from the steady erosion of various mass media industries without their replacement by other mass media—a change produced, as discussed in the last chapter, by the rise of the symbolic economy and post-Fordist practices. Digitization works very much in tandem with post-Fordism to make targeting narrow and specific audience segments, or niches, a central strategy of media industries that long profited by producing texts designed to be acceptable to broad and heterogeneous audiences. Shifts in media industries to targeting narrower audience groups have happened in the past; the trend away from mass toward niche media—a shift that the efficiencies of digitization aids considerably—is different from these past transitions, however, as no new "mass" medium is emerging.

Some of the earliest thinking on this issue can be found in Joseph Turow's book *Breaking Up America*, which considers this trend relative to the magazine and advertising industries.[17] Turow explains the value advertisers find from the more narrow targets of niche media and asserts that this trend will continue as a result. Turow warns of the creation of the "electronic equivalent of gated communities" rising up as a norm, as large media companies "separate audiences into different worlds."[18] Writing in the late 1990s, Turow forecast much of what we see across media industries today—what he describes as a shift in U.S. media in the balance among **society-making media** and **segment-making media**. Society-making media are "those that have the potential to get different cross-sections of the population talking to each other" (broadcast television in the network era may have been the quintessential example), whereas segment-making media are those that "encourage small slices of society to talk to themselves."[19]

Many of the ideas that media scholars have developed about the significance and power of media grew out of the norms of society-making media. Consider for example the change in the nature of television news. In 1980, 52.1 million viewers tuned in to one of the broadcast networks' three evening newscasts. By 2006, that number had fallen by nearly half to 26.1 million.[20] It isn't fair to say that in the intervening 25 years people became half as informed. Now, arguably, a range of segment-making news forms exist—everything from those network newscasts that are watched by much smaller audiences, to the news with a conservative spin offered by the FOXNews cable channel, to the not-quite-the-news (but pretty serious enterprise of media criticism, nevertheless) offered up by *The Daily Show with Jon Stewart*. This doesn't even take into account the array of news perspectives offered by radio, newspaper, or online venues, which allow even greater segmentation.

The concern raised by Turow is similar to the possibility that technology scholar Nicholas Negroponte wrote about a newspaper of the future called *The Daily Me*, which would be customized to individual interests, and that probably now looks a lot like a Yahoo home page.[21] This prospect of "individualized news" is something that has elicited both considerable excitement as well as concern. On one hand, the prospect of news or other media that is personally relevant is attractive to those who seek to reduce the time spent searching for material of interest. On the other hand, such a means of access reduces the likelihood of using media to broaden our horizons beyond established interests and the ability of news services to function as agenda setters that tell audiences what is important.

This fragmentation of audiences has considerable consequences for both the operation of media industries and for the role of media as a force in culture and society. In terms of media industries, the reality that audiences have spread across so many media outlets has changed the nature of many media businesses. Media industries utilize different strategies in this era in which a broadcast television show is "successful" if it reaches 15 percent of those watching television as opposed to the 40 percent needed in the network era. One particular consequence is that media industries create content to reach subgroups of populations instead of the mass audience. Amanda Lotz's research on the rise of female-centered television dramas beginning in the late 1990s offered one such lesson. Throughout television history, there had been few successful drama series centering on a female character until the mid 1990s—a point by which significant fragmentation of audiences had occurred. This fragmentation made targeting a more narrow population (such as women) a viable competitive technique in a way that was different from the competitive practices in an earlier era, when male members of the audience were perceived as the program decision makers during prime time.

Fragmentation changes the strategies of media industries, and as a result, also requires reassessing the role of media in society. In some ways, a fragmented media system would suggest that any single piece of media would be less powerful because it is less widely shared. On the other hand, potentially positive society-making functions are also lost. Perhaps it might be difficult to imagine the negative consequences of fragmentation—especially when we experience more personally relevant media as a gain. As a society we've become increasingly accustomed to operating inside our fairly personalized gated informational and entertainment communities, and those of us privileged enough to attend or work for universities probably have more media targeted toward us than is the case for many others. Personally, we've noticed moments of surprising disjuncture when we are jolted out of our familiar media community to see what is "normal" in other media and are reminded that our worldview is just one of many. While this is purely an anecdote, the consequences of fragmentation of media remain key concerns over which coming generations of media scholars will struggle.

Convenience

Another contribution of digital technologies can be categorized as convenience. Indeed there is nothing inherently convenient about digitization—rather, media users experience the efficiency of digital recording and transmission as an advance in the convenient use of technologies. Whether in the portability of vast quantities of music, the efficient storage of DVRs and DVDs, or the quick and ready access to searchable print media online, we can see digital media making media use more convenient.

Digitization also has given us tools to make accessing the growing range of content now available more convenient. Aspects of digitization allow the creation of metadata that helps us sort and search the media we come in contact with, whether through interactive programming guides (IPGs) now common to digital cable systems, various smart search technologies and recommendation engines found in iTunes and retailers such as Amazon.com or NetFlix, or sophisticated print search possibilities available through databases and search engines. This is a fortunate gain, as the amazing expansion in choice of products becomes somewhat meaningless without tools to order, sort, and find media of interest.

Another component of digitization is the way it allows content to be removed from its previous source to allow greater audience control. Whether it is a matter of downloading a radio show or segment as a podcast, recording a television show to a DVR, reading a newspaper online or on a portable device, or buying a film on DVD, some media industries are embracing the ways digitization can enable consumers to use media products in increasingly varied ways. These changes then feed back into the operation of media industries—in how they seek to profit, in their practices for creating media products, in their presumptions of the constructed audience—to yield adjustments in operations.

COMING CHANGE

The consequences of digitization have been reconfiguring the operation of the media industries for over two decades now, yet it remains impossible to know how much industrial practices will continue to be adjusted as a result. Looking forward from the vantage point of 2010, we would expect to see four further consequences in coming years: greater fragmentation, cheaper and cheaper production costs, the development of business models based on spatial rather than temporal distribution windows, and increasing surveillance of users to counter problems of fragmentation.

Our forecast of greater fragmentation is based more on the user experience than the situation of particular industries. For example, in coming years, we probably won't see many more television channels (at least in the manner that we are currently accustomed to thinking of channels) or additional newspapers or magazines built around print editions. However, there is a good likelihood for the development of more on-demand television offerings, which will likely be organized in something more akin to a folder (in the manner that you are used to sorting things on your computer) than as the channels we have known. The consequences of digitization will similarly continue to reconfigure print industries as fewer industries maintain hardcopy print productions, but the possibilities of online distribution may actually further fragment audiences if these industries can find a viable financial model.

Certainly, across media industries the basic costs of production will continue to fall as compression technologies improve and allow more and more memory and functionality in computers. We may never really appreciate these as gains, however, as the potential cost reductions may quickly be offset by continued expansion in the quality and sophistication of digital imagery and sound that lead us to continue to desire newer and more advanced versions of technology. Although it may be difficult to imagine how video games could get any more lifelike or the production quality of film or television could be significantly augmented, there remain largely unexplored realms of virtual reality and 3-D that may become increasingly commonplace, rather than remaining purely science-fiction. Indeed, now that high-definition has taken hold, the buzz in television industry manufacturing has turned to 3-D.

We would also expect that the media industries will develop a better sense of viable business models that will come to dominate their operation in a digital era in the very near term. The global economic crisis beginning in 2008 certainly began pressuring these industries to reevaluate many of their experiments with new distribution and financial models as advertising dollars became increasingly difficult to access, especially without provable results. Like contemporary industry workers, we are not sure what economic model or models might ultimately work, as we remain very much in a period of innovation and experimentation despite the pressures of the larger economic environment. One thing we would expect is that pricing becomes more variable, based on spatial rather than temporal dimensions. What we mean by this is that the old mechanisms for creating artificial scarcity such as tiering the release of films through different distribution windows that feature *timing* releases will become increasingly obsolete as what the industry terms "day and date" release (availability in all these places at the same time or nearly same time) becomes more common. The U.S. media industries also historically have released content domestically, and then waited a period of weeks or months before releasing it in international markets. These windows too are becoming narrower as concerns about piracy lead to near simultaneous international debuts.

Finally, we would expect surveillance to become an increasingly common social issue and potentially a strategy by which media industries attempt to build their digital era business models. One of the advantages of digital distribution of media from an industry perspective is that it often provides expanded opportunities for the distributors to know things about their audiences. For example, digital cable boxes can report fine-tuned data about precisely what channel is watched when, when you channel surf, how long you stay on a channel and when you begin turning again, that is of great value to those trying to design media products. Also, online distribution of video features much greater ability to report how and when the content is watched, and even information about the viewer that may be gathered by "cookies" as well as information about your viewing habits or search history. All of this information is exceptionally valuable to distributors who seek to sell audiences to advertisers, and it may well be the case that advertisers are willing to pay as much for 10 viewers if they have detailed information about them as they would have paid for 100 or even 1000 relatively unknown viewers in another era. While the expanded mechanisms for audience surveillance are of great value to the media industries, users may raise legitimate concerns about this new access to their lives and seek greater privacy controls—or may decide that relinquishing personal data and an expectation of privacy is a worthwhile exchange for continued "free" access to various media products and services.

CONCLUSION

This chapter has assumed the ready availability of the Internet and a host of other digital technologies that are increasingly taken for granted by some populations as though they are as common as running water and fresh air, but even though their use may be common in our daily lives, it is important to remember that the revolution in media production, distribution, and use being wrought by digitization is not a uniform experience around the globe. Indeed, one of the new interesting measures of global comparison is the rate of Internet availability and the sophistication of the digital technologies deployed. The United States has long perceived of itself as a leader of technological development, but it increasingly lags behind because of its lack of comprehensive national policy and willingness to leave development, innovation, and implementation in the hands of commercial interests.

Some argue that digitization and all that it presents provide a challenge to top down models of industry operation that long have organized the industries that we have discussed here. While we would acknowledge that digitization is driving innovation and challenging these older models of media industry operation, we would also first note that those top down models were overly-determinist even before digitization (a problem we've attempted to assuage with the Industrialization of Culture framework). We would also note that it is probably too early to assert that digitization will lead to a fundamental reordering of power in the media industry in the long term, despite its ample consequences for industry operation. Following the argument of Harvard Business School professor Debora L. Spar, we think it is important to acknowledge that we have only witnessed the beginning stages of the influence of digital technologies on the media industries.[22] Spar draws parallels between the current moment and the revolution the Internet seems to be delivering with similar moments in the introduction of other media technologies. The situation borne out over and over is that after initial periods of innovation, commercialization, and creative anarchy, rules are imposed that significantly contain the revolutionary potential that once seemed inherent.

Different structural conditions—those matters of technology, regulation, and economics that we discussed at length earlier—are playing an important role in establishing norms and possibilities for media industry operation and media use in the digital era. The scope of change that digitization makes possible for media industries is stunning. Although seemingly just a matter of technology on the surface, this chapter has illustrated how digitization affects all aspects of making, distributing, using, and financing media, as well. Significant adjustments in media-industry norms have already occurred, and yet the reordering of norms remains far from complete.

QUESTIONS

1. Try to count all the ways you depend on digital media for simple, taken-for-granted conveniences in just one day. Did you post a photo to a social networking site? Did you enjoy the convenience of carrying hundreds of songs with you on your MP3 player? Were you able to access many of your library's resources from your dorm room? Did you watch a video clip sent by a friend at another school? All of these activities are made possible by digital technology, and your ability and desire to do such things are changing the operation of the media industries.

2. As noted in this chapter, the Internet has created problems for print media. Why do you think people have come to believe information distributed online should be free—and do you think this can (or should) be changed? Can you think of a new business model for newspapers and magazines that might allow them to benefit from this development? Might an iTunes for newspapers or a

Netflix for magazines be helpful? What are some of the benefits and problems that might be associated with such models?

3. Consider the source you use most frequently for news. Is it society-making or segment-making media? If it is the former, how does it define society? If it is the latter, how would you characterize the segment it caters to? Think specifically about the type of news it presents, and how it presents it, to back up your claims. Now, consider the same questions in relation to entertainment media you consume.

4. Think of a media text you have in both physical and digital form, such as a song you own on CD and as an MP3 file. Why do you have the text in more than one format? Which do you use more often—why? What are the pros and cons to each delivery technology? Are there some types of media texts that you want only in physical format or only in digital format? Why?

5. Think about Chris Anderson's idea that direct-pay media might want to consider giving away content free and generating revenue through other forums, such as pop stars making money from performances rather than music. What are the advantages and disadvantages to this approach? Consider different ways this idea could be implemented across various media industries—what could be given away and what could be used to generate profit? Might it work easier for some industries than others? Is there media that can't be free—why?

FURTHER READING

Many recent publications explore the "new" media being created digitally, although attention to their nascent industries is rare and the very newness of their topics makes it difficult to know which books will serve as classic references. Nevertheless, Nicholas Negroponte's *Being Digital* (New York: Vintage Books, 1995); Henry Jenkins' *Convergence Culture: Where Old and New Media Collide* (New York: New York University Press, 2006), and Jay David Bolter and Richard Grusin's *Remediation: Understanding New Media* (Boston: MIT Press, 2000) deal with issues related to digitization broadly.

There are also several newer works attempting to make sense of media in a digital world. Much of this work is preliminary, but provoking. See Chris Anderson's *The Long Tail: Why the Future of Business is Selling Less of More*, rev. ed. (New York: Hyperion, 2008) and *Free: The Past and Future of a Radical Price* (New York: Hyperion, 2009).

For more on how contemporary media companies exploit the possibilities for surveillance as a way to increase profits, see Mark Andrejevic's "The Work of Being Watched: Interactive Media and the Exploitation of Self-Disclosure," *Critical Studies in Media Communication* 19, June 2002, 230–248.

NOTES

1. RIAA, 2009 Year-End Shipment Statistics, http://www.riaa.com/keystatistics. php?content_selector=2008-2009-U.S.-Shipment-Numbers, accessed Oct. 20, 2010.

2. Joseph R. Dominick, Barry L. Sherman, and Fritz Messere, *Broadcasting, Cable, the Internet, and Beyond: An Introduction to Modern Electronic Media,* 4th ed. (Boston: McGraw Hill, 2000), 48.

3. Henry Jenkins, *Convergence Culture: Where Old and New Media Collide* (New York: New York University Press, 2006), 3.

4. Chris Anderson's *The Long Tail: Why the Future of Business is Selling Less of More,* rev. ed. (New York: Hyperion, 2008).

5. Ian King, "Business Big Shot: Arianna Huffington, Online Entrepreneur," (London) *Times Online,* Nov. 21, 2008, http://business.timesonline.co.uk/tol/business/movers_and_shakers/article5201252.ece; accessed April 9, 2009.

6. Joseph Turow, *Media Today* (New York: Routledge, 2008), 391.

7. Ibid., 400–401.

8. John Caldwell, *Televisuality: Style, Crisis, and Authority in American Television* (New Brunswick: Rutgers University Press, 1995).

9. Edward Jay Epstein, *The Big Picture: Money and Power in Hollywood* (New York: Random House, 2006), 22.

10. Ibid., 165.

11. Ted Tschang and Andrea Goldstein, "Production and Political Economy in the Animation Industry: Why Insourcing and Outsourcing Occur," paper presented at Industrial Dynamics, Innovation and Development conference (2004), Elsinore, Denmark.

12. Ibid., 348.

13. In addition to the original Long Tail article in *Wired* and the 2006 book of the same name, Anderson maintains current examples of the concept on his webpage, http://www.thelongtail.com/.

14. See Chris Anderson, *Free: The Past and Future of a Radical Price* (New York: Hyperion, 2009).

15. Chris Kohler, "SXSW: Wired Editor Chris Anderson's *Free* Will Be Free," *Wired. com,* March 17, 2009, http://blog.wired.com/underwire/2009/03/anderson-kawasa.html (accessed April 2, 2009).

16. Richard Perez-Pena, "The Times to Charge for Frequent Access to Its Web Site," Jan. 20, 2010, http://www.nytimes.com/2010/01/21/business/media/21times.html (accessed Feb. 24, 2010).

17. Joseph Turow, *Breaking Up America: Advertisers and the New Media World* (Chicago: University of Chicago Press, 1997).

18. Ibid., 2.

19. Ibid., 3.

20. Journalism.org, "Evening News Viewership by Network: 1980–2006," www.journalism.org/node/1346 (accessed Jan. 15, 2008).

21. See Nicholas Negroponte, *Being Digital* (New York: Vintage Books, 1995).

22. Debra L. Spar, *Ruling the Waves: Cycles of Discovery, Chaos, and Wealth from the Compass to the Internet* (New York: Harcourt, 2001).

CHAPTER 11

—

Globalization

In 2009, Nintendo released the European and American versions of *Lux-Pain*, a graphic-novel-based videogame for its handheld DS platform, in which the main character, Atsuki, seeks to save the inhabitants of Kisaragi City from a mysterious force known only as Silent. Hailed as innovative for its creative use of the DS' touch screen, its impressive anime-inspired graphics, and its carefully evolving storyline that features eight different possible endings, *Lux-Pain* has also been widely panned by critics and fans because of its awkward translation, egregious spelling errors, and poor localization, including uncertainty about whether the game is set in Japan, the United States, or elsewhere. As such, *Lux-Pain* provides a quintessential example of how globalization has changed the media we consume, as well as the promises and perils that globalization poses for media industries.

Lux-Pain's developer, Killaware, is a Japanese-based gaming company with a multinational staff of ten developers. Though based in Japan, the company targets teenage and young adult gamers in East Asia, Europe, and North America, specifically aiming at both young men and young women. As such, its developers try to draw on global cultural trends, such as anime, which are popular with this transnational target market, rather than on trends that are specific to an individual national market. Killaware, then, is not a Japanese company with international operations, and *Lux-Pain* is not a Japanese cultural export; instead, both the company and the text are inherently transnational.

Still, despite its transnational characteristics, *Lux-Pain* and its developer had to navigate the remaining complexities of global cultural difference, the most obvious of which is language differences. That is, in order to exploit its global markets and ride the wave of global trends, the company needed to find a way to overcome the vast differences that separate its targeted consumers in East Asia, Europe, and North America. **Localization** is the term that most people in the media industries use to describe this process of unmooring media texts from their immediate cultural surroundings and securing them in another locale. Localization includes language translation, as well as the translation of settings, such as Kisaragi City, narrative techniques, characters, allusions, and more. The commercial and popular success of a global text like *Lux-Pain* depends crucially on how well done this localization is.

Lux-Pain, then, is a perfect example of how the structures of the global media industries have run ahead of the textual strategies necessary to make global media a reality. Slowly, the industry has developed a range of strategies to try to deal with the persistence of global cultural differences, especially how those differences make the popularity of texts even more unpredictable than in national contexts. Put another way, globalization increases the **nobody knows** principle of the media industries. Ironically, the very strategies that the industry uses to deal with uncertainty can also sink a potentially popular text when they are poorly executed, as was the case with *Lux-Pain*.

* * *

Globalization refers to a variety of complex and sometimes contradictory social and economic developments that have been taking place for centuries. The contemporary form of **media globalization**, which aims to spread as widely as possible the considerable risks and rewards of commercial media, has been driven by the economic changes of **post-Fordism** and, more immediately, by the efforts of global advertisers to develop markets for their products around the world.

Along with post-Fordism and digitization, globalization is one of the forces that are presently working to reshape the media industries at every level of the Industrialization of Culture framework. For instance, as we noted in Chapter 3, the growth of global markets for media commodities of all types has exploded since the 1980s due to the introduction of new distribution technologies, and these developments have required the creation of a single, international entity that can enforce **intellectual property** rights, the World Intellectual Property Organization (WIPO)—a change in regulatory conditions that affects every media industry. On the other hand, at the level of industry practices, creators of film, television, games, and popular music all need to take into consideration international audiences and local adaptations when producing content.

The *Lux-Pain* example may lead you to conclude that globalization, as a force for change, is already well established in the media industries. While this is true in certain sectors of the industry, such as videogames and blockbuster films, which tend to earn more revenues from international markets than domestic ones, other sectors such as newspapers and television are still predominantly domestic in character, at least in the United States. As we explore in this chapter, however, various aspects of both of these media industry sectors are increasingly global in terms of the workers they employ, the texts that they produce, and the markets where they sell those texts. Of course, one of the main drivers of globalization today is the shift to digital media detailed in the last chapter; given the inherently global nature of the Internet (the fact that anyone, anywhere, can connect to a website anywhere else in real time), as digitization continues to change the media industries, the forms and practices of globalization that we discuss here may change profoundly as well.

WHY HAS GLOBALIZATION BECOME SO POPULAR?

Globalization takes advantage of the **long tail** of media commodities that we discussed in Chapter 10, which allows corporations to continue to profit from them for years to come, as well as the creation of global consumer markets, advertising, and worldwide communications networks that make it possible to coordinate and time promotions and releases across the globe. Commercial media organizations have long recognized the economic advantages of globalization, but only in recent years have the economic benefits been so great for most industries that they have actively sought to develop business and textual strategies designed to exploit global markets.

So, any explanation of why globalization has become so popular has to begin with changes in the media industries. We have already covered a number of these changes in Chapter 9, namely, the slow demise of the mass audience and the loss of control over channels of distribution, which have led all sectors of the media industries to focus on leveraging popular texts across multiple media and multiple territories. Equally important, however, has been the global spread of advertising agencies. These agencies facilitate globalization in several ways. First, they design advertising, find appropriate media outlets, and buy ad time around the world for products with a global reach, such as TBWA Worldwide's long-standing ads for Absolut Vodka, which feature the product's distinctive bottle, shown in Figure 11.1.

Second, advertising agencies identify particular population segments around the world and help develop media outlets and cultural products that encourage a

Figure 11.1 Absolut Vodka—an international brand.

sense of global community among them. Finally, the international expansion of advertising agencies has required the development of global communications infrastructures, such as broadband Internet, which has spurred other forms of media globalization. In this way, even those segments of the media industries that are not advertiser supported may now take advantage of communications networks that were subsidized in whole or in part by advertising agencies and their clients.

Worldwide, hundreds, perhaps thousands, of advertising agencies have international operations, but the most dominant global agencies that carry the most prominent, most lucrative, and most powerful advertising campaigns are generally owned by one of four major holding agencies that together accounted for nearly $35 billion in revenues in 2008. These agencies are Omnicom Group ($13.4 billion in 2008 revenues), WPP Group ($7.5 billion in 2008 revenues), Interpublic Group ($6.9 billion in 2008 revenues), and Publicis Groupe ($6.9 billion in 2008 revenues).[1] Together, these agencies generate slightly more than half of their revenues from U.S.-based operations, and the remainder from abroad.

Global advertising agencies work hand in hand with global corporations, global media conglomerates, and global telecommunications companies to cultivate and exploit markets for media culture around the world. For instance, the advertising agency Arnold, which is owned by the sixth-largest global ad agency, Havas, developed a promotional campaign for McDonald's franchises in the Pacific Rim that offered Justice League dolls with meal purchases in New Zealand, Australia, Singapore, and elsewhere to help promote the Warner Bros. movie *Justice League: The New Frontier.* The movie, in turn, was based on comic book characters owned by DC Comics, a subsidiary of Warner Bros. Here, then, is a global, multi-corporation attempt at **synergy**, with its core commodities centered around media texts. For many people, this is precisely the type of advertising-manufacturing-media integration that the word "globalization" conjures up, and for whom such arrangements raise serious concerns about how these synergies affect culture and human rights around the globe. We will cover these concerns about "cultural imperialism" later in this chapter, along with other perspectives about the wider social significance of media globalization. At the moment, though, we just want to point out how important these kinds of massive commercial undertakings are in shaping the world of global media.

At the same time, globalization takes place on a much smaller scale, as well, such as the recent explosion of cheap Nigerian video films that have become popular throughout the developing world. Although these smaller-scale operations depend to some degree on the **telecommunication infrastructures** that global conglomerates have laid, they also draw on much older global trade routes, and their social implications are probably quite different from those of their large, Western commercial counterparts.

BARRIERS TO MEDIA GLOBALIZATION

As the *Lux-Pain* example demonstrates, the production, distribution, and exhibition of global media texts face a variety of hurdles that domestic texts generally do not. Among the more obvious and difficult hurdles are language and cultural differences among potential consumers. Related hurdles involve national and international regulations that block or reroute global cultural flows in various ways. In response to these challenges, media companies with global aspirations have developed a variety of business practices, including emphasizing universal elements in texts, co-producing content, localization, branding, and direct investment in foreign markets in an effort to give imported content privileged access to potential consumers.

Cultural Barriers

The degree to which cultural differences serve as hurdles to media globalization differs among types and genres of media. Local news is probably the least transferable of all media content, while instrumental music is probably the most transferable. All other types and genres of media content fall somewhere in between these extremes, and different media content has led to varying levels of globalization and different adaptive strategies across industries and genres.

Some industries, such as Hollywood and popular music, have arguably been globalized for more than a century. Others, such as the magazine industry, have a handful of global brands, such as *Maxim* and *Cosmopolitan,* that carry international and local content, along with a much larger number of domestic titles in most countries. The main distinction between media content that can and cannot travel well abroad is the degree to which that content relies on language to communicate. In movies, for instance, action films that tell their stories largely through visuals tend to travel well across cultural barriers, while romantic comedies that rely heavily on verbal humor tend to have difficulty reaching audiences beyond their immediate language markets. The exception to this rule seems to be popular music, which can often overcome language barriers because listeners are more interested in the music tracks. Still, history is littered with examples of songs being reformatted from one language to another in order to increase their popularity. The German popular music industry in the 1950s and 1960s, for instance, relied heavily on translated versions of popular American hits, rewritten and sung by German bands, such as Werner Overheidht's version of Elvis Presley's "Heartbreak Hotel," entitled "Hotel zur Einsamheit" or "Hotel for Loneliness."[2]

Language differences are, of course, one of the most difficult challenges for any media product to overcome in global markets. On the other hand, language differences do not coincide perfectly with national boundaries, so language can actually help encourage international media trade. Perhaps the best example of this phenomenon is media trade in Latin America, where the vast number of people speak Spanish and trade in all types of media is well-established and long-standing. Generally speaking, however, language differences make trade difficult and, as we mentioned in Chapter 8, entire industries have grown up around the world to translate media from one language to another.

While the example of language differences may be obvious, other kinds of cultural differences can be equally as difficult to overcome, and language is no guarantee of cultural similarity. For instance, the extended song-and-dance routines in Hindi films, popularly known as "Bollywood," are off-putting for many non-Indian Americans, while they are the main lure for the audiences in other parts of the world who have made Bollywood the world's second-largest film industry. These cultural differences boil down to differences in expectations that moviegoers have of how a film's story will unfold, as well as expectations about film genres, namely, the expectation among viewers raised on Hollywood that only musicals involve singing and dancing. Cultural differences such as these can either weave together or keep apart audiences in different nations or language groups. Most of these differences and similarities have deep historical roots that have evolved over time.

Culture, then, acts as a channel for worldwide flows of media texts. Observers use the term **geocultural markets** to refer to these transnational media markets that are based on culture rather than national boundaries. Unlike national boundaries, however, one cannot easily draw a map of the world that shows where cultural boundaries begin and end. Instead, the identification of cultural similarities and differences is more of an act of imagination and interpretation than cartography. For one thing, culture works at many different levels, so that different societies may share some cultural elements, but not others. Depending on which of these cultural elements specific media texts activate, those texts may or may not find willing audiences abroad. For instance, the predominantly Islamic members of the Commonwealth of Independent States, which have long-standing historical, political, and folk culture ties with non-Islamic members, instead import media heavily from Turkey, Iran, and Saudi Arabia because of shared religious cultures. In addition, media flows can call attention to cultural similarities that otherwise might go unexplored, such as the shared sensibilities, gender politics, and economic challenges in Latin America and Eastern Europe that the popularity of Latin American telenovelas in Eastern Europe calls attention to.[3]

Technological and Regulatory Barriers

Communications infrastructures and government regulations often pose additional hurdles for media corporations with global aspirations. Communications infrastructures helped propel the wave of television globalization in the 1980s, as nations around the globe added cable and satellite television channels. At the same time, cable, satellite, and Internet delivery platforms remain quite unevenly developed around the globe, frustrating attempts by large corporations to get access to the world's audiences. National-level regulations also helped pave the way for the globalization of television, as country after country opened its broadcasting market to commercial competition, especially in Europe. At the same time, many countries have retained quotas on percentages of foreign content on television channels, especially content of American origin. These content quotas date back to the early days of the film industry, when a number of European nations established them to protect their domestic film industries from Hollywood dominance after World War I. Today, many foreign governments employ such quotas, along with co-production funding that helps defray production costs (see below), and limits on foreign direct investment in media production, distribution, and exhibition sectors.

For its, part, the U.S. government has worked hard to help American media conglomerates expand abroad. Throughout the decades, but especially beginning in the 1990s, the U.S. government represented Hollywood's interests in bilateral negotiations with other nations, securing the studios the right to purchase movie theaters and multiplexes abroad, as well as protection of intellectual property rights, among other concessions. Ironically, many of the protectionist measures that nations currently use to try to protect their domestic media industries were widespread during the development of American film and broadcasting industries. Obviously, national governments in many parts of the world believe that domestic media industries are central to their interests. Different **mandates** lead, of course, to different perceptions of how those industries serve state interests— public mandates, for instance, see the media industries as helping to cultivate an informed citizenry, while commercial mandates see them as contributing to economic growth—but all present-day nation-states work hard to protect and improve the state of their media industries on the world stage.

The United States and the West in general have been quite successful in their efforts to promote their media industries worldwide through regulatory innovations. First, as we already mentioned, the United States in the 1980s and 1990s succeeded in convincing several countries to privatize their media environments, cutting subsidies to publicly funded media outlets and forcing them to compete against commercial ones. Far more important, from the perspective of Hollywood, has been the development of global intellectual property regimes that favor the interests of powerful nations and industries. As we discussed in relation to copyright in Chapter 4, **intellectual property** is an old idea whose purpose is to guarantee that people who come up with ideas can't have them stolen by someone else; in its purest form, it's a legal guarantee that authors, inventors, researchers, and others get to keep the right to determine how their intellectual efforts get released to the general public, and who gets to profit from them. Most observers believe that, without intellectual property rights guaranteeing that someone can profit from their ideas, the best and brightest people might not enter fields as diverse as media, computer programming, and crop research—or, basically, any form of intellectual or creative work.

So, in its origins at least, intellectual property is designed to be a cultural and social virtue. In today's world, the international intellectual property rights, including media texts, are generally held by commercial entities, and the creative forces behind them have little control over how media texts are shared with the general public. Instead, intellectual property rights generally serve the interests of commercial companies trying to maximize profits. As Hollywood has become more and more reliant on global revenues, it has likewise sought to crack down on illegal **piracy**, or the buying and selling of illegally produced copies of television shows, films, computer games, software, music and so forth. As we mentioned in

Chapter 4, Hollywood's claims about how much money it loses worldwide due to piracy are probably overinflated, because a large number of people who buy pirated copies of media products probably couldn't afford to purchase them at standard prices. For this reason, a number of people think that piracy is a relatively minor problem for global media conglomerates; instead, the organizations that suffer most from piracy are small operations that operate on a shoestring budget, for whom every sale is crucial. In addition, some countries, most notably the People's Republic of China, have been reluctant to crack down on piracy because such **parallel economies** employ a large number of people. In short, the legitimate economy of some countries might suffer if the parallel economies built on illegal piracy were shut down.

OVERCOMING BARRIERS TO GLOBALIZATION

While globalization may conjure up images of people everywhere drinking Cokes, eating at McDonald's, listening to Michael Jackson, and watching *The Simpsons*, in reality, a host of barriers stand in the way of media corporations that want to make money from abroad—even the largest, richest, most seasoned media conglomerates. Century upon century of cultural development, as well as national regulations, differences in infrastructure development, and international regulations all stand between content producers and audiences abroad. Of course, the media industries have also had decades of experience in developing ways to overcome these barriers.

Although the barriers we have discussed shape potential media flows in obvious and subtle ways, the priorities of media conglomerates, advertisers, and other powerful actors often clash with those cultural differences. In the early 1990s, media baron Rupert Murdoch developed a pan-Asian satellite service dubbed Star that was designed to reach affluent, English-speaking viewers across Asia with programming from the United States, Europe, and Australia. Murdoch, however, quickly ran up against the incredible cultural diversity of the Asian Pacific-Rim region, as well as different time zones, communications infrastructures, and national political climates, all of which conspired to scuttle his plans for a worldwide satellite service. Undeterred, Murdoch decided to split his satellite service into different feeds serving different parts of Asia; partnered with local television producers, managers, and channels; and worked to bring his operations more in line with the technological and political realities on the ground in countries where he is most active.[4]

Rupert Murdoch's difficulties with Star TV in Asia point to both the complexities of global media operations and the persistence of large media conglomerates with aspirations to expand around the world. While the lesson in Murdoch's case was that media conglomerates have to work with the grain of political, technological, and cultural realities in order to be successful, it is also the case that large media conglomerates and their handmaidens in advertising and promotion also have a sometimes powerful influence on audience tastes, including worldwide audience tastes. Perhaps the best example of this power comes from Hollywood films. For more than a century, Hollywood has spent lavishly on costuming, set design, special effects, and stars in an effort to develop and sustain a signature Hollywood "style" of moviemaking. Although this style has changed through the decades, it still retains widespread recognition around the world, and tends to set the technical standards against which movies everywhere get measured. That is, even audiences in small countries with weak economies critique their domestic film industries for lacking the technical standards of Hollywood, even when those standards are prohibitively expensive.

Observers of global media often take one of two extreme positions with regard to globalization's broader social implications: either they celebrate the ways in which contemporary global media permit and encourage cultural diversity, or they lament how global corporate behemoth's are homogenizing the world's cultures. The more accurate position lies somewhere between these extremes. Undoubtedly, commercial media outlets do more than work with the grain of established cultural patterns to inform and entertain people with similar interests and cultural backgrounds, as the Star TV example demonstrates. Instead, these industries actively *promote* the convergence of popular media tastes across national boundaries and constantly seek out and try to exploit perceived similarities. In other words, transnational media operations do not simply reflect the cultural diversity of the globe, nor do they impose their own cultural order on the globe; rather, they simultaneously *reflect and impose* global cultural patterns.

Global Promotions and Buzz

As we discussed in detail in Chapter 7, worldwide distribution windows are increasingly being synchronized so that media audiences everywhere can consume the same texts at the same time. This strategy of simultaneous worldwide release is particularly evident in the film, gaming, and magazine industries, and less so in popular music. In the television industry, simultaneous release is becoming more prevalent, but it is stymied by concerns about piracy and the lack of coordination among distributors and exhibitors.

Simultaneous release permits distributors and exhibitors to generate worldwide "**buzz**" about new releases, as potential consumers read blogs, watch television, read entertainment magazines, and talk with friends and family abroad about the newest films and video games. The hope among industry insiders is that all of the talk and excitement that simultaneous release generates will get consumers everywhere more excited about the movie or game than they otherwise would be. Because promotions are centrally controlled and planned, they can also be cheaper to produce than if different promotional campaigns were developed in each market. Moreover, tie-ins such as toys and action figures can also be shipped and stocked at the same time all over the world, again cutting down potential costs. Finally, and perhaps most importantly, simultaneous global release can cut down on illegal copying, because most media piracy attempts to take advantage of lags in release times to sell pirated copies in a market before the official release of a product.

With regard to globally distributed magazines, simultaneous release helps generate sales by promoting and reporting on prestigious global events. For instance, local versions of global fashion magazines that cover fashion week in Paris need to be released soon after the event, before potentially interested readers find the reports elsewhere. We could make similar observations about online content, newspaper reports, and television programs built around these kinds of seasonal, global cultural events. To take another example, news reports about the winner of the Cannes Film Festival get transmitted almost simultaneously around the world as soon as the announcement is made.

The synchronized release of certain kinds of media texts adds to the perception that we are living an increasingly globalized world, one in which tastes and trends transcend national boundaries. Of course, it's important to remember that these seemingly global phenomena fit the needs of the industries first and foremost: they help fight piracy, they cut promotional and advertising costs, they streamline ancillary promotional campaigns such as action figure giveaways, and they generate higher sales in early windows than would staggered-release windows. Simultaneous release, then, is a clear example of a successful attempt by large media conglomerates to use their reach and their muscle to increase the popularity and sales of their products. The creation of buzz surrounding the newest releases is one strategy for trying to overcome cultural differences among media consumers worldwide, and one that avoids, rather than confronts, the problems associated with cultural difference. Other strategies seek much more actively to work with, rather than against, cultural realities.

Co-Production

One of the most successful formulas for balancing cultural realities with the desire to exploit international markets has been international **co-production**, which refers to a business arrangement in which production staff and creative workers from more than one country work together on a project with the aim of distributing the final product in each participant's home market and, perhaps, beyond. Co-production has been particularly prominent in film and television, and less common in popular music or print industries. Likewise, gaming has only recently begun to develop its own international co-production models, but this is primarily a way for smaller producers with different core competencies to work together to bypass the large game publishers, rather than a strategy to break into different international markets.[5]

In television, public service broadcasters in Europe, North American, and the Pacific Rim were among the first and most active proponents of international co-production, dating back to the early 1980s when many of them began to face competition from domestic commercial competitors. Co-production became a way for such broadcasters to defray costs and maintain production by working together with similar institutions in different countries. In theory, co-production provides an opportunity for a multinational group of creative people to work together to create programming that transcends national differences. In practice, at least in the early years of this strategy, partners had difficulty imagining what kinds of television programs could overcome those differences, and they tended to rely heavily on stories derived from classic works of fiction or historical events that affected the world as a whole, or at least each country in the target market. The problem with these strategies was that they often led to such watered-down programming that few audience members found them interesting enough to watch. In Europe, this led observers to coin the derisive term "Euro-pudding" to describe the seemingly simplistic and unappetizing mixture of cultures and creative forces.

As the years have passed, however, co-producers have gotten better and better at identifying good partners and projects, at the same time that extensive work with one another has led to a degree of cross-cultural understanding among producers that results in more culturally relevant programs for viewers. In particular, Canadian companies and the public service broadcaster the Canadian Broadcasting Corporation, or CBC, have become significant players on the international co-production market. Canadian commercial players are appealing to foreign co-production teams because of their close proximity to the U.S. market and the track record of success that the Canadians have getting programs picked up in the United States, which remains the largest and most lucrative national television market. Producers from around the world who hope to get their programming aired in the United States often seek out Canadian co-production partners for these reasons.[6]

Meanwhile, co-productions between the CBC and other broadcasters with public mandates, especially in Europe, are a way for these broadcasters to maintain their distinctive television storytelling techniques in an increasingly globalized and commercialized media environment. Let us be clear about this: public service broadcasting everywhere has been under assault for the past three decades because 1) it is inherently national, not international, and 2) it is publicly rather than commercially funded. While commercial broadcasters and their proponents have long insisted that public service broadcasters do not offer much that is distinct in their programming, and that they should be limited to only those types of television that commercial outlets cannot produce, Canadian media scholar Serra Tinic has demonstrated how very different public service broadcasting stories are from their commercial counterparts, even when they tackle the same topical material. Using the example of two made-for-television movies based on the global sex trade involving Eastern European women, Tinic shows how a commercial Canadian-U.S. co-production blames the entirety of the sex trade on a single individual, namely a Russian mob boss, while a co-production by the CBC and the UK public-service broadcaster Channel 4 on the same topic ultimately blames global capitalism, American business, and the United Nations for the trade. Taken together, these two examples nicely delineate the different reasons behind—and consequences of—commercial and non-commercial international co-productions.[7] Even in the realm of global media, it seems as though the mandate of a media outlet influences the kind of content we are likely to receive.

Localization

Like co-production, localization is strategy that global media organizations have developed to try to overcome the barriers that worldwide cultural difference pose to international flows of content. Localization refers to a range of institutional and textual arrangements that rework foreign content to be more culturally relevant for domestic viewers. Dubbing and subtitling are forms of localization, as are rewriting and re-recording popular songs in the local language with local pop stars. Unlike co-production, which is generally limited to the film and television industries, media industries of all types make use of localization.

Localization stems from the recognition that all media products, even those designed by global conglomerates, have to compete with a different and unique mixture of rivals in every local market. Consequently, global media organizations tend to have **devolved** operations in each market, in which local decision makers have a good deal of control over the production and distribution of content. At the same time, however, decision makers at headquarters want to maintain some degree of brand consistency and quality across all markets. Different organizations solve this dilemma of how to retain consistency while providing enough "play" to remain competitive in numerous different markets in different ways. Disney, for instance, tends to run almost all decisions through headquarters before they are finally approved, even down to such details as how each of its characters will sound in each market, while MTV allows local executives in lucrative markets a fairly free hand in programming, talent selection, scheduling, and so forth.

At minimum, however, most global media companies offer some degree of local control to decision makers, once they have been trained in the practices and cultures of the parent company. Fashion magazines, for instance, must of necessity localize their content, because of fashion differences and different competitive mixes in each market, at the same time that some degree of global consistency in content and branding is necessary to take advantage of global fashion trends and advertiser dollars. Before they are allowed to take the reins of the local version of the magazine, local editors of fashion magazines such as *Marie Claire, Elle*, and *Vogue* are sent to train at the magazine's headquarters, where they learn how to design photo layouts, stories, and overall issue themes that fit with the magazine's general brand. In addition, editors around the world participate in planning each new issue, again ensuring consistency across locally branded editions.

Localized versions of global fashion magazines offer good examples for exploring the patterns of similarity and difference in media content that localization strategies create. Fashion magazines feature a combination of fashion photo shoots, fashion-related articles, and news and gossip about the fashion industry, along with a large amount of advertising. The centerpiece of each issue is known as the "fashion well," which consists of about forty to fifty pages of photo shoots, uninterrupted by advertising, featuring the latest fashion designs. Each photo layout is titled and themed to give it coherence. While this overall structure remains consistent across each local edition, local editors have some discretion over which specific photographs to use, how to lay them out on the page, and how to translate the sense of the theme and the title of each photo shoot. Meanwhile, both feature articles and fashion news include local content as well as material that appears in other local editions. In other words, much of the *content* of the local version comes either from local fashion writers or from selections that local editors make from a range of foreign content options, while more senior editors and executives at the magazine's headquarters largely set the *format*.[8]

This replacement of imported forms with local content happens in other industries as well, and is at the heart of what it means to "localize" media. In television, one of the commonest ways that this localization happens is through the reproduction of local versions of popular TV **formats**, such as the multiple national versions of the reality show *Big Brother*. In film and popular music, this phenomenon is less clearly directed by centralized institutions seeking to "push" their content abroad, and more by media producers seeking to "pull" formulas from foreign cultures. Of course, in practice, the "pull" of media producers depends on the "push" of media institutions. For example, musicians around the world have found rap music to be an effective vehicle for their own creative expression, and the adaptation of rap music cannot be dismissed as mere copying of foreign music. Still, the distribution circuits of the global media industries brought rap music to these places in the first place, and only later were they adapted for domestic purposes.[9] To put it another way, there is a reason that, say, black Colombian music has not become the preferred format for youthful rebellion around the world the way that rap music has, and the reason for the discrepancy is that no global media industry exists to exploit black Colombian music.

The situation of local adaptation of global formats is somewhat different in film, as well. As with music, local creative talent tends to "pull" moviemaking formulas from abroad to help with storytelling and visual engagement. In some instances, these directors, writers, and actors have trained in Hollywood and made their names there. For instance, the global blockbuster *Red Cliff*, produced and created in mainland China by successful Hollywood director John Woo, tells a distinctly Chinese story about one of the foundational historical myths in Chinese society. The story is told in such a manner—with clear villains and heroes, a climactic battle scene, and romantic overtones among male and female characters—and uses such a variety of visual techniques—including the Chinese and global cinema star system; the construction of elaborate, historically accurate sets; and the use of special effects and spectacular battles to grab the viewer's attention—that is clearly identifiable as a global blockbuster, because it follows a formula that we have come to associate with those kinds of films.

Outsourcing

Each of these examples demonstrates how economic conditions have been altered by globalization and how these alterations have affected the practices of media distribution and production. When it comes to production, a related force—outsourcing—has also wrought profound changes. Outsourcing refers to the process whereby certain elements of production are completed somewhere overseas in order to take advantage of cheaper labor conditions and government subsidies. For instance, in 2005, 47 percent of Hollywood movies designed primarily for a U.S. market were filmed in the United States, while only 17 percent of scripted television series were shot domestically.[10] Typically, only certain elements of production get outsourced, particularly those elements that require the greatest degree of labor and the slightest degree of creativity.

The print media, particularly journalism, might seem more immune to outsourcing because of language demands and the need to be familiar with fast-changing local and national developments. Newspaper reporting has begun to succumb to outsourcing as well, however, as reporters in poorer nations with large English-speaking populations, such as India and Singapore, increasingly write articles for national and local newspapers. Typically, these reporters receive basic facts from string reporters in the local market, and they then write and e-mail their finished copy to editors at the local headquarters. Layout, design, and copyediting functions are also sometimes outsourced. In all of these instances, the lure of outsourcing is primarily the cost savings of hiring cheaper production workers. Moreover, the global communications infrastructure, especially the Internet, makes communication with foreign labor cheap and relatively quick while also permitting domestic supervisors to maintain a good deal of control over foreign workers.

Much as in the general economy, outsourcing of media production has generated a good deal of heated debate in the United States. At issue are the loss of high-paying, unionized American jobs; the quality of production work done cheaply abroad; and human rights concerns about underpaid laborers in poor countries. Toby Miller et al., for instance, claim that global outsourcing has led to a "New International Division of Cultural Labor," whereby Hollywood contributes to the disappearance of cultural diversity worldwide, as cultural workers abroad are forced to labor away on Hollywood projects rather than making their own, culturally-distinct media.[11] Tinic, however, has discovered that television producers in Vancouver, one of the main locations of runaway Hollywood production, use the money that they get from working on Hollywood projects to tell their own stories that are distinct to the region.[12] Still, it is quite apparent that outsourcing has weakened the positions of the various creative guilds and professional associations vis-à-vis media industry executives and management.

Globalization from Below

As we have already suggested, the dynamics of globalization tend to involve both an industrial "push" from above and a cultural "pull" from below. To be successful, the global efforts of media organizations have to integrate both of these forces, pushing their content in places that are pulling in the same direction. Putting this into the context of the Industrialization of Culture framework, remember how culture provides the background for all of the levels of the framework, suggesting how important culture is as a force that shapes both the operations of the media industries and the texts that they produce. Outsourcing is perhaps the clearest example of globalization from above. Because it involves production, not distribution or consumption of media content abroad, cultural forces play very little role in decisions about outsourcing; that is, as long as foreign media workers have the necessary skills to do the work, their cultural similarities to (or difference from) the domestic market make little difference, although the example of using reporters in English-speaking countries should serve as a reminder that cultural considerations are never absent. At the other end of the spectrum are a host of relatively disorganized global media operations that rely most heavily on the cultural preferences and practices of consumers who pull media texts from abroad.

The circulation and consumption of media texts that are not driven by powerful global media conglomerates, or **globalization** from below, take place across all media industries, typically through informal, and sometimes illegal, channels, and as such they are hard to characterize in any systematic or overarching way. From a commercial perspective, however, the overriding consideration of all of the types of globalization from below that follow is that, in order for them to turn a profit and remain in business, they generally must be built on legitimate national media industries. Without such a base to support the industry, they cannot in the first place produce texts, which the foreign consumers later pull toward them to consume.

One of the most prominent examples of this type of globalization from below in today's media world is the film industry in Nigeria, often referred to as "Nollywood." Depending on how one measures it, Nollywood is either the second- or the third-largest movie producer in the world, and its products, known as video films, circulate throughout the globe, especially in Third World countries where illegally pirated copies feature prominently in media stalls at large market bazaars. Nollywood producers have perfected a business and production model in which costs are contained by using extremely fast shooting schedules, usually one or two weeks, and cheap production techniques, such as shooting on video rather than film. Films are released on DVD for home viewing and in small viewing houses simultaneously, and they quickly spread through piracy throughout the country, the region, and the world. Only in the days and weeks before they lose control over the distribution of pirated copies can Nollywood producers make money, but this is enough to keep the industry afloat.[13]

Despite the popularity of Nollywood and the visibility it has received among industry insiders and academics, the business model is difficult to reproduce elsewhere because of its heavy reliance on domestic revenues. Still, the line between legitimate and illegitimate global media markets is somewhat fuzzy, and other media companies with varying degrees of legitimacy sit up and take notice of developments such as Nollywood, as they seek to understand, organize, and exploit the markets that Nollywood video films have opened up. For instance, in New York and elsewhere in the United States, the U.S. direct-to-home satellite service Dish Network has begun carrying Afrotainment, a digital channel built around the popularity of Nollywood films.

THE COMMERCIAL AND SOCIAL CONSEQUENCES OF GLOBALIZATION

Expanded Markets and Innovations

Imagine hundreds of millions of untapped Chinese media consumers. They have little access to media and entertainment, but their difficult life conditions make them ideal candidates for the kinds of escapist pleasures we associate with many media products. They may not have much money to spend individually, but as a group, they represent a huge potential market. They are, in many ways, a media market yearning to be tapped. Such are the ideals—one might say delusions—that drive media organization to seek overseas markets for their products, markets that can allow them to continue to exploit the long tails of those products in more and more places for longer and longer periods of time.

However, as we have suggested, globalization of the media industries entails more than savvy salesmanship and bookkeeping: globalization is both an economic and a cultural process, and these two forces are just as often in conflict as they are in harmony. The early dreams of media moguls luring hundreds of millions of new consumers simply by setting up a satellite feed have been replaced by a range of institutional practices that work with the grain of cultural difference, rather than against it. This has led to a growing variety of international opportunities for producers, distributors, and exhibitors of media content.

It has long been a truism that American media corporations exported a good deal to international markets, but imported little. The exception to this rule was the popular music industry, which has long imported musical styles, talent, and recorded music from abroad. Generally speaking, however, American media imports have traditionally been quite low: foreign films have tended to show up only in specialty theaters, mostly in larger cities; television channels in the United States have typically imported only about 2 percent of their entire program schedules; and only a handful of foreign newspapers and magazines have generally been available, particularly those in languages other than English that are aimed at recent immigrants.

Today, however, all of this is changing, and television has been perhaps the most profoundly affected medium. Reality formats, created in Europe and Australia, have found their way onto cable channels and even prime-time network TV. The powerhouse program of recent years, Fox Broadcasting's *American Idol*, for instance, is a format of the British series *Pop Idol*. And localized versions of scripted foreign series have become commonplace as well, including such well-known series as *The Office* and *Ugly Betty*. Foreign production practices have begun to show up in less obvious places as well, such as the efforts in the mid 2000s by American soap opera producers to incorporate the storytelling techniques of Latin American telenovelas in an effort to attract both young and Latino audiences. In all of these instances, we see television producers trying to take advantage of inno-vations made elsewhere to create programming that is fresh and appealing.[14]

Not only do today's television programs incorporate foreign styles and pro-duction practices, they also are increasingly funded with foreign money, with over-seas investors picking up distribution rights in their own markets and sometimes beyond. In other words, American television programs are increasingly designed for global viewers. Fox Television Studios, producer of such cable hits as USA's *Burn Notice*, has recently eliminated **deficit financing** of production through upfront investment by international co-production partners. Fox and its partners produce entire episodes and try to sell them to the networks. To date, their most successful property has been the short-lived ABC series *Defying Gravity*, but Fox has high hopes for this funding process in the future. Its willingness to entertain this financing model—and the willingness of the networks to buy the show—demonstrates just how globalized American television production is becoming.[15]

Media industries in other countries, meanwhile, have been dealing with these kinds of globalizing pressures for decades. While innovation may be the positive side of this coin, the negative side has been characterized as the loss of one's dis-tinct national culture and its replacement with a global commercial culture that values consumption over everything else. New media technologies such as satel-lite television, Internet distribution, and digitization in general have only sped up these processes of change, leading to a great deal of concern and speculation about the possible deleterious effects of media globalization among scholars, policy makers, and concerned citizens. From a practical standpoint, however, the media economies of the world's nations have now become so entangled that it would be extremely difficult to begin to pry them apart. In many ways, the genie of global-ization is already well out of the bottle.

Cultural Imperialism versus Cosmopolitanism

Concerns about the influence of foreign cultural values, particularly consumer-ism, have figured prominently in debates about media globalization, particu-larly in policy debates about limiting the import of American film and television programming that have taken place across the globe. Such concerns about **cul-tural imperialism**, or the domination of local cultural values by more powerful American values, are common in academic and popular discussions about media globalization. When we see children in China flocking to McDonald's for their birthday parties or poor workers in Nigeria foregoing food to buy Adidas shoes, it is hard not to wonder about the serious negative consequences of exporting our media, our media systems, and the values they contain. At the same time, the glo-balization of media points to and encourages other forms of cultural identification that we might view more positively.

Cosmopolitanism is the idea that the recognition of similarities and respect for differences among the world's people can diminish war and suffering, and some observers have suggested that media globalization can help create that recognition and respect. For instance, a film like *Hotel Rwanda,* about the Rwandan civil war in the early 1990s and subsequent genocide against minority Tutsis, not only brings knowledge of the horrors of that conflict to international viewers, but it also demonstrates the humanity of ordinary Rwandans in ways that may cause viewers to be more understanding and sympathetic. Obviously, the era of instantaneous global communication is one in which cosmopolitanism can thrive. At the same time, it is important to remember that people in large swaths of the globe have very little access to these powerful new means of communication, and at best are objects whose stories find their ways around the globe, rather than consumers of global media who themselves have the opportunity to become more cosmopolitan.

Connecting Dispersed Communities

Another consequence of media globalization has been the establishment and maintenance of **diaspora communities**, or groups of people, often defined by ethnicity or national origin, who live in various different countries but maintain cultural connections with one another. Chinese and Indian diasporas are probably the largest communities globally, and in country after country, one can find media outlets tailored to these communities as well as a vibrant cultural exchange among them. Such media serve generations within the diaspora in different ways. Those who grew up in China or India before emigrating may embrace the international availability of media as a way to maintain connection with a familiar culture. Their children, however, who might have no firsthand experience with their parents' culture, might use media to learn about their parents' culture, yet particularly embrace media that give voice to their own experiences of negotiating among cultures.

Various changes in the media industries have altered the availability of media for diasporic communities. In the case the Indian diaspora living in the United States in the 1970s, visual media were primarily circulated through film prints exhibited in community centers. This required the diasporic community to come together physically to enjoy familiar media. In the 1980s, these screenings gave way to videocassettes that were often circulated through South Asian grocery stores. In some places that had large diasporic communities, weekly public access television series were produced and distributed to other communities as well. In the 1990s, the availability of satellite television made it possible to receive packages of Indian television channels around the world. Also, late in the decade, the technology boom led to many India-related dotcom companies designed to aid members of the Indian diaspora that sought to connect with Indian culture. The Internet enabled real-time engagement with the films, songs, and controversies of the moment, eliminating the lag time of analog technologies. Thus, shifts in technology that allow affordable international distribution and changes in industry practices that recognize the commercial value of diasporic and international audiences have reconfigured media texts.

In addition, media globalization can allow groups that have little historical connection to imagine themselves as members of a larger diasporic community. For instance, in the 1980s, the Maori minority in New Zealand imported

African-American culture and political sensibilities as a way to understand their own oppression and struggle for greater rights and respect, despite the fact that the Maori are of Samoan, not African, descent.

CONCLUSION

Undoubtedly, globalization has increased consumer choices in certain parts of the world, although access to media and communication technologies as well as domestic *and* global media culture are quite circumscribed in much of the globe. A good deal of debate exists, however, about the social and cultural consequences of those choices, particularly the degree to which those options merely increase consumerism around the world and undermine global cultural diversity and integrity.

Perhaps the most important thing to remember about globalization is that, in order to be profitable, globally circulated media must fit the demands of both the large corporations that push media abroad, *and* local consumers who pull foreign media texts toward them. As we have suggested throughout this chapter, large corporations, particularly advertisers, try extremely hard to mold the desires of transnational consumer segments to fit the needs of the industry, but these efforts are only occasionally successful. Consequently, the contemporary media industries have developed a wide range of business practices designed to take advantage of, rather than destroy, cultural differences.

Finally, we have seen that significant debates exist about the social consequences of media globalization. While some insist the globalization is destroying the world's cultural diversity, others claim that it is preserving diversity. As with much we have discussed throughout these pages, we believe that such positions are too extreme. While we do not want to dismiss or apologize for the power of massive media conglomerates to shape society and culture, neither do we want to underestimate the resilience, adaptability, and stubbornness of cultural practices and traditions. Ultimately, the social and cultural consequences of media globalization vary among different countries, different groups within countries, and even among different individuals.

QUESTIONS

1. Imagine that a major U.S. media figure, such as Tom Cruise or Madonna, has hired you to help him or her appeal to more international markets in the future. What specific strategies might you recommend in order to localize his or her media texts? Would certain aspects remain the same while others change based on different markets—why? Think about the different ways localization can occur in a variety of media industries and across a number of different media texts.

2. Identify a U.S. media text that you feel would have consequences that are more cultural imperialist than cosmopolitan (or vice versa) if it were exported around

to other countries. Why do you think this would be the case? Do you think it is a case of either/or—or do you think the consequences could be mixed? How? Now think about a media text created in another country that has been imported to the United States and consider those potential consequences. How are they different from or similar to the consequences you imagined with the exported media text?

3. Discuss the advantages and disadvantages of a windowed release versus a simultaneous release, as discussed in the seventh and present chapters, respectively. Think of a media text and then consider what a company might gain by staggering release dates around the world instead of releasing it everywhere at the same time. What might be sacrificed with a simultaneous release—and vice versa? How does "buzz" factor into both strategies?

FURTHER READINGS

A wide range of books and articles exist on media globalization, only a fraction of which we can include here. For more on Western domination of world media markets, see Miller et al.'s *Global Hollywood 2* and Daya Kishan Thussu's *International Communication: a Reader* (London: Routledge, 2010). For an example of globalization-from-below, see Moradewun A. Adejunmobi's "Nigerian Video Film As Minor Transnational Practice," *Postcolonial Text,* 3 (2007). For studies of outsourcing in the media industries, see *Global Hollywood 2* and Ted Tschang and Andrea Goldstein's "Production and Political Economy in the Animation Industry: Why Insourcing And Outsourcing Occur," DRUID Summer Conference (2004), http://www.druid.dk/conferences/summer2004/papers/ds2004-92.pdf (accessed Feb. 27, 2010).

The breadth of work on globalization in the television and film industries is too numerous to do justice to here, but for news media see Daya Kishan Thussu's *News As Entertainment: The Rise of Global Infotainment* (Thousand Oaks, Calif: Sage, 2007), and for the globalization of rap music see Tony Mitchell's edited volume *Global Noise; Rap and Hip-Hop Outside the USA* (Middletown, Conn.: Wesleyan University Press, 2001).

NOTES

1. Rupal Parekh and Bradley Johnson. "Adworld has new king in Sir Martin Sorrell. (Cover story)." *Advertising Age* 80, no. 9 (March 9, 2009): 1–19. *Academic Search Elite,* EBSCO*host* (accessed Sep. 17, 2010).

2. Uta G. Poiger, "Postwar German Popular Music: Americanization, the Cold War, and the Post-Nazi Heimat," in *Music and German National Identity,* ed. Celia Applegate and Pamela Potter (Chicago: University of Chicago Press, 2002), 134–150.

3. Timothy Havens, "Globalization and the Generic Transformation of Telenovelas," *Thinking Outside the Box: Television Genres in Transition,* ed. Gary Edgerton and Brian Rose (University of Kentucky Press, 2005), 271–292.

4. Michael Curtin, "Murdoch's Dilemma, or 'What's the price of TV in China?'" *Media, Culture & Society,* 27 (2005), 155–175.

5. Phil Elliott, "Is Co-production the Future?" *Gamesindustry.biz* (June 1, 2009), http://www.gamesindustry.biz/articles/is-co-production-the-future (accessed Feb. 25, 2010).

6. Serra A. Tinic, *On Location: Canada's Television Industry in a Global Market* (Buffalo: University of Toronto Press, 2005).

7. Serra A. Tinic, Between the Public and the Private: Television Drama Global Partnerships in the Neo-Network Era," *Television Studies After TV*, ed. Graeme Turner and Jinna Tay (London: Taylor & Francis, 2009), 65–74.

8. Brian Morean, "More Than Just a Fashion Magazine," *Current Sociology,* 54 (2006), 725–744.

9. Tony Mitchell (ed.), *Global Noise; Rap and Hip-Hop Outside the USA.* (Middletown, Conn.: Wesleyan University Press, 2001).

10. The Center for Entertainment Industry Data and Research, "The Global Success of Production Tax Incentives and the Migration of Feature Film Production From The U.S. to the World, Year 2005 Production Report" (2006), http://www.ceidr.org/2005CEIDRReport.pdf (accessed Sep. 17, 2010).

11. Toby Miller et al., *Global Hollywood 2* (London: BFI Publishing, 2005).

12. See note 6 above.

13. Onookome Okome, "Nollywood: Africa at the Movies," *Film International,* 5, no. 4 (2007), 4–9.

14. See note 3 above.

15. Joe Flint, "Studio's New Take on Cost Cutting," *Los Angeles Times* (Nov. 14, 2009), http://articles.latimes.com/2009/nov/14/business/fi-ct-fox14 (accessed Feb. 22, 2010).

Glossary

A la carte refers to the option for cable subscribers to pick whichever channels they want and pay a fee per channel, rather than being forced to select from packages determined by cable providers.

A-list/B-list issue refers to the arbitrary, yet significant, variation among the talent involved in media products. The financial consequences of a decision to select a well-known talent (A-list) to star in or make media productions over a relatively unknown talent (B-list), who may offer just as good of a performance for a smaller salary, is not absolute or consistent in a way that such decisions often have economic consequences that can be calculated.

Above-the-line refers to costs and workers that are unique to each media production, rather than costs and workers that the organization maintains from project to project. Generally, above-the-line workers are creative staff, while **below-the-line** workers are technical or support staff.

Access refers to one's ability to use or receive media and communication services.

Adaptive strategies are conventional practices that media organizations have adopted to help make commercial media production more predictable and help defray risks.

Agency is the amount of control media industry workers have over how and what they do, allowing them to be meaningful actors in how their companies operate and in the creation of media products.

Affiliates are the individual television and/or radio stations that make up a broadcast network.

Analog is a non-digital method of recording that stores signals in a manner that represents the message using a direct facsimile, or an "analogy," of the original (e.g., audio tapes, vinyl records).

Anti-trust regulations are laws, handled in the United States by the Department of Justice with the Federal Trade Commission, intended to prevent too much industry consolidation.

Ars longa is the long economic life of media-industry products. After an initial period when a company loses money on a media text such as a TV show, the media text may continue producing profits for decades through avenues such as syndication.

"Art for art's sake" is an attitude pursued by many creative workers in the media industries whose primary incentive is not necessarily to make media texts that are likely to make the most money, but to make the story they really want to tell.

Artificial scarcity is a practice used by industries, involving windowing and price differentiation, to control where, when, for how long, and at what cost people may experience a media product.

Audimeter is a device designed by media audience-measurement firms that records which channel a television or radio set is tuned to.

Auxiliary practices refer to a category of "secondary" or "supporting" roles and practices in media industries, including critics, agents, and audience-measurement companies.

Below-the-line costs and workers are those that tend to carry over from project to project, including the costs of production and postproduction, as well as workers who are primarily involved with the technical aspects of media production.

Bicycling is a media distribution strategy that involves transferring physical copies of media texts from exhibitor to exhibitor.

Block booking is a practice once used by film studios that required independent theaters to agree to take a block of studio-selected films (often films that were not very desirable) if they wanted to get the big new studio film with top talent.

Boutique media firms are small firms, typically with a small number of employees, that specialize in one particular segment of media production, distribution, or exhibition.

Brands refers to particular characters, story worlds, or recognizable elements of texts that can be exploited across multiple media, sometimes referred to as transmedia storytelling.

Broadcast flag prevents digital recording from television, or involves mechanisms that prevent us from freely moving purchased audio files among devices or recording them to a physical medium.

Broadcasting permits a single transmission to reach hundreds, even thousands, of listeners with the same message at the same time, through the utilization of radio waves of the electromagnetic spectrum to transmit voice (radio) or voice and video (television).

Buzz refers to the excitement generated around a particular media text, whether that excitement involves only those who work in the industries or society at large.

Carryover effect is an exhibition strategy of television broadcasters that encourages viewers to watch a new program by airing it immediately after a popular program, in the hope that viewers will stick around watch the new show.

Casual work is hiring independent workers on a project-by-project basis, rather than hiring them on long-term contracts. It is an increasingly popular cost-cutting strategy of commercial media industries.

Circumscribed agency is a perspective that assumes that the choices we make in our lives are not wholly our own, but neither are they simply imposed upon us by outside forces.

Commercial mandate is the primary goal, or reason for being, of a media industry that values the earning of profits.

Common carriers are telecommunications companies, such as the telephone company, that simply carry content, rather than originating it themselves.

Communications technologies are mechanical or electronic innovations that permit human beings to communicate with one another in ways that differ from our natural abilities.

Complex professional era refers to the period beginning in the 1950s during which creative workers became salaried employees of organizations devoted to creating culture. These organizations have grown steadily larger, more diversified, and more global, and they rely on workers with highly specialized skill-sets.

Conditions refer to the economic, regulatory, and technological realities that media industries operate within and that are larger than any individual entity or organization.

Conglomeration generally refers to the increased dominance of companies involved with many different products or services (i.e., the same companies that air the shows on their networks also produce the shows in their studios).

Consolidation of ownership describes the concentration of many media industry operations into the hands of just a few companies, resulting in less competition.

Constructed audience is the audience—its characteristics, likes, and dislikes—imagined by creators and those throughout the industry during the making of media.

Content aggregators are organizations that select and bring together an assortment of media texts in order to sell them to exhibitors or consumers.

Content regulation governs what can be included in media texts. Typically, these regulations are based on social unacceptability or they enforce copyright.

Conventions are agreed-upon ways of creating media texts, including the use of particular genres, narrative techniques, and strategies of organization. See also **formulas**.

Convergence describes the new connections among media enabled by digitization, in terms of technical language, cultural and technological forms, media products, communication systems, and the media industries themselves.

Co-production refers to a business arrangement in which production staff and creative workers from more than one country or organization work together on a project.

Copyright refers to legal protection for creators of original works (e.g., music, poetry, books) from those who might distribute others' work, passing it off as their own and profiting from it.

Corporate image advertising is a style of advertising that was used to advance corporate image, rather than to focus on the attributes of the product. It was common during the sponsorship era of broadcasting.

Cosmopolitanism is the idea that the recognition of similarities and respect for differences among the world's people can diminish war and suffering, a notion that some suggest can come about through media globalization.

Cost plus is a system to finance the creation of television programs in which a producer brings an idea to a network, and, if the network wants to develop the idea, the network pays the cost of production plus a fee or profit to the producer.

Creative Commons refers to a nonprofit movement, founded by Lawrence Lessig, responding to the possibility of the digital age—for both sharing and producing media. Those who establish a Creative Commons (cc) license for their work waive some of their rights in order to more easily allow others to share and build upon their work while still maintaining some rights.

Creative industries is the term most often used among businesspeople and politicians to describe those segments of the economy devoted to making and selling creative products. The designation includes what we define here as media industries, as well as a number of other industries. See **symbolic economy**.

Creators are typically the people who hold the guiding creative vision of a media text.

Critical scholarship starts from the assumption that the current arrangement of societies is unequal, and often focuses on documenting those inequities.

Cross-promoting See **transmedia**.

Cross-ownership refers to ownership of companies in multiple media industries, such as in newspapers and broadcast stations.

Cross-subsidize means to use profits from one business activity to cover losses in another, a common practice in media **conglomerates**.

Crunch time is a period of intense work during which people work as many as eighteen hours a day, usually in order to meet a deadline.

Cultural determinism is the belief that that the cultural uses of a technology determine how that technology influences industry and society.

Cultural imperialism is the theory that media globalization leads to the destruction of local cultural values by more powerful ones.

Cultural interventionist policies seek to encourage voices other than those of commercially motivated media and can take the form of content and structural regulations. These policies encourage the production of media believed to have some sort of pro-social effect.

Culture refers to the artifacts of expressive culture that the media industries produce (e.g., films, newspapers) as well as to the specific social practices, values, mores, and hierarchies associated with a particular group of people.

Data mining is a term that captures industry wide perceptions about how valuable information about consumers' habits has become for today's businesses.

Deficit financing is a television-industry process whereby production studios lose money in making series during the first few years—even if their show is a hit. While it loses money making the show, however, the studio (which licenses rather than sells the show to a network) maintains a possibility of other revenue streams through secondary markets.

Demographic refers to a narrow subsection or segment of the entire population. See also **niche**.

Deterministic approaches to studying media industries tend to explain the behavior of media industries through a single aspect, such as the industry's mandate or technology.

Delivery technologies is a term Henry Jenkins uses to distinguish the means of facilitating distribution (e.g., tapes, CDs, MP3 files) of media content (e.g., recorded sound).

Devolved media operations refers to a corporate organizational structure in which decisions are made by local executives, rather than executives at headquarters; it primarily refers to companies with international operations.

Diaries are small notebooks that audience-measurement companies send to a sample of viewers, who are then asked to fill it in, by writing down everything they watch over a two-week period, and then return it by mail.

Diaspora communities are groups of people, often defined by ethnicity or national origin, living in various different countries but maintaining cultural connections with one another.

Differential promotion refers to the fact that distributors tend to shower praise, attention, and money on only a small fraction of the products they acquire—specifically, those they believe have the greatest potential to become hit.

Digital see **digitization**.

Digital distribution refers to the physical transmission of media texts in a form that is computer readable, as opposed to **analog** forms. Digital distribution permits compression of media texts into much smaller files than their analog counterparts.

Digital divide refers to the gap between those who have access to and facility with new technologies (the "information rich") and those who do not (the "information poor").

Digital reproduction allows users to generate exact copies of original media files.

Digital rights management (DRM) refers to technological enforcers of copyright that control use of media in many different ways (e.g., limiting the amount of time a digital file works, preventing printing or saving of files). Much of the legal support for DRM can be found in the Digital Millennium Copyright Act of 1998.

Digitization refers to a technical process or a technical specification describing the way media are recorded and/or transmitted; digital media are those media that translate the content of media—be it images or sound—into digital code, a language of ones and zeroes.

Direct pay is a source of revenue generated from payment from audiences (e.g., film admissions, movie rentals, magazine purchases) and so, in these instances, media industries need to convince their audiences that their products are worth paying for.

Disaggregation refers to unbundling media texts from their traditional distribution platforms and permitting them to circulate in other platforms, such as taking songs from a CD and offering them for sale individually over an Internet music site.

Distribution/distributors involves transporting completed media texts from their sites of production to the places where they will be exhibited or retailed to audiences, as well as the range of business activities that this process entails.

Distribution windows See **windowing**.

Diversity of voices is the regulatory goal aimed at making sure media regulation fosters an environment in which more, rather that fewer, have access to expressing themselves through media.

Dominant ideology is often thought of as "common sense" or just the way things are. It describes systems of belief that are widely shared in a society at a moment in time, which come to take on extraordinary power because they are normalized by everything from schools, to religious organizations, to the content of popular media such as television.

Downstream windows are distribution channels that occur later in time than **upstream windows**; i.e., DVD release of a film subsequent to its theatrical release.

Dual product markets is an economic concept referring to the two layers of sale that occur in media industries: a media company offers a media product (e.g., a radio playlist, a prime-time lineup) to an audience, although the economic transaction comes from selling the audience to an advertiser.

Dual revenue streams refers to two sources of financial support for an industry: advertiser support and some subscription or direct payment by the media user.

Duopolies occur when two or more stations in the same market are owned by a common entity.

Duopoly rules which were repealed in 1999, prevented a single organization from owning more than one broadcasting station in a single market.

Economics refers to those features of funding and paying for media, such as how a text is funded (investment, deficit financing), how its costs are recouped— whether through advertising, user payment, or sale in other markets, as well as issues of industry structure (ownership) and the impact of broader economic changes on the media industries.

Economies of scale refers to the economic advantage that companies may gain by consolidating their operations. They are achieved when the average cost of a good decreases in accordance with expansion in product output.

Edge refers to a media text's or genre's ability to establish clear taste boundaries among demographic groups.

Exhibition/exhibitors is the process of making finalized media texts available for consumers, whether through a film theater, a television station, a radio station, or a retail store.

Fair use allows for exceptions to use of copyrighted material. Established by the 1976 Copyright Act, the provision allows for limited copying or use of a product that is protected by copyright so long as it is in accord with a few key conditions, such as criticism, comment, news reporting, teaching, scholarship or research.

Federal Communications Commission (FCC) is an agency of the U.S. government that is charged with enforcing the regulatory provisions that govern many media industries, particularly broadcast and cable television, telephony, and some aspects of the Internet.

Federal Radio Commission (FRC) the precursor to the Federal Communications Commission (FCC), established the commercial norm of broadcasting by requiring broadcasters attain a license to use the airwaves.

Federal Trade Commission (FTC) regulates many aspects of the Internet and the advertising industry. For instance, along with the Department of Justice, it oversees the practices of all industries and ensures that companies do not develop unchecked or monopoly power.

Financial Interest and Syndication Rules (also known as Fin-Syn) refers to rules in effect from 1970 to 1995 that prohibited television networks from owning a stake in their prime-time programming. Because networks were prevented from producing much of their own programming, considerable competition existed in the industry.

First Amendment guarantees that "Congress shall make no law...abridging the freedom of speech, or of the press...," providing most media with substantial protection regarding the content of what they produce.

First-copy costs are the expenses required to make the first copy of a media good.

Flexibility describes the structure of the media industries today, which is far more adaptable than in the past; the way we access media, which allows us more control over where, when, and how we consume texts; and also employment practices, such as the use of casual, contract labor rather than full-time, unionized employees.

Flow refers to one of three media-industries models proposed by French media theorist Bernard Miege, and includes radio, television, and, as he described in 1989, "new media." It produces "a continuous flow requiring daily contact and the development of audience loyalty."

Fordist/Fordism refers to the type of mass production organized by Henry Ford, which emphasizes centralization, standardization, long-term profit horizons, and durable goods.

Formal self-regulation refers to an industry's self-imposed rules limiting or categorizing content. Typically developed through industry consortiums, although often with no formal enforcement mechanism. For example, the MPAA's movie rating system.

Formats See **Formulas**.

Format sales refers to a particular practice in which the premise, characters, and norms of a media text (e.g., *Who Wants to Be a Millionaire*) are sold for production in another country.

Formulas are known attributes in the design and production of a media product that have been successful in the past and are utilized to manage risk and uncertainty when selling the product to audiences. These include the use of known products (e.g., sequels), known talent (e.g., A-list stars), standard features (e.g., television shows are either thirty or sixty minutes long), and formats (e.g., Top 40 radio stations).

Fragmentation refers to a shift away from mass-media use to niche-media use in the digital era.

Franchises are cable companies that serve as the sole service provider for a community. They are often owned by companies that own numerous systems across the country.

Genre is a category that popular media texts generally must fit to help guarantee that it will find an appropriate and willing audience. See **Convention**, **Formula**.

Geocultural markets are transnational media markets that are based on culture rather than national boundaries.

Governmental mandate refers to media systems that are designed primarily to fulfill governmental ends, particularly propaganda; usually, we find these mandates in nations with authoritarian governments.

Gross sales refer to the total revenues a company makes prior to deducting costs of production, distribution, marketing, and overhead.

High-definition television (HDTV) describes a revision to the established standard of the U.S. television picture from 480 to 1,080 scan lines.

Hollywood accounting is the casual term used to describe a manner of accounting for the costs of production (mainly through "overhead" charges) that reduces the net profits of creative products to a loss so as to avoid payment of royalties or percentages of net profit.

Horizontal integration is the conglomeration of various companies at the same level of the value chain, such as a company purchasing multiple production studios.

Ideologies are worldviews, or the social common sense of our time. Most media scholars believe that the media are important purveyors of ideologies. See also **Dominant ideology**.

Indecent refers to a type of speech that is prohibited on the airwaves at certain times but that is not subject to prior restraint. The FCC defines indecency as "language or material that, in context, depicts or describes, in terms patently offensive as measured by contemporary community standards for the broadcast medium, sexual or excretory activities or organs."

Independents are media entities that either self-finance the creation of their products or solicit investors to pay for production, such as filmmakers who are unaffiliated with a company that also owns a network or film studio.

Industry lore refers to "common sense" ways of doing things among media industry executives and workers, including ideas about what consumers want, what trends are hot, etc. Typically, industry lore is based more on perception and convention than on research.

Informal self-regulation refers to self-imposed narrowing of the universe of possible texts that industry workers impose to remain commercially viable. These often come from "industry lore" about what is or isn't profitable. Although fairly intangible, these are the most stringent regulations upon media content.

Intellectual property in its purest form, is a legal guarantee that authors, inventors, researchers, and others keep the right to determine how their intellectual efforts get released to the general public and who gets to profit from them.

Intentional overproduction involves deliberately producing more cultural texts within an industry than are likely to succeed in the hope that a few will become "hits" and make up for the financial losses of all the "misses." This is a strategy intended to manage the uncertainties in the marketplace.

Just-in-time production is the effort to produce goods as close as possible in time to the moment they are purchased.

Known product See **Formulas**.

Known talent See **Formulas**.

Lead-in effect is an exhibition strategy of television broadcasters that, through the construction of the program schedule, encourages viewers to watch a particular program by airing it immediately before a particularly popular program in the hope that viewers will tune into the popular show early and see at least a few minutes of the prior show. See also **Carryover effect**.

Libraries are the collections of available texts that distributors have for sale, typically including texts from a range of producers.

License fees are paid to media producers in exchange for the right to distribute and sell media texts.

Lobbyists represent the interests of media industry sectors to the FCC and Congress. These associations, such as the Motion Picture Association of America (MPAA), attempt to influence policy by using their funds to persuade the FCC and the legislature to make sure new policies help rather than hinder their businesses.

Localism is a regulatory goal that guides the creation of media policies and regulation that enable media that originate from the community served.

Localization describes the process of unmooring media texts from their immediate cultural surroundings and securing them in another locale, including language translation, translation of settings, and narrative techniques.

Long tail is a concept coined by *Wired* magazine editor Chris Anderson that describes the value media industries can find outside of the blockbuster. It describes the slope to the curve of graphing Pareto's principle, or the "80/20 rule," which shows in most industries that 80 percent of the profits are made from 20 percent of the products (the blockbusters). Also see **Pareto's Principle**.

Loss leader describes an activity or product of a media industry that is known to be unprofitable but that is advantageous to the industry in other ways.

Magazine-format advertising is an advertising strategy that replaced the single-sponsorship model as the norm on television. In the magazine-format model, advertisers typically purchase thirty-second spots in a portfolio of shows rather than paying for the entire production costs of a program (single sponsorship).

Majors is a general term referring to the dominant players in any given media industry that typically exhibit some degree of **vertical integration**. Examples include the major Hollywood studios, the major record companies, and the major videogame publishers. In television, the "major" broadcast networks were commonly referred to as the Big Three.

Make-goods is the industry term for additional advertising time or other remuneration made to an entity that does not get whatever value was guaranteed for its purchase. For example, in the television industry, an advertiser is often guaranteed a certain number of viewers by the network. If the network doesn't deliver, it then gives the advertiser other spots to make up the deficit.

Mandate is the primary goal, or the reason for being, of the media industry. An industry may have a commercial, non-commercial, or mixed mandate.

Market-professional era is the second of three distinct periods in cultural production that began in the nineteenth century, when trade and industry became increasingly important dimensions of the overall economy and a new class of businesspeople began to gain power and disposable income in Western societies. During this time, individual artists and producers began to sell their wares on newly developing cultural markets.

Market research is a category of research usually conducted prior to and during the development of products. Researchers take media products at various stages of completion and elicit responses from members of targeted demographic groups (through, for instance, surveys, focus groups, and other specialized techniques) in an effort to integrate audience preferences more fully into the final product, thereby increasing sales.

Marketing and distribution costs include the cost of having films printed and shipped to theaters and the cost of having records, tapes, and CDs made and shipped to stores, as well as the costs related to promoting media texts to distributors and consumers.

Mass customization is a process that focuses on producing commodities that are more tailored to local market conditions than their mass-production predecessors. It calls attention to the fact that these commodities are still produced in factories for large numbers of people, not crafted for individual consumers, but that they are more tailored to buyer preferences than mass-produced goods.

Mass media are media organizations that are designed to appeal to the widest possible group of consumers.

Media activist groups are generally nonprofit, grassroots political organizations that lobby on behalf of media users.

Media culture refers to the products that the media industries create. See **Text**.

Media globalization refers to economic practices of the media industries that aim to generate profits across national boundaries, in an effort to spread risks and take advantage of the **public good** nature of media texts.

Mixed mandate systems exist in media industries in which a vital public system remains, but in which a commercial system has developed alongside it.

Monopoly refers to organizations that operate without competition in their respective industries, typically with governmental approval. See **natural monopoly**.

Natural monopolies refers to the perception that some industries can only operate efficiently and profitably if they are controlled by a single **monopoly** organization. They often receive greater regulatory oversight as a consequence.

Network neutrality, or net neutrality is the principle that Internet service providers not discriminate among messages or users and that they pass along all messages at equal speeds and that users be able to access all webpages regardless of their service provider.

Newspaper-Broadcast Ownership Rule was relaxed in 2007 to permit a company to own newspapers, television stations, and radio stations in the same market under certain conditions.

Niche refers to a particular segment of the consumer population, rather than the entire mass population. It refers to both audience segments and media designed to target those segments.

"Nobody knows" is the idea that it is much more difficult to predict what features will make a media text a success or failure than in most other industries.

Non-commercial mandate refers to media industries whose main goal is something other than commercial profits. Types of non-commercial mandates include public, community, alternative/DIY, and authoritarian mandates.

Objectivity refers to the idea that journalists should report news stories without bias or interference. It is often thought to be important for the proper functioning of democratic societies.

Obscene works as defined in the 1973 Supreme Court case *Miller v. California*, are those "which, taken as a whole, appeal to the prurient interest in sex, which portray sexual conduct in a patently offensive way, and which, taken as a whole, do not have serious literary, artistic, political, or scientific value." This ruling emphasized the idea that different communities are likely to have varying definitions of obscenity. Because obscene works are not protected by the First Amendment, they are subject to prior restraint.

Oligopoly refers to an industry that is dominated by a small number of companies that effectively block additional competitors from entering the market. Compare **monopoly**.

Outsourcing is a labor practice that seeks to hire workers in the cheapest possible labor markets in order to save money. It has become more possible and more popular because of the rise of instantaneous, worldwide communications networks.

Overhead costs are the expenses required to maintain media institutions. These costs are not isolated to a particular product but are required to maintain the infrastructure used by media industries such as film studios or record labels.

Overstocking involves carrying a wider range and number of media texts than an organization expects to sell in an effort to manage risk.

Owned and operated stations, or O&Os are individual stations, usually located in large cities such as New York and Los Angeles, owned by a network.

Ownership caps are legal restrictions on the number of media organizations a single entity may own.

Parallel economies are illegal markets, also called "black markets," that specialize in the trade of illegal copies of media texts. See **piracy**.

Paramount Decree was the outcome of *United States v. Paramount Pictures, Inc.*, a 1948 anti-trust case decided by the Supreme Court. It ended the vertical integration of the film industry by forcing the "Big Eight" studios to divest themselves of the theaters they owned.

Pareto's Principle refers to the "80/20 rule," which shows that in most industries 80 percent of the profits are made from 20 percent of the products.

Patronage era refers to the first of three distinct periods in cultural production, when the dominant way of funding creative goods was for patrons to commission artists, musicians, playwrights, and so forth to create cultural texts for their particular needs.

Payola refers to the music-industry practice of distributors giving cash and other gifts to DJs in order to get them to play their songs and rave about them on the air.

Peer-to-peer networks are informal connections among computer users by which they, often illegally, share digital media files.

Penny presses were cheap, commercially funded newspapers in the nineteenth century that began to reach a truly national readership and were read by a wider cross-section of the population, most notably working-class immigrants.

People Meter is a technology introduced by audience-measurement company Nielsen in 1987. It expanded the ability of audimeters, adding a mechanism to report who was in the viewing audience. In the early 2000s, Local People Meters were introduced in large cities to provide overnight data about local television stations.

Pilot episodes are the initial episode of a television program, which serve as a kind of testing ground for networks to evaluate whether to order additional episodes.

Piracy is the buying and selling of illegally produced copies of copyrighted media texts.

Planning costs include acquiring creative goods (e.g., the fee a studio pays to secure a script) and are often risky expenditures, as they often involve monetary or time commitments that are never repaid because many media goods aren't ultimately created.

Platform windows are a media distribution strategy that involves releasing a text in one location or medium in an effort to build **buzz** before releasing it more widely.

Point-to-point media and technologies are designed to facilitate interpersonal communication between individuals, rather than among institutions and audiences. Compare **mass media**.

Political economy of media refers to a common scholarly approach to studying media industries that focuses primarily on the economics of supply and demand, the drive of large conglomerates to dominate markets, and the role of governments in protecting and supporting commercial media enterprises.

Post-Fordism/Post-Fordist is a historical period that comes after **Fordism**, when media industries have become more important for overall economic growth, **just-in-time production** has replaced mass production, and consumers are targeted as **niches** rather than as mass audiences.

Power with regard to media industries, refers to the capacity to shape operating conditions, prevalent business practices, and **industry lore** by means of both persuasion and outright control.

Practices is an umbrella term that includes a broad range of individual workers, their roles, and the day-to-day routines in which they participate. This book organizes practices into three types: creative, distribution and exhibition, and auxiliary.

Price differentiation is the fact that the cost to see a movie or other media text is different depending on where and when you see it. For instance, seeing a movie now in the theater is about $10, but it will cost only about $3 if you wait to rent it.

Prior restraint is the prevention of circulation of content, as granted by rulings of the Supreme Court. This is allowed only if the content is obscene.

Private good is something that, once consumed, is unavailable to other consumers, as opposed to a **public good**.

Privately held media companies are typically managed by a family, do not issue publicly traded stocks, and are not subject to the same disclosure rules as publicly held companies.

Product placement refers to the practice of inserting products into entertainment content as a form of advertisement.

Production costs are all the expenses involved in the actual making of a media product.

Professional organizations work to internalize certain expectations about appropriate and inappropriate industry operation.

Propaganda refers to efforts by governments to use the media to persuade citizens, usually to believe something inaccurate.

Prosumer incorporates both the media "producer" and "consumer," acknowledging that consumers are increasingly involved in the production process from the beginning, and many prosumers are active producers of media texts themselves.

Public domain designates content as "public property" because a copyright has expired and so one no longer needs to pay the originator for rights of use.

Public goods refer to something that is not destroyed or used up in the process of consuming it. For instance, watching a television show typically doesn't prevent someone else from also doing so; as opposed to a **private good**.

Public interest, convenience, and necessity refers to the requirement that U.S. broadcasters must serve specified public needs in return for their licenses.

Public sphere is a phrase, coined by German social theorist Jürgen Habermas, that refers to the unique space for public debate that the mass media can provide in modern societies.

Publicly held companies are those that anyone can buy stock in and that consequently have a responsibility to stockholders to protect their investment. They are also subject to a variety of government regulations that require disclosure of financial details and particular accounting.

Publishing refers to one of three media industries models proposed by French media theorist Bernard Miege, and includes books, music, films, and videogames. Such media are characterized by their production of "isolated individual works" that are purchased by individuals. Particularly key here is that 1) audiences purchase distinct works (unlike the written press model), and 2) that these media tend to be mainly financed through direct pay by audiences, rather than primarily advertiser supported.

Pure demographics refer to segments of the audience that are relatively absent from other demographic groups. For example,

"Real" audience refers to the actual people who consume a media text, including those who show up for a film or purchase a new song.

Regulation encompasses the creation of laws, guidelines, and rules governing the operation of media industries (production, distribution, and exhibition) and the enforcement of those laws, which often requires the creation of specific regulatory bodies. Most media industries face two types of formal regulation, those that regulate either content or industry structure.

Remediation is a process in which the aesthetic practices of a new medium influence the aesthetics of an older medium.

Reproduction costs refer to the expense of copying and distributing a completed media text to exhibitors and consumers.

Revenue models are the particular strategies that businesses employ to earn profits from media texts.

Rights are contractual permissions that **copyright** holders give to other organizations to sell their intellectual property.

Rights holders are the people or organizations that legally own media texts.

Rights period refers to the contracted length of time that a distributor or exhibitor can sell a media text.

Risk refers to the economic dangers that commercial media organizations face when trying to make money off of cultural texts.

Royalties are percentages of profits that media workers receive from the sale of media texts. Usually limited to **above-the-line** workers.

Safe harbor refers to hours between 10:00 p.m. and 6:00 a.m.—established by the FCC—when indecent content is allowed because broadcasters can reasonably assume children will not be in the audience.

Scale is the baseline of compensation and benefits for workers.

Secondary markets also referred to as **syndication**, are the entities—such as international networks, local and independent stations, and cable channels—to which studios sell their television shows after a particular amount of time in order to make a profit. Another secondary market is the release of television series on DVD.

Segmentation is the process of defining consumers and audiences into **demographic** groups.

Segment-making media a term coined by Joseph Turow, refers to media that "encourage small slices of society to talk to themselves."

Simultaneous release refers to synchronized worldwide distribution windows, allowing media audiences everywhere to consume the same texts at the same time.

Single sponsorship refers to the onetime norm of the television industry in which one advertiser was associated with a program, paying all of the costs of production as well as fees to the network and advertising agency.

Social panics are widespread outcries of hysteria related to fears about media effects, most commonly surrounding concerns about the consequences of sexual and violent content and their potential influence on children.

Society-making media a term coined by Joseph Turow, refers to media "that have the potential to get different cross-sections of the population talking to each other" (e.g., broadcast television in the network era).

Sponsorship model of advertising involved a single sponsor paying the costs of production and a fee to the network for airing the show. This model dominated U.S. broadcasting during the radio years and into the early years of television.

Standard features See **Formulas**.

Standards and practices is the office charged with maintaining television network policies about content and making sure that the show being prepared for the network will not result in any kind of legal action through, for instance, indecent content or defamation.

Star system refers to the organization of many creative industries today, in which a small number of highly visible talents wield considerable power over the creative process. Compare **studio system**.

Station group refers to an entity that owns stations affiliated with various networks located in cities around the country.

Studio system refers to an organizational model prevalent in the film industry from the 1920s through the 1950s, in which the major Hollywood studios controlled both the creative and the business processes of the film industry. Compare **star system**.

Subscription is a form of payment in which a media user provides a source of revenue for the media outlet. Subscriptions may be a media entity's sole source of revenue (e.g., HBO) or may be paired with advertising support (e.g., most magazines).

Sunk costs refers to the fact that media goods typically require all of their costs in order to create a single copy of the media good. They then have low marginal costs—or further costs required to make additional copies of the original. This differs from most manufacturing industries.

Surrogate consumers are the middlemen involved in media distribution and exhibition. They operate on the consumer's behalf when winnowing down the thousands of media products that are available on the market to a manageable, albeit limited, number for consumers.

Symbolic economy refers to those kinds of commodities and industries that primarily serve communicative, informational, or entertainment-related functions, such as the media industries, the fashion industry, and the telecommunications and computer industries.

Syndication See also **secondary markets**.

Synergy is a buzzword often used to describe a belief that, in conglomerating various media operations or companies, the combined value is greater than the sum of the individual parts due to the potential of cross-promotion enabled by owning multiple media—such as many different broadcast and cable channels.

Talent refers to media performers such as journalists, actors, and musicians.

Technical potentialities are inherent features of media technologies that make certain social uses more or less likely.

Technological determinism is a theoretical perspective that says that a technology's potentialities determine how that technology will affect the media industries and society. It attributes strong, nearly omnipotent, powers to the technologies that surround us. Compare **determinism** and **cultural determinism**.

Technological dystopianism is the idea that technological innovation brings about a chaotic, undesirable human society on earth.

Technological utopianism is the idea that technological innovation brings about an idyllic human society on earth.

Technology is an operating **condition** of the media industries; it refers to the mechanical and electronic means by which media **texts** are created, distributed, and exhibited.

Telecommunication infrastructures are the hardware that transmit media and point-to-point communication, including phone wires, cables, and wireless networks.

Telecommunications Act of 1996 lifted the limit on national ownership of radio stations and loosened other limits leading to a massive consolidation within media industries.

Transmedia storytelling or **brands** refer to particular characters, story worlds, or recognizable elements of texts that can be exploited across multiple media.

Upstream windows are distribution channels that occur earlier in time than **downstream windows**, such as theatrical distribution in comparison with prime-time network broadcast.

Value chain refers to the various activities that a media text passes through in order to become a commercial product; economic value gets added at each link in the chain. Links include production, distribution, and exhibition, each stage of which earns profits.

Vertical integration is a competitive strategy that describes the attempt to control every stage of media production, such as when television networks and studios are owned by one corporation.

Webisodes are episodes of a television series that are available only on-line.

Windowing refers to releasing new media texts on a staggered schedule, differentiated by medium or territory. This schedule is intended to build excitement about new media products in order to drive people to consume them and helps ensure that distributors can squeeze the maximum amount of profit possible out of media products.

Wire services collect and share, or sell, stories among news organizations and media outlets such as newspapers, television and radio channels, and internet websites. They operate as cooperatives, for-profit organizations, or government-funded entities.

Written press refers to one of three media industries models proposed by French media theorist Bernard Miege. It is similar to the publishing model, except in this case—that of media such as magazines and newspapers—the media produce a "series of commodities, purchased regularly." This difference is important because the constant product of written press industries means that they are financed differently because they just keep making the same thing—thus they aren't organized around a series of discrete products.

Index